THE POLITICS OF PROVOCATION: PARTICIPATION AND PROTEST IN ISRAEL

SUNY Series in Israeli Studies
Russell Stone, Editor

Gadi Wolfsfeld

THE POLITICS OF PROVOCATION: PARTICIPATION AND PROTEST IN ISRAEL

State University of New York Press

Published by
State University of New York Press, Albany

For information, address State University of New York
Press, State University Plaza, Albany, N.Y., 12246

Library of Congress Cataloging-in-Publication Data

Wolfsfeld, Gadi.
    The politics of provocation: participation and protest in Israel
    /Gadi Wolfsfeld.
        p. cm. — (SUNY series in Israeli studies)
    Bibliography: p.
    Includes index.
    ISBN 0-88706-768-9. ISBN 0-88706-769-7 (pbk.)
    1. Israel—Politics and government. 2. Political participation—
    Israel. 3. Radicalism—Israel. I. Title. II. Series.
    JQ1825.P359W65 1988
    320. 95694—dc19   87-24623
                                                              CIP

10 9 8 7 6 5 4 3 2 1

To Lauren and Noa

CONTENTS

	List of Figures	ix
	List of Tables	x
	Preface	xi
	Introduction	1
1.	The Changing Political Culture of Israel	6
2.	The Analytical Framework	29
3.	Who, What, and Why: Explaining Individual Participation	39
4.	Beyond the Numbers	72
5.	Explaining Collective Action	91
6.	Beyond the Collective Numbers	115
7.	Outcomes of Collective Action	149
8.	Conclusion	163
	Methodological Appendix	174
	Notes	186
	References	195
	Index	201

LIST OF FIGURES

1–1	Political Discontent in Israel	14
2–1	An Analytical Framework for the Study of Political Action Repertoires	31
3–1	Explaining Individual Political Action	40
3–2	Gender, Psychological Involvement, and Education	43
3–3	Ethnicity and Psychological Involvement	45
3–4	Resources, Attitudes, and Repertoires: A Model	55
3–5	Mobilization Attitude Profiles	59
3–6	Institutional Attitude Profiles	61
3–7	Resources and Skills Profiles	63
3–8	Social Background Profiles	65
5–1	Explaining Collective Political Action	97
5–2	Patterns of Mobilization: A Typology	101
5–3	Mobilization and Political Action Repertoires: Hypotheses	109
5–4	Collective Action Profiles	111

LIST OF TABLES

1–1	Changes in Israeli Political Orientations	16
1–2	Psychological Involvement and Institutional Efficacy	21
1–3	What Can You Do to Change a Law?	22
1–4	Institutional Action and Mobilized Action	25
1–5	Political Action Repertoires	27
3–1	The Effects of Psychological Involvement	48
3–2	Explaining Political Discontent	52
3–3	Explaining Orientations Towards Mobilized Action	54
3–4	Factor Analysis of Israeli Political Action	57
3–5	Institutional Action and Mobilized Action: Regression Analyses	70
5–1	Israeli Protest Groups: Distribution of Traits	93
5–2	Israeli Protest Acts: Distribution of Traits	95
5–3	Mobilization and Political Action: First Cut	107
5–4	Mobilization Type and Flexibility	114
7–1	The Correlates of Publicity	152
7–2	The Distribution of Success	155
7–3	Organization, Resources, and Success	157
7–4	Mobilization Type and Success	158
7–5	Extensiveness, Activism, and Success: Controlling for Interests	160
7–6	Disorder and Success	161
A–1	Statistical Attributes of Questionnaire Measures	179

PREFACE

One of the advantages of studying Israeli political behavior is the large amount of unexplored territory which is left to scout. This book is, in essence, the first study of political participation in Israel. It is hoped that the ideas which are presented will offer some insights into the rather unique nature of Israeli political culture.

It is a pleasure to acknowledge all those who helped make this work possible. The research which is reported within these pages was made possible through the generosity of the Shinbrun Fund of the Hebrew University and a grant from the Ford Foundation which was provided by the Israel Foundations Trustees.

I was fortunate to obtain access to two very important sources of data. I want to thank the Israeli Institute for Applied Social Science Research for allowing me to use information which was collected within their continual survey of Israeli society. The data for the cross cultural analyses in chapter 1 were provided by the *Zentralarchiv fuer empirische Sozialforschung (ZA)*. They were originally collected by individual institutions in each country for the study, "Political Action—An Eight Nation Study." Neither the original collectors of any of these data, nor the *ZA* bears any responsibility for the analyses or interpretation presented here.

I also want to acknowledge the department of political science at M.I.T. which provided a wealth of services and facilities during my sabbatical stay in Cambridge. A special thanks goes to Lucian Pye and Russell Neuman of that department who provided the moral, intellectual, and financial support which enabled me to complete this work.

I owe a special thank you to my gifted research assistant, Gil Askenazi, who diligently carried out the many and varied tasks which fell into his realm of responsibility.

Of the many colleagues who read this manuscript before its publication, I want to single out Elihu Katz and Bill Gamson. It was Elihu who suggested the final title for this book after my own efforts in this area had all failed. Bill's guidance and insights were quite remarkable, and his suggestions have certainly improved the final product.

I also want to thank other colleagues who were willing to spend some of their valuable time reading either part or all of the manuscript: Asher Arian, Samuel Barnes, Akiba Cohen, Avraham Diskin, Yitzhak Galnoor, Emanuel Gutmann, Sam Lehman-Wilzig, Peter Medding, Ira Sharkansky, and Ehud Sprinzak. I learned a great deal from all of their comments and criticisms but I must accept full responsibility for any failings in the work.

I also want to acknowledge the guidance and support of the editor of this series, Russell Stone. His enthusiasm for the project has been a great help to me.

Finally, I want to thank my initial proofreader, Lauren Wolfsfeld. She is living proof that despite their speed, machines will never read as well as humans.

INTRODUCTION

> If the democratic model of the participatory state
> is to develop in these new nations, it will require
> more than the formal institutions of democracy—
> universal suffrage, the political party, the elective
> legislature. A democratic form of participatory poli-
> tical system requires as well a political culture con-
> sistent with it.
>
> —*Almond and Verba (1963)*

This is a study of one nation's attempt to develop a participatory political culture. Israel is about to turn forty and it is a useful time to take stock. It is a country which is teeming with political movement. Citizens often find themselves moving from crisis to crisis and the political clock seems to be permanently stuck at the eleventh hour. Israelis always have a compulsion to talk about politics: more often they have good reason to shout.

In the past this need for political influence went largely unfulfilled. It was found in previous studies of Israeli political culture (Galnoor 1982; Etzioni-Halevy 1977; Arian 1971) that Israelis were frustrated spectators, with an extremely low sense of political efficacy. Israeli citizens are faced with a political system which is dominated by inaccessible political parties and a proportional electoral system whose strengths lie in the area of national unity rather than political accountability.

An important change has occurred in the political culture of Israel, starting in the early seventies. The age of protest arrived somewhat late to the country, but Israelis have adopted it with a vengeance. When compared with other countries it is the only one in which protest is the first course of political action. Although much of this behavior offers a welcome opportunity for political access and communication, other aspects are indicative of an alarming contempt for the rule of law, and even a potential danger to the stability of democracy in Israel.

The politics of provocation is a cultural syndrome in which direct action becomes the predominant means of making demands on government. A strategy of provocation is based on a belief that politicians are much more likely to respond to pressure than to persuasion. It is perhaps best illustrated by the saying, "It's the squeaky wheel that gets the oil."

A political culture based on political provocation is a far cry from the civic culture described in Almond and Verba's (1963) classic work. The underlying belief system is more likely to be characterized by political cynicism than trust: few have faith in the formal channels of access. On the other hand, citizens have no wish to replace the system; they do not question its basic legitimacy. They seek responsiveness, not revolution.

The political action repertoires which characterize the politics of provocation tend to reflect this distinction. They are often rude and disruptive but rarely uncontrollable. The disorder and violence which accompany such protests is primarily designed to nettle the authorities into action, not coerce them. The primary weapons are the mass media and public opinion, not rifles and guns.

TOWARDS A COMPREHENSIVE THEORY OF POLITICAL ACTION

This study is not only about Israel. Although the politics of provocation seem to be especially prevalent in this country, the underlying logic should also be applicable to other settings. To facilitate such applications a conscious effort has been made throughout this work to also deal with more general questions about the roots of political action. It is hoped that the work will also contribute towards a more general theory of political action.

An instrumentalist view of social science theory is taken here: theories are seen as "tools of inquiry . . . designed to suggest, stimulate, and direct experiment" (Kaplan 1964). The goal of the present study is to contribute to the considerable progress which has already been made in the field. There is an emphasis on the integration and specification of existing theory although attempts are also made to develop and test new ideas about political action.

The efforts in the area of theoretical integration are an attempt to contribute towards a more unified model by bridging the gap between a number of research traditions. Until recently, for example, studies of political participation and protest have been carried out separately. There is increasing evidence, however, that the similarities between these two modes of behavior outweigh their differences. The study of individual political behavior has also been mistakenly separated from the study of collective action. Yet it is clear that any comprehensive model of political action must deal with both the individual and the collective level of analysis.

The theoretical framework which is developed in this work is not intended to serve as such a model. Rather, it is hoped that the general logic which underlies the model and the empirical investigation which accompanies it will encourage others to develop more dynamic models of political action. Because of these intentions a great deal of emphasis is placed on the "exceptions to the rules." Hopefully, the study raises at least as many questions as it seeks to answer.

SOME GUIDING PRINCIPLES

The theory and the methods used in this investigation are based on certain premises which should be enunciated. The first supposition is that citizens are rational actors whose political behavior can best be understood by examining their level of political resources, their need to be involved in politics, and their evaluations of the political system. Individuals and groups may not always make perfect judgments, but decisions are based on their best attempts to make sense out of the information available to them. There is ample opportunity to corroborate this thesis.

The second assumption is that only an interdisciplinary approach to political action can offer an adequate explanation of behavior. There are psychological, sociological, and political reasons for political behavior and social scientists must strive for a more unified approach to the issue. This demands not only a dedication to interdisciplinary theory, but also a willingness to adopt a variety of methods.

The final guideline relates to a dilemma which faces all of those engaged in empirical research: the choice between precision and vision. The level of caution used in research often determines the scope of observations. Social scientists who emphasize precision are most concerned with the issue of statistical control. They are wary of any conclusions based on small samples, case studies, and qualitative analysis. Researchers more interested in vision, on the other hand, take a more holistic approach and have little patience for "number crunchers."

In this study we try to have our cake and eat it, too. The quantative and qualitative perspectives each offer important insights into Israeli political action. The narrower focus of statistical analysis allows us to formulate specific hypotheses about political action, whereas qualitative interviews and case studies provide a deeper understanding of both the model's limitations and how it relates to the political context of Israel.

ORGANIZATION OF THE TEXT

The need to contribute towards the development of a more general theory of political action and the attempt to better understand the political culture of Israel are the two goals which dictate the plan of argument for this book. The discussion moves back and forth between theory and context, in an attempt to arrive at a more powerful explanation of political action.

The first chapter is devoted to depicting the setting for the study. It documents the dramatic change in political attitudes and behavior which have occurred in Israel and offers cross-cultural evidence about the ways in which the political culture of Israel is relatively unique. An attempt is made to describe the beliefs, attitudes, and behaviors which serve as the cultural foundation for the politics of provocation in Israel.

The second chapter has a more general intent and clarifies the theoretical underpinnings for this particular study. An analytical framework is presented which is designed to explain both individual and collective political action. It is argued that the roots of all political behavior can be understood by looking at variations in background, mobilization, and evaluations of the political system. Both individual and collective political actors, it is argued, choose repertoires which reflect these differences.

In chapter 3 the framework is adapted to explain individual political action. A rational choice model is developed and tested which should be applicable to most Western democracies. The evidence provides strong support for the claim that people choose an action repertoire which best reflects their particular set of motivations and attitudes. The analysis also offers important evidence about which Israelis are the most likely to participate in both institutional and mobilized forms of political action.

In chapter 4 the analysis of individual behavior is an attempt to go beyond the statistical analysis presented in chapter 3. In-depth interviews allowed respondents to talk about their political experiences in their own terms. The interview transcripts offer important insights into both the strengths and weaknesses of the theoretical model. They also provide a deeper understanding about how Israelis relate to their rather unique world of politics. The picture which emerges is not an encouraging one.

A model of collective action is developed in chapter 5 and it follows the same logic as the model used to explain individual participation. The specific variables and the method of inquiry are different, but both analyses are based on an attempt to explain how political action repertoires are affected by differences in background, mobilization, and evaluations. The major theme of the chapter is that strategic choices about protest can best be understood by examining group needs, which are related to varying patterns of collective mobilization. A typology of protest groups is developed and tested in this chapter which should be of some use to those interested in more general questions about collective action.

A return to the context of Israel through the case studies is presented in chapter 6. The protest leaders interviewed for this section were very forthcoming in describing the rules of the game and their own interactions with other protest groups, the press, and the authorities. The group portraits provide a wide range of alternative interests and tactics, including some comparative material on groups protesting against the withdrawal from Sinai and those opposing the war in Lebanon. In addition to offering a useful application for the model, these materials illustrate the ways in which Israeli authorities inspire the politics of provocation.

The analysis presented in chapter 7 provides a finishing touch to the empirical analysis. The discussion centers on the outcomes of collective action and, once again, deals with both the specifics of Israel as well as more universal questions. The descriptive materials illustrate that Israeli protesters have an extremely high rate of success, a finding which helps explain why so many citizens prefer this route to political influence.

There is also an attempt in this chapter to deal with more general questions by focusing on the correlates of group repression, publicity, and success. Patterns of collective mobilization not only affect how people act, but also how others will react. Protest leaders make choices on the basis of assumptions about expected costs and benefits and the empirical data presented offer a rare opportunity to test those assumptions.

In the final chapter the most important lessons from the study are summarized and the implications for both social scientists and policy makers are described.

Chapter 1

THE CHANGING POLITICAL CULTURE OF ISRAEL

This chapter is devoted to placing the political culture of Israel in perspective. The discussion is divided into three sections. The first section offers a brief historical overview which will describe the early political culture of Israel. This period was dominated by paternalistic party machines which had a veritable monopoly on the control of political communication. A variety of political, social, and economic forces led to a gradual change in this pattern and by the late sixties the stage was set for the emergence of a very different political culture.

The second part of the chapter employs a variety of empirical data to detail the emergence of provocative politics in Israel. During the seventies Israeli citizens expressed an increasing sense of discontent with government leaders, a growing need to be involved in politics, and a lack of faith in institutional means of redress. Political protest became the preferred means of political participation and there was a startling rise in the number of demonstrations and acts of civil disobedience.

The third and final section places these developments within a cross-cultural perspective. The political culture of Israel appears to offer a rather significant case for those studying political action. When compared to citizens in eight other Western countries, Israelis have the highest level of psychological involvement and one of the lowest levels of faith in government efficacy. Israel is also the only country where protest has become the first course of political action.

The two perspectives offered then, are those of time and culture.

Whereas the historical context provides important insights into the roots of Israeli political action, the cross-cultural perspective tells us the ways in which Israeli political culture is unique.

A BRIEF HISTORY

To understand Israeli political culture, it is critical to first deal with its development and change. Unlike most such descriptions, the present analysis attempts, where possible, to examine the development from the perspective of the citizen. Although national surveys have only been carried out consistently since the sixties, enough is known about the early years to give at least a partial picture of how Israelis related to their political system.

Before Independence

It is useful to begin the discussion by considering the socio-political background of those who founded and propagated the Zionist movement in the late nineteenth century. As a political movement, Zionism was created by politically conscious Jews struggling to deal with the ideological positions of their time. They were certainly not representative of either the Jewish or the non-Jewish population as a whole. The vast majority were "enlightened" Jews from urban communities in Europe who had long since left the confines of the ghetto.

If those who joined the Zionist movement were atypical in their level of political consciousness, those who actually settled and stayed in Palestine needed an even greater degree of ideological commitment. Facing the hardships of any pioneers, those who remained in Israel were ". . . self-selected, possessing the stamina, the inner resources of the belief in Zionism, and the desire to recast the Jew as a productive worker which were necessary to survive" (Shimshoni 1982, 16). Certainly not all of the newcomers were fervent ideologists, but the process of mobilization and immigration during those early years suggests an unusual percentage of political activists. As Arian (1971) put it: "The political elite of the country arrived *before* the masses were there to lead".

The political culture of this early period was probably most influenced by the arrival of what is known as the second *aliyah* (wave of immigration). Forty thousand Jews arrived between 1904 and 1913 and the ideological principles which characterized that group have long since become central themes in the political symbolism of Israel. They were committed to both socialism and a return to the land, and founded the first *kibbutzim* (collective settlements). These early settlers saw themselves as revolutionaries (Fein 1967), and thus political discussion and ideological debate were an integral part of their lives.

During the time of the British mandate, these skills became crucial. The pre-independence Jewish community in Palestine, known as the *Yishuv*, established many of the political institutions of a sovereign state. The citizens were asked to pay taxes, elect a national assembly, and even serve in the military (Horowitz and Lissak 1968), and most complied willingly. This sense of volunteerism was a central part of the early years and created the foundations for the state to be. The Peel commission of 1937 described the Yishuv as ". . . a highly educated, highly democratic, very politically minded, and unusually young community" (Horowitz and Lissak 1968, 19).

The most important political institutions established were the political parties. As detailed in the work of Horowitz and Lissak (1978), the first organized parties were those formed by the workers, which were distinguished as ". . . an educated and politically conscious group" (70-71). Due to the fact that political parties preceded the existence of the state, they took on a wide variety of tasks, supporting their members in the areas of culture, employment, health, and welfare.

The parties also established elaborate means of political socialization which helped guarantee the loyalty of members from cradle to grave. As children, they would attend a party school and after school participate in the activities of the party youth groups. Once eligible, they would be recruited into the appropriate military unit and upon completion of their service most likely read the party newspaper. The party machine permeated almost every aspect of a person's life and facilitated stable ideological identifications and commitment. For all intents and purposes, the party was the state and citizenship was defined by party membership.

By far the most successful political machine was that created by *Mapai*, which was formally established in 1930 through a coalition of two workers' parties. The party during these early years both offered and encouraged political participation, as described by Medding (1972):

> Contact between leaders and followers in the 1930s tended to be based upon personal acquaintance, and was informal, direct, and fairly regular. Party leaders visited party branches throughout the country to discuss the vital issues with the rank and file . . . Direct contact with

party leaders as well as actual participation in decisions created a sense
of intimacy and warmth within the party, a feeling of equal partnership
in a gemeinschaft-like fellowship. Informality and the absence of
clearly defined or written rules of party organization and procedure
were the norm (86).

Medding's description offers the image of an almost idealistic political culture with both eager and active participants and a responsive
political elite.

There is another aspect of political action in the Yishuv which is
also worthy of note. In 1939, the British, reversing previous policy, is-
sued the White Paper which seriously restricted Jewish immigration
to Palestine. Although the political parties had cooperated with the
British until that point, the change in policy set the stage for a new
mode of political mobilization. Jews in Palestine were forced to turn
to illegal means of demonstrating, massing arms, and bringing in illegal immigrants. This struggle against the British is seen as one of
the critical steps towards independence. The use of direct action and
civil disobedience is given a very special place in Israeli history. The
parallel between these pioneers and modern protesters is often used to
justify modern cases of public disorder.[1]

In sum, the political culture of the Yishuv was characterized by
three major developments which determined the pattern of politics
for modern Israel. Most important was the establishment of a strong,
autonomous party machine, which was designed to both distribute
services and rapidly mobilize the entire public. Secondly, the public
was both highly educated and politically conscious, and from all indications had a high level of participation in party politics. Finally, the
culture was one where the struggle against the British tended to
glorify the use of direct action as a means to gain political independence.

The Early Years of Statehood

The establishment of the state of Israel had an important impact
on all aspects of political culture, although some developments took
longer than others to take effect. First, the role of the party was now
subservient to that of the state. The insistence of Ben Gurion (the first
Prime Minister) on the principle of *mamlachtiut* (statism) insured
that many of the parties' powers in the area of education, housing,
welfare, and the military were drastically reduced. The transfer of
power to the state was a gradual one and in the early years the public

bureaucracy was plagued by the same party patronage under a different name. Eventually, however, the civil service did grow independent of the parties, a fact which drastically reduced their ability to dispense favors.

A second factor which changed the nature of the party was the rapid growth in the population. Between 1948 and 1951, 700,000 Jews came into Israel, doubling the Jewish population (Arian 1975). This remarkable development changed the nature of the party dramatically and political parties in Israel were forced to give up a good deal of the openness and intimacy which characterized the pre-state era. Party structures grew increasingly formalistic and distant. As Medding (1972) put it, "Above all, much of the sense of participation was lost: the participant had become, in the main, an observer" (87). Aronoff's (1977) study of the Labor Party describes how the party developed elaborate mechanisms for supressing any input from the party membership and activists. Elaborate rituals were developed to give the appearance of unity and tranquility and avoid any real conflict.

A third factor also had an influence on both the nature of the party and political participation: economic development. The rapid process of modernization brought about an increase in both urbanization and a shift to more independent life styles and occupations. Each of these trends had predictable influences on both the role of the party and the level of citizen involvement. The move away from small rural communities limited the party's ability to mobilize and socialize its membership. The process of bringing members together, communicating, and dispensing responsibilities becomes infinitely more complicated when people live as individuals rather than as a community. In addition, as pointed out by Galnoor (1982), the responsibility for the political socialization of both children and adults moved from the political parties to more independent agents such as family, school, place of work, and the expanding mass media.

In *Elite Without Successors*, Yonaton Shapiro (1984) offers yet another explanation for the weakening of the party machine. There was a large gap, he argues, between the founders of Israel who were born abroad and the next generation of leaders who were born in Israel. The older generation was unwilling to share political power with the new elite, causing many of those with the greatest potential to drift towards leadership positions in the military, industry, and the growing bureaucracy. Those who remained in politics were relatively unprepared to assume responsibility for managing the party.

It is important to stress that despite these trends, the Israeli political party remained in these years the only serious political broker in the state. This fact is probably best illustrated by the paucity of both pressure groups and protests. Israelis looking for alternative channels of political expression would have been hard pressed to find any. Direct action techniques, so popular in the time of the Yishuv, became rare. In the fifties, for example, there was only one protest of any historical worth; a 1959 uproar which took place in "*Wadi Salib*," a Haifa slum populated by North African immigrants.

Years of Transition

The sixties in Israel were a time of transition, as Israel became a "normal" Western society. The ideology of collectivism, although still prevalent, was being subsumed to a more individualistic life style and commitment. According to research from that period (Lissak 1964) the aspirations of young people were changing and there was a greater emphasis on personal mobility which would assure a better quality of life. The increasing availability of public housing also reduced the degree to which citizens were dependent on political parties.

There were other events in the sixties which set the stage for the change in Israeli political culture. The Lavon affair (1954–55) was a bungled espionage mission which led to the execution of two Egyptian Jews. The political fallout from the scandal led to a major crisis in the early sixties and was also related to Ben Gurion's final resignation in 1963. As Israel's first Prime Minister, Ben Gurion exercised a remarkable amount of control over Israel's affairs and his political demise marked the end of an era in Israeli politics.

Another, rather different, event which had an effect was the introduction of television in 1968. Television served as an important catalyst for protest. First, Israelis were able to observe the wave of protest which swept throughout Europe and the U.S. in the late sixties and early seventies. People clearly learn to expand their political action repertoires by watching the behavior of their peers. Secondly, television enabled even the smallest protest groups an unprecedented opportunity for mass exposure. Television is the most powerful of the mass media in this respect, and in Israel today, an estimated 77% of the population watch the evening news on the one national television channel.[2] Finally, television may also have had an effect on both the need to be involved and political discontent. Televised news reaches a much wider audience than newspapers.

The Israeli political culture was geared for metamorphosis.

THE EMERGENCE OF PROVOCATIVE POLITICS

The orientation of Israelis towards their political system has dramatically changed since those early years of independence. The evidence presented below points to three significant trends in the political culture of Israel, all of which have contributed to the politics of provocation. The first is an *increasing sense of political discontent* in reaction to the inability of successive Israeli governments to deal with Israel's many problems. The second change is marked by an *increasing need for political expression*: the level of psychological involvement of the Israeli polity has grown dramatically. The final, and critical, component of this process is the *decreasing sense of institutional efficacy*: more Israelis than ever before feel politically impotent.

These three trends lead to a perception of *blocked opportunities* (Paige 1971), which is seen as the motivational key to understanding the politics of provocation. A sense of blocked opportunities can be defined as a belief that institutional means of political access are either inaccessible to the average citizen or worthless. Citizens who are skeptical about the openness of the political system must choose between political apathy or direct action. When both psychological involvement and political discontent are also on the rise, then a greater number of citizens will choose protest; political actors follow the path of least resistance. As direct action and civil disobedience become more conventional, the politics of provocation begins to take hold.

Rising Political Discontent

It is not difficult to track the rise in political discontent in Israel during the seventies and early eighties. The period is marked by a staggering series of political blunders, scandals, and disasters which led to a growing sense of anger and frustration. The war of attrition with Egypt took place in 1969 and 1970 and the loss of life in that encounter put a quick end to the euphoria which had permeated Israeli society after the Six Day War (1967). Even more devastating to the national morale was the Yom Kippur War (1973) when the military was caught almost completely by surprise; which resulted in an extensive number of deaths and injuries. A new government was inauguratged in

1974 under Yitzak Rabin. This government was tainted not with war but corruption, and even Rabin himself had to resign over a financial indiscretion, shortly before the elections in 1977. The dramatic rise in Israeli political discontent during these years is documented in Figure 1–1.

The figures are based on a single question which was asked in an ongoing national survey of public opinion. The question asks how the government is dealing with the "present situation." The yearly percentage replying "Poorly" to "Very Poorly" serves as the indicator of political discontent.[3] Although only 8% of the population was dissatisfied with government performance in 1967, it reached an incredibly high point of 81% by the time the Labor Party was voted out of power in 1977.

The first Likud government had every advantage in regaining the people's confidence in the political system. Five months after Menachem Begin became Prime Minister, President Sadat of Egypt came to Jerusalem, an event whose effects on the Israeli public can only be described as euphoric. Yet, as can be seen, despite the first peace treaty with an Arab state, levels of public discontent eventually returned to their previously high levels. A good deal of this discontent was related to the deteriorating state of the Israeli economy. Apart from a convenient respite during the 1981 elections, the economic situation had deteriorated to a extremely dangerous level by 1984. The Lebanese War (1982) was just one more indication that Israeli governments seemed to be moving from failure to failure, at an extremely high cost to its citizens.

The rise in discontent between 1967 and 1984 had reached the point of a national consensus. The fact that such a high level of discontent has been expressed about both governments illustrates that these findings are not based on mere partisan sympathies. In a poll taken in 1984, 56% of the population expressed a negative attitude towards politics; only 30% responded in that manner to an identical question posed in 1973.[4]

In sum, there can be little doubt that the theme of rising political discontent has dominated the Israeli political culture of these years.

The Growing Sense of Blocked Opportunities

The other two factors which lead to the politics of provocation are a high level of psychological involvement and a low level of faith in institutional efficacy. Gamson (1968) also referred to the psychologi-

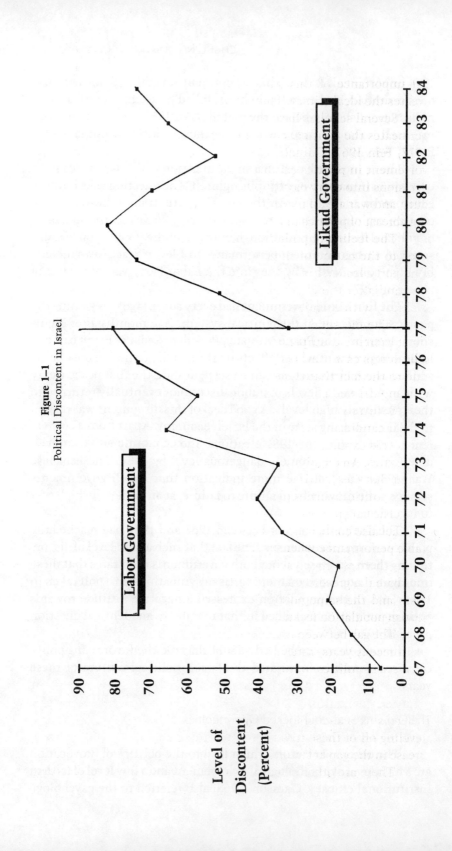

Figure 1-1
Political Discontent in Israel

cal importance of this particular combination, suggesting that it creates the ideal climate for protest.[5]

Several scholars have referred to this sense of frustration which permeates the political culture of Israel (Arian 1985; Etzioni-Halevy 1977; Fein 1967; Galnoor 1982). The high level of psychological involvement in politics can be traced to the obtrusiveness of political decisions into every day life. Decisions about prices, salaries, reserve duty, and war are all made by a highly centralized government. Keeping abreast of politics in Israel is simply a necessity of life.

The feeling of political impotence in Israel can best be attributed to the nature of the party structure and the electoral system. The party leadership is totally protected from the people, both before and after the elections. The party structure is extremely hierarchical, with each level electing and being responsible to the next level. The electoral system is probably, for national elections, the most extreme example of proportional representation in the world. The voters cast their ballots for parties rather than individuals and due to the fact that there is no regional representation, politicians have no defined constituencies. Israeli citizens have no representative to turn to in time of need and no way to even vote against a particular candidate.

This explains why so many Israelis feel negatively about political parties. An ongoing opinion poll by Mina Tzemach (Chazin 1985) found that 69% of the adult Jewish population believe that the role which political parties play in Israel is not an essential one.

The bargaining process which creates the coalition governments of Israel also contributes to this general sense of suspicion. The inevitable performance whereby small parties pressure larger parties into giving them an unrepresentative proportion of cabinet seats and funds lays bare the greedier side of politics. There are good reasons for cynicism and the same poll by Tzemach found that 59% of the adult Jewish population feel negatively about the Knesset itself.

The gap between involvement and efficacy has grown even greater in recent years, as can be seen in Table 1–1. Israelis are more interested in politics, want to discuss politics more than before, and express a greater need for political influence. There has also been a decrease in institutional efficacy: 51% expressed doubts in 1969, whereas 61% did in 1981.[6] Although there may be somewhat of a leveling off of these trends in the eighties, there has been a clear increase in the gap between involvement and efficacy.[7]

There are other pieces of evidence which point in a similar direction. Lehman-Wilzig (1983) asked a national sample why they thought protest was so popular in Israel. Out of a list of six possible responses, the reason chosen most often was, "The citizen does not have enough other ways to express his opinions to the authorities". A similar measure was used by the present author. Respondents were asked about the extent to which they agreed with the statement, "The main reason why people go to demonstrations is that there is no other way to influence the authorities." Sixty percent of those who had an opinion agreed with this idea.[8] A different version was also presented: the sample was asked whether or not they agreed that, "It's not nice to carry out illegal demonstrations or block streets but sometimes there is no choice." A relatively high 30% of those who gave an opinion agreed with this more radical notion.

Table 1–1
Changes in Israeli Political Orientations[a]

Question	1969	1973	Year 1977	1981	1984
1. Interested in Politics (Great Deal/Somewhat)		48%			62%
2. Discuss Politics (Great Deal/Somewhat)		39%	64%	57%	
3. Want to Have an Influence (Great Deal/Somewhat)		46%	65%	57%	
4. Can't Have Influence (Little, None)	51%	66%	66%	61%	

a. Apart from 1984 all figures come from Arian's (1972, 1975, 1980, 1983) election surveys. The 1984 figure is based on a national survey carried out by the author (see Methodological Appendix).

The Israeli political culture of the seventies and early eighties offers almost a perfect test of the blocked opportunities approach to political dissidence. The influence gap in Israel has clearly been growing and should lead to an increase in extra-parliamentary activities as an alternative to more traditional paths to political influence.

The Rise in Protest

This is exactly what has occurred. As Lehman-Wilzig (1981) has shown, by 1979 protest in Israel had risen to a level five times greater than that of 1960, with by far the highest rise occurring during the seventies. This set of data also shows that the role of the parties in such protests also declined and more and more protests were being organized by new interest groups.

Fewer people are turning to political parties. Arian's (1985, 106) election surveys show membership dropping from 18% in 1969 to 8% in 1984. The author's survey data reveals that although 17% of Israelis over fifty belong to a political party, a remarkably small 2% of those between eighteen and twenty–nine report such membership.[9] Although the effects of political maturity might narrow this gap, it is also a sign of the radical change in political action repertoires.

This emergence of a new form of political action has had important consequences for political discourse in Israel. The precedent was first set in 1971, when a group of Oriental Jews from impoverished neighborhoods joined together to form the Black Panthers. The protests against poverty were considered extremely violent at the time and a great shock to the political establishment. As a direct result of these protests, social welfare was moved to a much higher priority level on the public agenda.

Many groups followed, especially after the Yom Kippur War (Etzioni-Halevy 1977). The two best known groups organized during the seventies are *Gush Emunim* (The block of the faithful) (Newman 1985; Rubinstein 1982; Sprinzak 1981a) and Peace Now (Bar-on 1985). The importance of these groups lies in their being seen as legitimate representatives of the right and left in Israel. The fact that these extra-parliamentary movements were organized outside of the political party structure says quite a bit about the way the Israeli political culture has changed. By the time the Lebanese War broke out in 1982, new groups were being mobilized at a moment's notice.

Data collected for the present study suggested a certain leveling off in the number of protests carried out in the eighties, or perhaps a slight rise. Although it is difficult to compare the present set of results with those collected by Lehman-Wilzig (1981), the number of protests reported in the newspaper *Ha'aretz* were 157 in 1979, 154 in 1980, 108 in the election year of 1981, 154 in 1982, 161 in 1983, and 170 in 1984.[10] It is noteworthy that a similar leveling off was found in some of the psychological trends discussed.

Have the politics of provocation also led to an increase in the intensity of protest in Israel? Apparently not. Data from both the Lehman-Wilzig (1981) study and the present research have suggested that the proportion of violent demonstrations is better related to specific political circumstance than to long-term trends.[11] It would appear that there is no increase in the level of disorder and violence in recent years, despite the increase in discontent. If the blocked opportunity thesis is correct, the influence gap appears to lead to an increase in the amount of protest but not in its intensity.

It is also important, however to consider the half-empty part of the glass. First, although the proportion of disorder and violence has not risen, the absolute number of such acts has gone up. In addition, the proportion of such acts is hardly small. Using the data set collected for the present study, it was found that 30% of all acts of protest were illegal, 23% of all protest acts involved some type of public disorder, and 15% included some act of violence (the categories are not mutually exclusive).[12]

In addition the costs of breaking the law are rather low because the police are very reluctant to arrest protesters. Those who carry out illegal acts which are peaceful have about a 12% chance of experiencing at least one arrest. Non-violent disturbances lead to arrests in 24% of the cases and even the use of violence only leads to arrests in 37% of the acts. Group leaders, then, have a better than even chance of breaking the law with impunity. This may be one reason why the number of illegal acts in Israel appears to be so high.

It is true that many of these acts involve pseudo violence, such as informing the police before illegally blocking a road. Injuries were reported in only 19% of the disorderly and violent events and 70% of these were light injuries (see Appendix for coding). As futher described below, the politics of provocation are often based on a strategy of "uncivil disobedience."[13] Such acts tend to be rude and disruptive and different in spirit than civil disobedience, but intentionally fall short of uncontrolled violence. Nevertheless, the contempt for law and order which accompanies such acts establishes a normative environment which is potentially very dangerous.

Sprinzak (1987) argued that "illegalism" is endemic to the political culture of Israel and has always been encouraged by the political elite. Finding ways to bypass bureaucratic obstacles is a well-known tradition in Israel (Danet and Hartment 1972, Danet. In press). As the number of such acts grow, however, so may their impact. The climate of cynicism leads some to go beyond the normal limits of disobedience; fringe groups may be the most affected by the change in political temperament. It is no coincidence that the vigilantes of the eighties were the same people engaged in the creation of illegal settlements in the seventies (Sprinzak 1987; Weisburd and Vinitzky 1984).

There is then, both good news and bad news for Israeli society. On the positive side is the fact that new modes of political action are creating novel opportunities for political communication. Citizens who would have been shut out of the political process a few years ago are getting a real chance to be heard. There is, however, a social cost attached to this new political channel. The politics of Israel are characterized by an increasing number of direct actions which are either illegal, disorderly, or violent. Surely a more orderly form of communication would incur fewer risks for this relatively new democracy.

It is useful, in light of these findings, to compare the Israeli experience with that of other countries.

A CROSS-CULTURAL PERSPECTIVE

The concept of political culture is inevitably associated with the perspective of comparative politics (Almond and Verba 1963). It is difficult to measure the political orientations and behavior of Israelis without comparing them to citizens living in other countries. The concepts of high involvement and low efficacy, for example, can only be verified in relative terms. Making such comparisons is dependent upon the ability of researchers to be explicit in defining and measuring the concepts under study.

One of the most important studies of this type is *Political Action* by Barnes and Kaase (1979). Although the book deals with five countries, data was collected in a total of eight different nations during the mid-seventies: Great Britain, Germany, The Netherlands, Austria, the United States, Italy, Switzerland, and Finland. Some of the questions used in that study were given to a representative sample of 631 Israelis in December of 1984 (see Methodological Appendix). Although it is unfortunate that there is a gap of ten years between the surveys, there is reason to believe that the basic distribution of orientations and behavior did not change much in Europe or the U.S. during that time.[14] In any case it offers the best opportunity available to compare the political culture of Israel.[15]

The comparison will be divided into two major sections: political orientations and political behavior. Political orientations refer to beliefs about politics which characterize a given political culture. In keeping with the theme of blocked opportunities, this particular comparison will be focused on the gap between psychological involvement and institutional efficacy in the various countries and cultural assumptions about the ways in which demands are made on the political system. The ways in which beliefs are translated into action are described in the section on political behavior. The uniqueness of Israel is demonstrated by looking at levels of institutional action, mobilized action (protest), and political action repertoires.

Political Orientations

The politics of provocation, it was argued, are based on three components: high discontent, high psychological involvement, and low institutional efficacy. Although it was not possible to offer a comparison about levels of discontent, evidence about the involvement/efficacy gap is available. Psychological involvement was measured by asking respondents in all nine countries about the extent to which they "read about politics in the newspapers," "talked about political subjects," and tried to "convince others to vote as they did."[16] Institutional efficacy was measured by assessing the degree of agreement with three statements: 1) "I don't think public officials care much about what people like me think." 2) "Generally speaking, those we elect to Parliament lose touch with the people pretty quickly." 3) "Parties are only interested in people's votes, but not their opinions." The results of this comparison are presented in Table 1–2.

As can be seen, the intensity of psychological involvement in Israel is unequaled by that in any other country. Although some countries approach the level of reading about politics exhibited by Israelis, no group of citizens spends nearly as much time talking about politics or trying to convince others how to vote. Israel has, as claimed, a uniquely high level of psychological involvement.

Their level of institutional efficacy, on the other hand, is relatively low, although it varies among the three questions. In keeping with previous arguments, Israelis appear to be especially cynical about the responsiveness of the political parties. Only Italy has less faith in the parties and has a notably similar type of electoral system. Unlike citizens in Israel, however, Italians also have a relatively low level of psychological involvement.

Indeed, as might be expected from previous work (Almond and Verba 1963; Verba and Nie 1972; Verba, Nie, and Kim 1978), psychological involvement appears to be generally correlated with institutional efficacy. Although Israel has the highest level of involvement, however, it has the sixth highest level of institutional efficacy. No other country in the analysis exhibits such a disparity and this lends support to the claim about an influence gap in Israel.

A second piece of evidence is even more revealing about the ways in which the Israeli political culture is unique. Respondents were asked the following open-ended question (taken from Almond and

Table 1–2

Psychological Involvement and Institutional Efficacy

PSYCHOLOGICAL INVOLVEMENT	Israel	U.S.	G.B.	Ger.	Neth.	Aus.	It.	Swit.	Fin.
1. Reads about Politics in Newspaper	81[a]	76	67	74	66	59	38	67	63
2. Talks about Politics	81	65	47	43	52	45	34	49	52
3. Tries to Convince Others to Vote as Him	38	19	9	22	10	17	19	14	11
Mean Score (Grand Mean = 45.0)	66.7	53.3	41.0	46.3	42.7	40.3	30.3	43.3	42.0

INSTITUTIONAL EFFICACY	Israel	U.S.	G.B.	Ger.	Neth.	Aus.	It.	Swit.	Fin.
1. Public Officials Don't Care	39[b]	44	31	33	41	28	19	38	33
2. Those We Elect Lose Touch	23	30	27	21	26	21	12	27	22
3. Parties are Only Interested in Votes	21	38	29	38	44	26	16	35	26
Mean Score (Grand Mean = 29.2)	27.6	37.3	29.0	30.6	37.0	25.0	15.7	33.3	27.0

a. Involvement scores represent percentage of sample which responded "Frequently" or "Sometimes."

b. Institutional Efficacy scores are percentage reporting "Disagree Very Much" and "Disagree." The higher the score, the higher the sense of efficacy.

Verba 1963): "Suppose a law were being considered by the Knesset, which you considered to be very unjust or harmful; what do you think you could do"? It is useful to look at the responses to this question as a description of the first "avenues of influence" people consider. The results presented in Table 1–3 summarize the percentage in each country who responded "nothing," "contact leader," and "to demonstrate."

Table 1–3
What Can You Do to Change a Law?

COUNTRY[a]	Nothing	Contact Leaders	Demonstrate
Israel	40.4	5.4 (9.1)[b]	13.2 (22.2)
United States	14.5	65.4 (76.5)	.3 (.4)
Great Britain	33.7	52.8 (79.6)	.6 (.8)
Germany	41.4	12.8 (21.9)	4.9 (8.3)
Netherlands	45.2	5.4 (9.9)	3.6 (6.6)
Austria	54.9	4.0 (8.9)	2.9 (6.4)
Switzerland	17.8	3.6 (5.6)	.5 (.8)
Finland	42.9	10.2 (19.0)	.7 (3.3)
Mean	36.4	(28.8)	(6.1)
Median	40.9	(14.5)	(4.9)

a. This question was not asked in Italy.

b. The first percentage is based on the total number of responses, whereas the second is calculated among those who mentioned some type of action.

Twenty–two percent of all Israelis who said they could do something about an unjust law reported that they would demonstrate. This is the highest proportion in any country, and the only country where demonstrations were the most likely choice (apart from "nothing"). In keeping with the lack of personal representation in Israel, only 9% of those who chose a path of influence suggested they would turn to a political leader. Some other countries are even more unlikely to consider contacting a leader their first choice, but they would choose other alternatives. In Switzerland, for example, the modal choice was to initiate a referendum, whereas citizens from Austria mentioned petitions most.

It is also useful to compare the political beliefs in Israel with those held in the United States. Although both have high levels of psychological involvement, the United States has a much higher level of institutional efficacy than Israel. This level of faith in the political leadership is indicated in Table 1–3. Very few Americans say there is nothing they can do to change a law, and the vast majority first think about writing to their representatives in Congress.

Each culture has its own conventional paths of response, and for Israel demonstrations clearly fill this role. As will be seen, these orientations are also reflected in the nature of Israeli political behavior.

Political Behavior

Most previous studies of political participation in Israel are related to the period before the politics of provocation became dominant and mobilized action became so popular. Etzioni-Halevy (1977), based on data from the early seventies, came to the conclusion that Israelis were basically interested spectators due to their sense of being blocked from institutional participation. Galnoor's (1982) study deals with the nature of political participation in Israel until 1965. He claimed that Israelis tend to have high rates of responsive participation (voting) but rather low levels of committed (campaign work, unorganized initiatives) types of action. As indicated, Lehman-Wilzig (1983) was the first to point to a high level of protest activity in Israel but used survey questions which could not be compared to those used in *Political Action*.

It is important to be explicit about what is being measured in the present research. The definition of political action used in this study is taken directly from the classic work of Verba and Nie (1972): "Those activities by private citizens that are more or less directly aimed at influencing the selection of government personnel and/or the actions they take." The research does not deal with Israelis' voting behavior, which has been studied by others (Arian 1972, 1975, 1980, 1983; Caspi, Diskin, and Gutmann 1984). As amply shown by Verba, Nie, and Kim (1978) the act of voting is qualitatively different from all other forms of political behavior and the present concern is with less universal types of participation.

Institutional action refers to all types of political action which are organized within the established political institutions of a country. *Mobilized action* refers to all attempts to have an influence which are organized outside of the formal political system. As with any such definition, there are borderline cases which are not easy to categorize. How, for example, is contacting a politician through writing a letter distinguished from submitting a petition? Although some empirical evidence on this issue is presented later on, it suffices to say that when an individual writes to a representative, the only organization involved is the Parliament. Petition campaigns, on the other hand, are usually organized by some type of external pressure group. The definition of behavior as conventional or unconventional (Barnes and Kaase 1979) is based on implicit assumptions about the frequency of different actions, which, as is shown below, are questionable.

The data presented until now suggested that Israelis should have a high level of mobilized action and a low level of institutionalized participation. The results shown in Table 1–4 allow more specificity.

The level of institutional action is indeed, below average. Israelis exhibit a relatively low level of community work and attendance at political meetings and an especially low level of contacting public officials. Their level of campaigning, on the other hand, is about average. Israelis' extremely high level of psychological involvement is not reflected in their level of institutional participation. Once again the contrast with the United States is glaring. Americans have high levels of involvement, high levels of institutional efficacy, and high levels of institutional action: they are indeed citizens of the classic civic culture (Almond and Verba 1963).

Israelis, on the other hand, are more likely to convert their psychological involvement into protest, specifically demonstrations. Sixteen percent of all Israelis have participated in demonstrations, which is second only to the Italians, a result which parallels the results concerning the lack of faith in political parties. Equally important, the proportion of Israelis who have demonstrated is higher than for any institutional activity, other than community work (and, of course, voting). In this sense the use of demonstrations in Israel can be considered conventional political behavior.

The results with regard to the other forms of mobilized behavior do not offer any clear cut patterns. Although a relatively high 35% of Israelis have signed petitions, there are several countries in which this more passive mode of action is better developed. This may be due to the fact that petitions tend to be a borderline case of mobilized action, more dependent on the good will of political leaders.

As to the illegal forms of protest, it is difficult to make any serious comparisons, because of the small numbers involved and the assumedly low reliability of such threatening questions in surveys. In general, however, the percentage of Israelis who admitted to carrying out such acts seems to be very close to the levels reported in the other countries. Whatever the level of public sympathy for such acts, or the number of such acts which seem to take place, few Israelis reported having actually participated in such events.[17]

In light of the arguments made earlier, the more interesting question is whether or not Israelis participate in demonstrations in-

Table 1–4
Institutional Action and Mobilized Action

INSTITUTIONAL ACTION	Israel	U.S.	G.B.	Ger.	Neth.	Aus.	It.	Swit.	Fin.
1. Community Work	19[a]	38	17	14	18	14	19	21	33
2. Political Meeting	11	19	9	22	7	19	21	17	19
3. Contact Official	10	28	11	11	14	12	9	15	12
4. Political Campaign	8	15	5	9	3	6	7	10	7

MOBILIZED ACTION	Israel	U.S.	G.B.	Ger.	Neth.	Aus.	It.	Swit.	Fin.
1. Signed Petition	34.6	60.1	23.0	30.4	21.3	39.7	16.5	45.5	20.5
2. Demonstration	15.7	12.1	6.0	8.3	6.8	7.2	17.2	8.4	5.9
3. Refuse to Pay Rent/Taxes	1.7	2.5	1.9	.8	3.9	1.1	1.7	.7	.4
4. Wildcat Strikes	1.3	2.0	4.9	.9	1.7	2.0	1.2	.3	4.5
5. Sit-ins	1.1	1.5	.6	.1	1.4	.4	4.4	.6	3.9
6. Block Traffic	.8	1.3	1.2	1.6	1.2	1.4	2.0	1.0	.3
7. Damage Property	.3	.5	.5	.3	.3	.2	.5	.3	.5
8. Violence	.3	.9	.2	.3	.4	.2	.3	.2	.4

a. Percentage of sample responding "Often" or "Sometimes."

stead of using institutional processes. The politics of provocation occur when a significant proportion of citizens participates exclusively in direct action, due to their sense of being shut out of institutional modes of action. The psychological evidence is presented in a later analysis, but it is important to first establish the extent to which the politics of provocation are unique to Israel.

Respondents in each of the nine countries were divided into four action types on the basis of their political behavior. *Inactives* were citizens who didn't carry out any form of political action. *Conformists* were citizens who carried out exclusively institutional actions. They confined their political participation to one or more conventional types of activities: community work, political meetings, contacting an official, and/or participating in a political campaign. *Dissidents* were characterized by the opposite type of political action repertoire: they took part in at least one form of protest, but abstained from any institutional activity. The final action type, *Pragmatists*, exhibited the most interesting repertoire; they reported carrying out at least one type of activity from each mode of action. For the purposes of this particular analysis, signing a petition was not considered a form of political action.[18]

The four types represent then, those who don't participate in either form of action, those who choose between institutional and mobilized action, and those who take part in both. If political behavior in Israel is indeed ruled by the politics of provocation, Israelis should show a distinct preference for Dissidence over Conformity. The empirical evidence presented in Table 1–5 documents this tendency.

Israelis are more likely than citizens from other countries to use mobilized action as an alternative to institutional actions. A quarter of all Israelis who are active confine themselves to protest (mostly demonstrations), a figure unequaled in any other country studied. Israel also has the lowest percentage of Conformists, despite Israelis' high level of psychological involvement.

It is interesting to again compare the profiles of Israel with that of the United States and Italy. The United States, it will be remembered, was characterized as a classic civic culture (Almond and Verba 1963): high involvement, high efficacy and high institutional action. It is no surprise therefore that 74% of those who are active confine themselves to the traditional means of expressing their opinions, whereas only 9% are Dissidents.

Italy, on the other hand, was the only country with a higher rate of demonstrations, but as can be seen, a greater proportion of Italians (11.7%) combined this activity with some form of institutional participation. Although there appear to be many similarities between the case of Israel and Italy, Italians have a more diverse type of action repertoire.

Table 1–5
Political Action Repertoires

COUNTRY	TYPE			
	Inactive	Conformist	Dissident	Pragmatist
1. Israel	62.2	20.5 (54.2)[a]	9.4 (24.7)	7.9 (21.0)
2. United States	43.9	41.5 (73.9)	5.0 (9.0)	9.6 (17.1)
3. Great Britain	61.2	21.0 (66.0)	6.1 (19.3)	4.6 (14.6)
4. Germany	65.8	24.4 (71.3)	4.2 (12.4)	5.6 (16.2)
5. Netherlands	67.6	21.0 (64.8)	6.4 (19.8)	4.9 (15.2)
6. Austria	68.6	24.2 (77.9)	2.9 (9.2)	4.3 (13.6)
7. Italy	61.3	21.7 (56.2)	5.3 (13.6)	11.7 (30.2)
8. Switzerland	62.6	27.9 (74.9)	4.4 (11.8)	5.1 (13.7)
9. Finland	54.7	35.0 (77.3)	4.2 (9.3)	6.0 (13.2)

a. First number is based on percentage of all respondents, whereas the number in parentheses represents the proportion of those who carried out at least one political behavior (i.e., Inactives are excluded).

It is clear that modern Israel offers an important case for the study of political action. It is a relatively unique example of an intensely political society, where citizens have found a way to overcome institutional obstacles to political participation. The political party, which once monopolized Israeli politics, is no longer the only game in town. Israelis are no longer willing to play the part of interested spectators: a good deal of political involvement is now taking place in the streets.

The national perspective represents only the first piece in a more complex puzzle. The major problem with this level of analysis is that it deals in averages. This form of statistical shorthand often obscures as much as it clarifies. Other parts of the puzzle tell us more about who protests in Israel, why they do, and why some use violence whereas others do not.

The implications of these results, however, go beyond the borders of Israel. The themes which are developed are based on a rational choice approach to political action. The politics of provocation and blocked opportunities which characterize Israeli political culture are only one of many possible patterns of political behavior. What is needed is a more general framework to serve as a guide for explaining such variations. The second chapter is devoted to setting the foundations for just such a model.

Chapter 2

THE ANALYTICAL
FRAMEWORK

The subject of political action has, until now, been studied from two very different perspectives. The first is the study of political participation, mostly carried out by political scientists concerned with how individual citizens get involved in politics (for a review see Milbrath and Goel 1977). The early studies in this field (Milbrath 1965; Almond and Verba 1963; Verba and Nie 1972) emphasized the institutionalized modes of making demands and did not consider protest a form of participation. More recent studies (Barnes, Kaase, et al. 1979; Muller 1979), on the other hand, have pointed to the use of protest and even political violence as an alternative means of making demands on the political system. In support of this view they have pointed to the fact that the two modes of political action are correlated (Barnes, Kaase, et al. 1979).

Sociologists and social historians studying collective behavior have undergone a similar transition in thought (for reviews see Jenkins 1983: Eckstein 1980; Snyder 1978). Traditionally, such researchers (Durkheim 1951; Kornhauser 1959) considered protests and political violence as abnormal deviations from a perfect social order. The mass society approach claimed that the lost souls of society were often attracted to protest movements as a means of affiliation and a vent for frustration. The more recent work in the field, however, sees social conflict as inevitable and has turned the academic focus on the issues of how groups are formed (Olson 1965), the mobilization of collective resources (McCarthy and Zald 1979; Oberschall 1973; Tilly 1978), and strategies of protest (Gamson 1975). Labelled the *resource mobiliza-*

tion approach, this school of thought emphasizes the rational aspects of collective action: the "organization of discontent" (Snyder 1978).

Although they use different labels, the researchers from these two fields often use similar concepts to describe the political behavior of both individuals and groups. Both, for example, talk of the centrality of resources in establishing the potential for political action; each has its own version of the rational actor model in which participants weigh costs and benefits, and both schools of thought attempt to explain how background factors affect political action.

It is possible to use these similarities to build a general framework which aids in explaining both levels of political behavior. This attempt at theoretical integration is designed to provide a rudimentary outline for a more comprehensive theory of political action. The first section of this chapter is devoted to developing such a framework, whereas the second part deals with the methodological strategy of the study.

THE ANALYTICAL FRAMEWORK

The theoretical structure rests on four conceptual pillars, as illustrated in Figure 2–1. Background, mobilization, evaluation, and behavior are explanatory constructs which can be applied to a wide variety of social behaviors. They are set in logical order which is meant to suggest that each stage is dependent on (but not necessarily caused by) that which precedes it.

The model begins with the notion that actors are born into a social context which has a critical effect on the crystallization of interests and the mobilization of resources. The nature and extent of interests and resources establish a certain potential for political action. A strategy is then developed which is designed to realize interests through the best possible utilization of resources. The repertoire which is finally chosen reflects the limits determined by the actor's resources, the goals set by interests, and the evaluations about the political system.

An elaboration of these points shows how each of these ideas is well grounded in previous research findings about both individuals and groups.

Background

The effects of social background have been a central concern in studies of both political participation and collective action. The

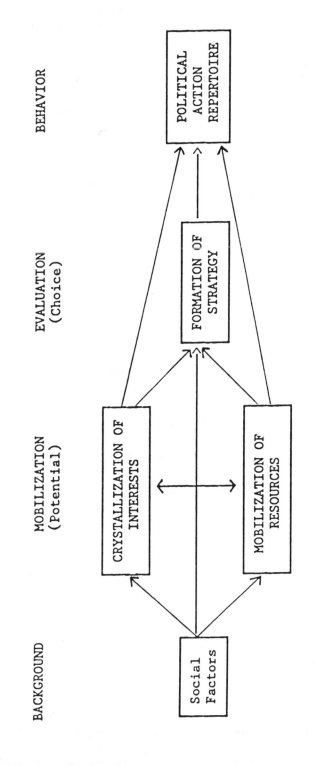

Figure 2–1
An Analytical Framework for the Study of Political Action Repertoires

model guiding Verba and Nie's (1972, 19) work is labelled the "standard socioeconomic model of political participation" and claims that socioeconomic status is the key to understanding both the extent and the mode of action. This finding has been replicated in every country in which the issue has been studied(Barnes, Kaase, et al. 1979; Verba, Nie, and Kim 1978).

Socioeconomic status is usually operationalized in such studies in terms of levels of education and income. Both of these factors have clear effects on the crystallization of political interests and the mobilization of resources. Citizens from more privileged homes are more likely to be exposed to political information and to form political attitudes (Almond and Verba 1963). These interests serve as a motivating force towards action. In addition, assets such as money and free time greatly aid the process of political mobilization.

Differences in social status also affect the ability of *groups* to mobilize. Protest groups organized by the poor, for example, have few resources to pool (Piven and Cloward 1979). They must elicit the good will of a third party, such as the general public, if they are to have any hope of influencing the authorities (Lipsky 1970).

The most important social factor for groups, however, is the level of internal organization of the population. Proponents of resource mobilization believe that organization is the necessary condition for both the mobilization of resources and sustained political action. Oberschall (1973) was one of the first to counter the myths of the traditionalists by pointing out that almost all action groups are formed on the foundations of some prior collective structure. The results of Gamson's (1975) study of American protest groups also illustrate the centrality of organization in any attempt to explain collective action.

Charles Tilly (1978) has developed the most detailed model of resource mobilization. He defines organization as "the extent of common identity and unifying structure among the individuals in a population." As with most social factors, a group's level of organization can change. In general, however, most groups are born with certain traits which define their limits of organization. Such factors as geographic dispersion, cultural differences, and demographic homogeneity all affect the internal structure of a group.

Organization has a direct effect on both the definition of collective interests and the mobilization of resources. The more organized a group, the more it can become "combat ready" (Gamson 1975) by establishing clear goals and gaining collective control over assets essential for sustained action. Just as socio-economic status provides the motivation and the ability for political participation, so organization is the key to developing a potential for collective action.

Social factors also have a direct effect on the formation of an action *strategy*. Attitudes towards participation are often based on cultural norms and expectations which serve as informational buffers for both individuals and groups. Such factors as age, ethnicity, and education all have an influence on the ways in which political actors make choices about political behavior. This is the reason why there is a direct line of dependency between social factors and the formation of strategy, as shown in Figure 2–1.

Mobilization

It is the process of mobilization which determines an actor's *potential* for political action. The analytical framework is focused on two aspects of that process: the mobilization of resources and the crystallization of interests. Each of these factors has significant effects on both the formation of strategy and the development of a political action repertoire.

The crystallization of interests is the motivating force behind both individual and collective political action. The literature on individual participation (Almond and Verba 1963; Verba and Nie 1972; Verba, Nie and Kim 1978) relates to two such interests: partisanship and civic-mindedness. Partisan interests drive citizens to participate in favor of specific political goals whereas civic-mindedness generates a more general need for political influence. The nature and extent of partisan and civic interests have been shown to have a direct influence on choices about political participation.

The quality of shared interests is the driving force behind collective mobilization. Members of a population join together to realize advantages or prevent disadvantages (Tilly 1978). During a period of mobilization, collective definitions of interests are disseminated among potential group members to create a sense of solidarity. The nature of shared interest affects group strategy and action.

Tilly (1978), for example, made a distinction between an offensive mobilization in which groups attempt to achieve new advantages and a defensive mobilization where group members try to protect themselves from harm. Each type of mobilization was historically associated with different forms of collective action. Such acts as food riots, tax rebellions, and draft resistance were employed as reactive tactics, whereas strikes were almost always used for the pursuit of new advantages.[1]

The mobilization of resources has also proven to be an important element in both individual and collective action. The difference between the haves and have nots is a theme which is stressed in both schools of thought. Resources have an effect on the crystallization of interests, the formation of strategy, and the nature of political action itself.

Wealth of any kind creates a new set of priorities, and often the preservation of resources becomes an interest in and of itself. In addition, actors with greater resources are likely to expand their interests when they have the luxury of choosing from a greater number of goals (McCarthy and Zald, 1977).

The level of resources also affects strategies of action. Those with limited resources rarely have many alternatives to consider. As Tilly (1978, p. 75) suggested, any type of mobilization is always the most expensive for the poor. Actors with expendable resources can develop political experience on a trial and error basis whereas those without such assets must rely more on intuition, as they are unlikely to have more than one opportunity to act (Wolfsfeld 1984a). A rational plan of political action must include a strategy which reflects the actor's level of resources.

The model claims that resources have a direct effect on political action, above and beyond any perceptions about interests and strategies. Those with resources can hire lawyers and media consultants or contribute to political campaigns. Those with political knowledge can give speeches and articulate demands, whereas the politically ignorant usually lack such skills. The wealthier the actor's store of resources, the richer the political action repertoire.

Evaluation: The Formation of Strategy

Almost all the modern literature on political action is based on a rational choice model of behavior. Although the definitions of costs and benefits may vary, the axiom of rationality can be found in research on both individuals and groups.

The proponents of rational choice among scholars of individual political action have had an especially important impact on the study of protest and violence. The choice between conventional and unconventional forms of political action is based on preceptions about the relative efficacy of each mode of action (Barnes and Kaase 1979; Wolfsfeld 1986a, 1986b). Muller and Opp (1986) have provided the most comprehensive model of rational choice and offer strong evidence about the ways in which individuals weigh the costs and benefits associated with political violence.

The notion of rational choice is also a central component of the resource mobilization approach to collective action. As Oberschall (1973) put it:

> The individuals who are faced with resource management decisions make rational choices based on the pursuit of their selfish interests in an enlightened manner. They weigh the rewards and sanctions, costs and benefits that alternative courses of action represent for them. (p. 29)

In his (1975) book, *The Strategy of Social Protest,* Gamson examined the ways in which groups struggle to find the optimal program for realizing collective interests. One of the more intriguing analyses centers on the "success of the unruly." The fact that collective violence is not always self-defeating offers another piece of evidence about the rationality of strategic choices.

Political Action Repertoires

Political action repertoires serve as the major dependent variable in this study. The term repertoire was chosen to reinforce the notion that political actors choose from a variety of participatory options, and each mode carries with it a set of appropriate skills and resources. The construct is also useful in reminding us that the various actions can be combined in a complex array of strategic styles.

Verba and Nie (1972) were the first to point out that political participation was not unidimensional: there are qualitative differences among the different modes of participation. Although these authors confined themselves to the more conventional types of participation, they emphasized the importance of understanding the variations in skills, motivations, and choices which are associated with each type of act.

Barnes, and Kaase (1979) took this notion one step further by looking at ways in which individuals created an action repertoire by mixing and matching both conventional and unconventional modes of behavior.[2] It was found useful, for example, to distinguish between citizens who used both conventional and unconventional modes of action and those who confined themselves to only one form of participation.

Tilly (1978) used the term repertoire in a more general sense. The range of group choice, he argued, is limited to those behaviors which are known in a given culture and time. The repertoires of a given society are related to factors such as "the daily routines of the population," their "accumulated experience with collective action," and "the pattern of repression in the world to which the population belongs" (p. 156). The term repertoire in this study refers to the set of political actions carried out by a given actor.

The major goal of this research project is to explain the political action repertoires of both individuals and groups. It is worthwhile to look at variations in political action from a number of perspectives. First, one wants to say something about the *extent* of political action, i.e., how much political behavior is actually carried out. A second concern relates to the *intensity* of a political action repertoire. Action choices range between legal and institutionalized forms of participation to outright violence. Finally, it is important to explain the relative *flexibility* of a repertoire. Why do some actors confine themselves to one kind of activity but others use a more varied approach to making demands? The theories presented later in this work attempt to answer just these questions.

Some Conceptual Gaps

The theoretical framework lays out a very large research agenda. It is important, however, to also clarify what has been left out. The most significant factors are effects which can be attributed to external forces and agents, which set the context of political action. Government authorities, for example, take actions which affect the mobilization and evaluations of both individuals and groups. Political leaders create threats and opportunities as well as raise and lower the costs and benefits of political action. Other actors, such as peers, the mass media, and rival protest groups also have important effects on political action repertoires.

It is useful to create an initial model, however, which establishes the basic laws of behavior before attempting to deal with interactive effects. The logic of this claim is based on the assumption that social interactions are best understood within a given cultural context. In the present study, the effects of outside forces are dealt with in the qualitative analyses which emphasize the issues and actors which are specific to Israel. Hopefully, some of the lessons from these sections can be incorporated into a more comprehensive model.

A second element which was not considered in the theoretical framework concerns the relationship between the individual and the group. The model deals with each actor separately by adapting a general theoretical framework to each level of analysis. It does not deal with the issue of how groups recruit individuals and gives only a very partial explanation about why individuals join groups.[3] The interaction between the two levels of analysis is an important subject, but goes beyond the scope of the present study.

THE METHODOLOGICAL APPROACH

The methodological strategy employed in the present study was based on three basic principles: multiple methods, multiple indicators, and direct definitions.

The first principle has already been discussed and is based on the assumption that no one methodology is ideal for the study of political action: each has its strengths which contribute to the overall pattern of results. This principle was implemented by using both structured and unstructured methods of data collection.

The two major methods used were a representative national survey of Israeli adults to study individual participation and an analysis of newspaper articles about protest groups. The survey was conducted in the spring of 1982, and the news articles covered protests which occurred between 1979 and 1984 (see Methodological Appendix).

In both cases, a sequential model (Louis 1982) was adopted whereby the quantitative data was collected first, followed by qualitative observations which provided a deeper understanding of social dynamics (Sieber, 1978). Approximately a hundred of those who had participated in the national survey were reinterviewed using a less structured interview. Similarly, after completing a rigorous content analysis of newspaper stories on protest activities, interviews were carried out with protest leaders to obtain a more detailed account of group resources, strategy, and action. This use of the complementary perspectives offered a degree of insight which would have been otherwise impossible.

The principle of multiple indicators was based on a similar set of assumptions. The survey questionnaire was built by using as many different questions as possible to measure the same underlying variable. Psychological involvement, for example, was measured using questions which asked about political interest, reading about politics in the newspaper, and discussing politics. Using more than one indicator assures a more reliable measure of the variables. Two different newspapers were used in the content analysis of protest groups. This allowed for an extensive test of the validity of the sampling sources.

It was also deemed important to operationally define the variables under study in as direct a manner as possible. Survey respondents were asked explicitly about motivations and beliefs; there was no need for camouflage or deception. A measure of institutional efficacy, for example, simply asked the respondents about the extent to which they believed that various acts (e.g., campaigning) were effective.

In the newspaper analysis, the code sheet was based almost entirely on information which could be taken directly from the article, with no interpretation on the part of the coder. Coders were often required to give to their work reliability scores which distinguished between data which was taken directly from the text and that which was based on inferences.

Despite the multitude of methods, not all the challenges presented by the general model could be met. Some of these limitations are inherent to the research methodologies employed, whereas others are a function of the more mundane, yet critical factor known as funding. The survey section is strongest in its attempt to measure and explain the ways in which people make choices about political action. It is weaker in dealing with the variables related to resources and interests. Similarly, although the group data is extremely detailed when it deals with the repertoires of collective actions, it is far less precise in characterizing the nature of collective resources or the dynamics of group strategy. In both cases, however, the qualitative material helps compensate for these weaknesses.

A final note is in order about the research strategy which guided this project. It is hoped that readers find that the study was as dedicated to exploration as it was to verification. Many of the findings were unexpected, but few were ignored. There was an attempt to fit each piece of empirical evidence into the complicated puzzle known as political action. Although there are still many pieces missing, the theories, hypotheses, and results of this study provide a good deal of information about their shape and size.

Chapter 3

WHO, WHAT, AND WHY: EXPLAINING INDIVIDUAL PARTICIPATION _____

What types of Israelis get involved in politics? Why do they do it? Why do some Israelis only participate in one type of action, whereas others particiapte in many? How can the psychological roots of the politics of provocation best be explained? These are the questions grappled with in chapters 3 and 4. The model presented in the last section serves as an explanatory map which points towards some answers. A more detailed version of the map is needed before starting out on our journey into the realm of individual political behavior. The map is presented in Figure 3–1.

The diagram offers a convenient outline of the logic behind the chapter. The constructs which are underlined in the figure are considered essential to the model, whereas other variables are specific indicators used in the present study. The list is not intended to be exhaustive, but does provide a significant test of the model. The two variables set in parenthesis could not be measured directly, but their effects can be inferred from other pieces of evidence.

The map also provides a guide to the organization of the chapter. The first section deals with the relationship between social background and mobilization, the second is concerned with understanding how people make evaluations and develop a stragety of action, and the final part explains how these orientations are translated into political behavior.

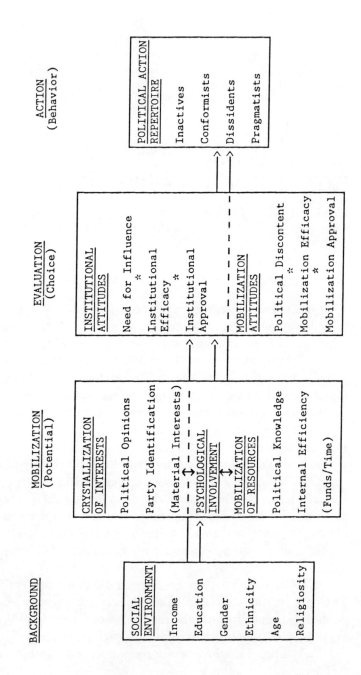

Figure 3–1
Explaining Individual Political Action

BACKGROUND AND MOBILIZATION: DEVELOPING A POTENTIAL FOR ACTION

The model presented in Figure 3–1 emphasizes the importance of social background in explaining who gets involved in politics. All the variables used to explain differences in Israeli involvement are taken directly from studies carried out in other countries. Income, education, gender, ethnicity, age, and religiosity have all been found to have a significant effect on both institutional participation (Milbrath and Goel 1977; Verba and Nie 1972; Verba, Nie, and Kim 1978) and mobilized action (Barnes and Kaase 1979; Muller 1979).

The model is especially indebted to Verba and Nie's (1972) work in which it is claimed that *psychological involvement* in politics is the central variable explaining the potential for action. A lack of psychological involvement makes it difficult for certain citizens to participate in the democratic process. Such individuals are less likely to read or talk about politics and less likely to develop political opinions.

The degree to which these tendencies are determined by social differences are an important indicator of political equality. If certain ethnic groups take less of an interest in politics, they are less likely to make political demands and less likely to have an impact on policy (Verba and Nie 1972). The question of who is to blame for political apathy is really secondary. The important question is whether or not certain Israelis are born with an inherent disadvantage in political potential.

The measure of psychological involvement used in this study was based on three questions in the national survey. The first asked how interested the person was in politics, the second how much they read about politics in the newspaper, and the third how often they talked about politics, among their friends. The three indicators were designed to tap a need for political information, the search for information, and the use of information.

Socioeconomic Status

The effects of certain social differences appear to be universal. As discussed earlier, socio-economic status (usually measured through education and income) has been found to affect the level of political involvement in every country in which it has been studied (Milbrath and Goel 1977; Verba and Nie 1972; Barnes and Kaase 1979). Israel is no exception to that rule and the two strongest correlates of psychological involvement in politics are education (r = .28) and income $(r = .26)$.[1] Such class differences bring many other advantages such as free time and the ability to speak and write well. If individuals have no political interest or knowledge, however, these factors will rarely come into play.

Gender

The more interesting questions about differences in political concern the effects of factors such as gender, ethnicity, and religiosity. Here the effect would be expected to depend more on cultural variations. Although most European women exhibit significantly less involvement than men, for example, the gender gap in America appears to be negligible (Verba, Nie, and Kim 1978; Welsh 1977; Barnes and Kaase 1979).

Are Israeli women less psychologically involved in politics than Israeli men? One of the earliest goals of the founders of Israel was to eliminate such differences between the sexes. Israeli women have served in the army from the beginning of the state. The differences between men and women coming from Eastern background, however, were quite dramatic, especially in terms of the division of labor (Bar-Yoseph 1978). Previous studies on political socialization (Adoni 1979) and women's representation in the political elite (Bar-Yoseph, 1978) both suggested that Israeli women are less likely to be politically mobilized than men.

To test this proposition the levels of psychological involvement for men and women were examined from three different levels of education and the results are presented in Figure 3–2. The raw values have been transformed so that the mean score is zero. Any positive score indicates a level of psychological involvement which is above the national average, whereas a negative score indicates that the group has less involvement than most other Israelis.

Israeli women from every educational level exhibit significantly less psychological involvement in politics than men. The most surprising result is that even college educated women are less involved than their male counterparts. The best explanation for these differences probably lies in the process of political socialization: Israeli children learn (like others) that politics is a predominantly male concern. Whether for reasons of socialization or conscious choice, many Israel women withdraw from the game of politics before they begin.

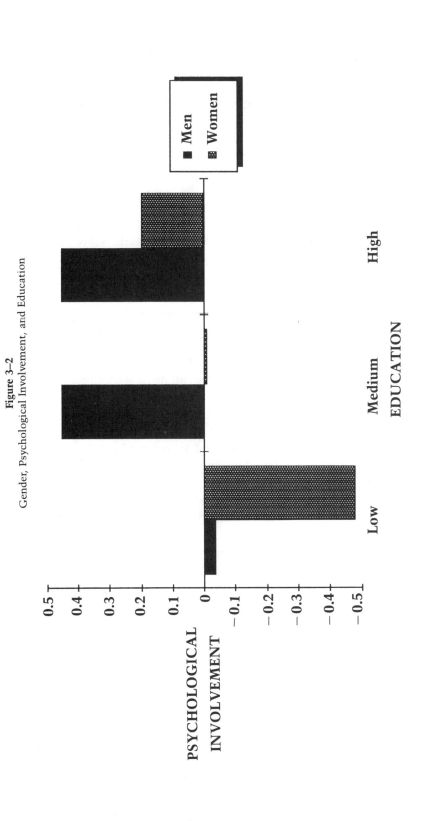

Figure 3–2
Gender, Psychological Involvement, and Education

Ethnicity

The importance of ethnic differences in Israeli society are obvious to even the most casual observer of that country. The major social distinction made about Israel concerns the differences between Ashkenazic Jews, whose cultural background can be traced to Europe or America, and Sephardic Jews, whose roots lie in Northern Africa and Asia. The differences between the two groups range across many social dimensions: Ashkenazic Jews tend to be better educated, less religious, and have smaller families. Most of the Sephardic families in Israel immigrated after the state was formed and many express a resentment about discrimination by the Ashkenazic elite.

The division between the two ethnic groups also has political overtones. Whereas the Ashkenazic Jews tend to support the more socialist and liberal political parties, most Sephardic Jews tend to vote for more right wing parties. The rise of the right in Israel is often attributed to demographic trends which show an increasingly large number of Sephardic voters (Arian 1985). It is clear then, why so much of the work on Israeli political behavior deals with these ethnic divisions.

The distinciton between Ashkenazic and Sephardic Jews is, however, somewhat misleading. Over 50% of the population of Israel was born in that country (Statistical Abstract of Israel 1985) and many are third generation Israelis. The intermarriage rate has been constantly increasing and the most recent figures show that about 26% of all Israelis marry outside their ethnic group. It is important to keep these facts in mind when ethnic differences in political orientations and behavior are examined.

Respondents to the survey were divided into the seven ethnic categories which are used in most national surveys in Israel. The categories are based on either the subjects' place of birth, or (if born in Israel) the father's place of birth.[2] The results are presented in Figure 3–3 and the scores have again been transformed to have a mean of zero. Presented in the figure are both the raw scores of each group and the adjusted scores which reflect the effects of controlling for education (i.e., holding education constant).[3] There are significant differences among the groups, even after controlling for education.

The distinction between Ashkenazic Jews and Sephardic Jews appears too simplistic. It is true that those born in Africa and Asia have the lowest level of involvement and that those with fathers born in Africa also score low on this measure. Children born in Israel of Asian parents, however, have a higher level of psychological involve-

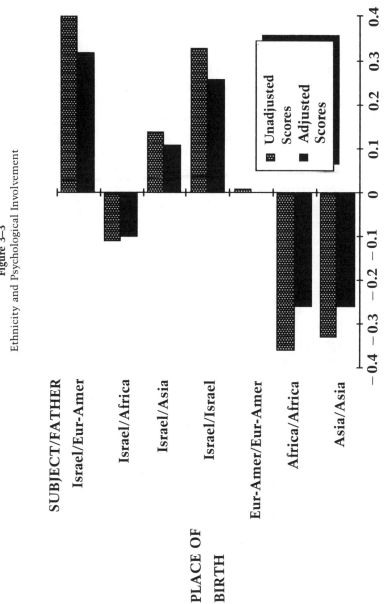

Figure 3–3
Ethnicity and Psychological Involvement

ment than respondents born in Europe. Furthermore, second generation Israelis, a group often ignored in such analyses, has the second highest level of psychological involvement. Indeed, four out of the five groups who were born in Israel have levels of psychological involvement which are above the population average, but none of those born abroad achieve this level.

A division based on place of birth seems to offer a more accurate portrait than one which looks at ethnicity alone. A native-born Israeli probably enjoys a number of advantages in political mobilization over the immigrant. Language skills, social ties, and a deeper sense of belonging all ease the way towards psychological involvement in politics.

These results could also be understood by considering different processes of political socialization. If, as is believed, such orientations are set at an early age (Merelman 1986), Israeli children are likely to undergo a very intensive brand of political socialization due to the impact of politics on every-day life. European children are also more likely to be exposed to political opinions than those born in Africa or Asia. Whatever the reason, an explanation based on place of birth tells more about differences in potential than one based solely on the distinction between Ashkenazim and Sephardim.[4]

Religiosity

Religiosity is the final social influence and one which is especially important within the political culture of Israel. The divisions between secular and religious Jews are in many ways much more significant than those defined by ethnicity (Liebman and Don-Yehiya 1983). Some of the bitterest political debates in Israel revolve around religious issues. Many secular Israelis resent laws such as those which forbid public transportation on the sabbath and which grant Rabbis control over marriages and divorces. Religious citizens express moral and political indignation over the lack of respect for Jewish law in Israel. Many religious Israelis have also been active in movements such as Gush Emunim, which oppose the return of any of the occupied territories.

In other countries, religious citizens tend to be less involved in politics (Barnes and Kaase 1979). It might be questioned whether this finding also applies in Israel, given the strong link between religiosity and politics. The results of the national survey, however, showed that the religious in Israel are, indeed, less psychologically involved in politics.[5] Whatever the impressions gathered from the media, there is a conflict between leading a religious life and being involved in politics.

Age

There is no relationship between age and psychological involvement in Israel. In contrast to the findings in other countries the youth of Israel have just as much potential for political action as their elders. As shall be seen, however, age does determine how that potential is translated into behavior.

Taken together these findings offer a valuable inventory for separating between Israelis who are rich in political information and those who are poor. The Israeli most likely to be psychologically involved in politics is a secular male born in Israel of Western parents who has achieved a higher education and an above average income. The least likely candidate is a religious female born in either Africa or Asia with less than a high school education and a poor income.[6] As is shown later, however, potential does not always translate directly into action.

Mobilization Through Involvement

What are the consequences of having a higher level of psychological involvement? According to the model presented earlier, psychological involvement serves as the catalyst for both the mobilization of informational resources and the crystallization of political interests. The process of mobilization also leads to evaluations of the political system and the development of a political action strategy. This is why involvement is seen as the key to political potential.

To test these assumptions, the survey contained a number of questions concerned with resources, interests, and evaluations. Informational resources were measured by a simple political knowledge test (given to the smaller sample), two questions about the respondents' understanding of the political concepts of left and right, and two questions measuring internal efficacy (e.g., subjective competence). The crystallization of political interests was measured through a question which asked about the degree to which respondents "tried to convince others how to vote." Finally, the degree to which a citizen made evaluations of the political system was based on separating those who did and did not give opinions about the political environment, government responsiveness, or their approval of various types of political acts.[7]

The results presented in Table 3–1 confirm the assertion that psychological involvement is a key factor in developing a potential for political action. There is a fairly strong correlation between involvement and informational control. The uninvolved citizen is unlikely to have neither the motivation nor the resources for participation and is unlikely to be a full partner in the democratic process.

Table 3–1
The Effects of Psychological Involvement

	The Mobilization of Resources		
	Political Knowledge	Left/Right Understanding	Internal Efficacy
Psychological Involvement	.26	.35	.36
(N)	(108)	(980)	(968)

	The Crystallization of Interests
	Opinion Leadership
Psychological Involvement	.41
(N)	(1,003)

	Political Evaluations		
	Political Environment	Efficacy of Actions	Approval of Actions
Psychological Involvement	.24	.23	.23
(N)	(900)	(932)	(932)

Some Other Factors

There are other variables, apart from psychological involvement, which affect both the crystallization of political interests and the mobilization of resources. The poor and the aged have an inherent interest in welfare benefits, for example, and their checks at the end of the month tell them more about this interest than any newspaper story. Furthermore, even those who want to make demands on the government may lack the physical resources to participate in any type of action. As shown in Figure 3–1, social forces have a direct impact on these two elements of mobilization, independent of their correlation with psychological involvement.

In the present context only one such relationship which is especially relevant to the present context is mentioned: the relationship between social background and political identification. The potential for political action is determined not only by having opinions, but also by the substance of those beliefs, by partisanship as well as civic-mindedness. Those generally opposed to the party in power, for example, are more likely to protest than those who identify with the government.

At the time of the survey, the government in power was formed by a coalition of the right-wing Likud party and several religious parties. The social differences between those who voted for and against the government are well documented (Shamir and Arian 1983; Caspi, Diskin, and Gutmann 1984) and some have been alluded to in earlier discussions. The citizens in Israel who generally support the leftist opposition parties tend to be Ashkenazic, better educated, less religious, and older. The effects of social differences on political identification are an important illustration of the link between social background and political interest and should be kept in mind as in the next stage of explanation.

STRATEGIES OF ACTION: EVALUATIONS AND CHOICE

The Components of Strategy

The findings presented up to this point generally have shown that inequalities in Israel resemble those found in other countries. Despite the unusually high level of psychological involvment in the politics of the country, the differences within the population run along familiar social dimensions. To understand the sense of frustration which leads to the politics of provocation it is necessary to move from the stage of mobilization to that of evaluation. It is here, when Israelis attempt to form a rational strategy of action, that understanding of the psychological roots of dissidence can begin.

In the model presented in Figure 3–1 the need to distinguish between *institutional and mobilization attitudes* is emphasized. This distinction is rooted in a central theme of the study: there is a qualitative difference between decisions to participate in institutional behavior and decisions associated with protest. An explanation of these differences begins by establishing the components of each set of attitudes.

The formulation of the present study is based on Ajzen and Fishbein's (1980) psychological model in which it is stated that attitudes towards any behavior can best be understood by examining three factors: the degree to which an individual *values outcomes* of that behavior, beliefs about the *likelihood of such outcomes*, and perceptions about the *social norms* associated with the behavior. In simpler terms, a person's attitude towards any act is determined by the degree to which he or she believes the action is worthwhile, likely to succeed, and socially acceptable.

Muller's (1979, 1982) work was the most explicit attempt to apply this model to the study of political action. His "expectancy-value-norm" theory was an important contribution to the field and offered a powerful tool for explaining the evaluations associated with both legal and illegal modes of action. The logic of the present effort runs along similar lines, but offers the alternative distinction between instutional and mobilized behavior.[8]

Returning to the elements presented in Figure 3–1, attitudes towards institutional actions are defined in terms of the *need to have political influence, institutional efficacy,* and *institutional approval* (Wolfsfeld 1985b, 1986a, 1986b). The need to have political influence is a useful way of summarizing the motivations associated with such acts as campaigning, attending a political meeting, or working in the community. The goals of such acts are general, and usually long range; the outcomes which are valued are often more personal and subjective.

As discussed earlier, institutional efficacy relates to the individual's beliefs about the efficacy of working within the system. Whatever the citizen's desire for political influence, he or she must also believe that it is possible. Many citizens share the belief that nothing comes out of political participation and this has a direct impact on their attitudes towards institutional action.

The final component of institutional attitudes is institutional approval. Although few citizens are morally opposed to institutional politics, some groups do have ideological objections to working within the system and others see all forms of politics as dirty. The concept of civic duty is also likely to vary among different social groups. The extent to which citizens internalize these norms should also affect their attitude toward institutional politics.

The elements which explain attitudes towards mobilized action are very different than those which have been discussed until now. Whereas institutional attitudes are general and longterm, mobilized attitudes are usually specific and short-term; an orientation towards institutional politics is mostly positive and proactive whereas the disposition associated with protest is usually negative and reactive; finally, institutional acts are almost universally approved but mobilized acts remain controversial.[9]

These points become clearer when we consider the major moti-

vation of those who protest: *political discontent.* Discontent expresses a need for change, a dissatisfaction over the current state of political affairs. Whether the resentment springs from economic issues or
ideological ones, the demands are more concrete, precise, and conten-
tious.[10] The level of anger will have a clear effect on attitudes towards
mobilized action.

Mobilization efficacy is an evaluation about the chances for successful protest. Whereas internal efficacy refers to a person's subjective competence, mobilization efficacy is based on an assessment of
political reality. Those who express faith in such tactics are making a
statement about the power of groups, about the need to organize, and,
to a certain extent, the need to circumvent the formal political structure. Such beliefs are based on both personal experience and observations about how other protest groups fare.

Questions about *mobilization approval* also affect attitudes towards direct action techniques. Despite the growing popularity of protest in recent years, a significant proportion of citizens in all Western
countries remain morally opposed to such tactics (Barnes and Kasse
1979). This normative component forms a central part in any decision
to engage in such actions, especially when it involves breaking the
law or engaging in violence.

It is important to note that the three components of an attitude
towards action can not be easily isolated. People's level of discontent
is likely to have an affect on their level of mobilization approval and
their beliefs about institutional efficacy will also influence their
sense of institutional approval. The attitude towards a mode of action
is the final result of the interaction among the three components:
value of outcome, beliefs about the likelihood of the outcome, and
norms about the behavior.

Origins of Strategy

The distinction between institutional attitudes and mobilization attitudes is also apparent when the origins of each set of beliefs is
examined. Whereas the civic attitudes associated with institutional
action are rooted in pyschological involvement, attitudes towards
mobilized action are best explained by looking at social and cultural
differences within Israel. This finding reinforces the notion that institutional attitudes are more general and stable, whereas mobilized
attitudes are more specific and temporal.

The relationship between psychological involvement and civic
attitudes is well documented in Verba, Nie, and Kim's (1978) work. In

fact psychological involvement itself is defined as a civic attitude. The Israeli data also supports this notion and psychological involvement is correlated with the need for political influence $(r = .26)$, institutional efficacy $(r = .18)$, and institutional approval $(r = .31)$.[11] None of the various differences in social background had any independent effect on institutional attitudes.

The origins of mobilization attitudes, on the other hand, are unrelated to psychological involvement. A positive attitude towards protest is based on political identifications and social environment. Political interests are clearly the most important element determining the level of discontent and although such interests will remain fairly stable over time, the amount of discontent can change as quickly as an Israeli government. Level of discontent was measured using a variety of questions designed to measure both general and specific kinds of dissatisfaction.[12] The major correlates of discontent are presented in Table 3–2.

Table 3–2
Explaining Political Discontent

	Category	N	Unadjusted Scores	Adusted Scores[a]	Beta Weight	F
Political Identification[b]	Left	75	.67	.57		
	Center	256	−.12	.02	.45	92.94
	Right	356	−.46	−.42		
Religiosity	Religious	110	−.34	−.27		
	Traditional	255	−.23	−.10	.16	10.30
	Secular	322	.30	.17		
Education	Less than High School	311	−.25	−.16		
	High School	253	.09	.04	.16	12.30
	College	123	.44	.30		

a. Scores were adjusted for the effects of the other independent variables. The adjusted scores for political identification, for example, represent the level of discontent when religiosity and education are held constant.

b. Political Parties were categorized as follows: Right = Likud, Tchiya; Center = National Religious Party, Agudat Yisrael, Tami, and Telem; Left = Labor Alignment, Citizen's Rights, and Shinui. Note that all center parties were members of the government at the time of the survey.

Political interests clearly dominate the analysis: party identification is the most important indicator of discontent. The degree of religiosity and the level of education also have an effect on political discontent, above and beyond those which can be attributed to their correlation with party identifications. Ethnic divisions do not have an independent effect. This finding is a significant one in that it once again contrasts with the usual assumption about the importance of ethnicity in explaining Israeli political behavior.[13]

The temporal nature of this relationship can be illustrated by considering what differences would have emerged if the survey had been carried out when the Labor party was still in power. Those who identify with the right would have exhibited the greatest level of dissatisfaction. The origins of discontent depend on which groups feel threatened.

Beliefs about the efficacy and acceptability of mobilized action are probably more stable, although they too vary over time and culture. The case of Israel again offers an important illustration of this point. Mobilization efficacy and mobilization approval were measured directly by asking the participants about their views on the effectiveness and acceptability of a variety of political actions. The activities used to build the mobilization efficacy and mobilization approval scale included responses about legal demonstrations, settling without permission, organizing a petition, occupying a public office (sit-in), disrupting traffic, and using political violence. For the purposes of this particular analysis one overall scale was used which combined responses about efficacy and approval and the major correlates of mobilization beliefs are presented in Table 3–3.[14]

The Israelis with the most positive evaluations towards protest are young, leftist, educated, and religious. The effects of the first three factors are certainly not unique to Israel; the acceptability of protest is a rather modern phenomenon and the young, the college educated, and those on the left of the political spectrum stand in the vanguard of direct action (Barnes and Kasse 1979; Muller 1979).

The fact that religious Israelis express such positive opinions towards protest is unusual: the religious in other counties are usually the most reluctant to use protest techniques (Barnes and Kaase 1979). The most negative evaluation about mobilized action was expressed by those Israelis who consider themselves traditionalists, whereas the secular population exhibited an average score on these scales. The traditionalists are, therefore, the only true conservatives on this issue.

It seems that the religious in Israel have views on direct action which reflect the events of recent years. A large number of religious groups have achieved a good deal of success through the use of demonstrations and civil disobedience. Gush Emunim has served as the prime example by forcing several governments to sanction the creation of illegal settlements on the West Bank.

Table 3–3
Explaining Orientations Towards Mobilized Action

	Category	N	Unadjusted Scores	Adusted Scores[a]	Beta Weight	F
Age	18–29	217	.32	.31		
	30–49	293	.02	.01	.24	23.17
	50+	224	−.34	−.31		
Leftism	Left	126	.39	.40		
	Center	236	−.05	−.02	.19	13.90
	Right	372	−.10	−.12		
Education	Less than High School	288	−.25	−.15		
	High School	308	.11	.05	.13	6.79
	College	138	.27	.20		
Religiosity	Religious	99	.23	.25		
	Traditional	272	−.22	−.13	.12	5.82
	Secular	363	.10	.03		

It is important, however, to view these results about mobilization attitudes in perspective. Respondents were asked about the degree to which they "would be willing to break the law to achieve justice." The only background factor which proved to be significantly correlated with approval of this statement was age. The young in Israel are the least intimidated by legal barriers. Although the college educated and religious public may be more willing to use protest, they apparently draw the line at breaking the law.

These then, are the origins and the ingredients of strategy. Institutional attitudes are general in both their origins and their substance. Those with a high level of psychological involvement in politics have a greater overall need to have an impact on the political system and a greater faith in their ability to do so using institutional means. Mobilization attitudes, on the other hand, are more specific, temporal, and culturally based. Those who develop a complete strategy of political action have crystallized a set of attitudes towards each mode of action. They have formed both a general and a specific set of orientations and it is the interaction of these two strategic components which best explains actual behavior.

POLITICAL ACTION REPERTOIRES

The stage is now set for the final act in this particular play. Quite a bit is known about the actors: their backgrounds, their motivations, their inclinations, and their expectations. How an actor behaves in rehearsal, however, is not necessarily indicative of what will happen in the actual performance. Potentials and strategies are not always converted into action.

The concept of repertoire is used to indicate that political actors choose a mode of political actions which reflect their own particular skills and evaluations. A political action repertoire is not seen as a fixed set of responses for every political issue, nor is it assumed that it will expand in any particular direction.[15] These behavioral scripts all revolve around certain basic themes, but are open to revisions due to changes in political circumstances. Given sufficient threat, for example, even the most conservative citizen will take to the streets.

The model, should, however, tell quite a bit about the ways in which background, mobilization, and evaluation are translated into political action repertoires. Individuals develop patterns of political behavior which reflect all these factors. The effects of background are further considered somewhat later; the claims about the effects of mobilization and evaluation are summarized in Figure 3–4.

Figure 3–4
Resources, Attitudes and Repertoires: A Model

| | POLITICAL ACTION TYPE | | | |
	Inactives	Conformists	Dissidents	Pragmatists
Resorces/Skills	–	+	+	+
Mobilization Attitudes	–	–	+	+
Institutional Attitudes	–	+	–	+

The four ideal types presented in chapter 1 are used: Inactives, Conformists, Dissidents, and Pragmatists. These types certainly do not exhaust the list of behavioral options, but they do serve as a useful means of organization. The Inactives and the Pragmatists represent two extreme points on a continuum, whereas the Conformists and the Dissidents represent two points in between.

The Inactives never really make political evaluations. They may vote, but they are unlikely to even think much about politics between election campaigns. The variations among the three active types, on the other hand, can be attributed to evaluational differences. The Conformists have positive attitudes towards institutional action and negative attitudes towards protest, whereas dissidents hold exactly the opposite views. Pragmatists have positive attitudes towards both modes of behavior.

The Pragmatists illustrate that despite the differences between the two sets of attitudes, they are not incompatible. People can combine a general need for influence with a specific feeling of discontent and come to the conclusion that both modes of action are effective and legitimate. As their name implies, Pragmatists alter their behavior in accordance with political circumstances.

Conformists and Dissidents have more limited repertoires. Their attitudes reflect polar opposite views of the political world. Conformists feel good about the political system and their ability to have an influence; they reject the use of protest. Despite their high level of psychological involvement, Dissidents are cynical about government responsiveness and are brought to protest through their discontent and their faith in direct action.

The model was tested using three separate analyses. The first operation was designed to explore the basic dimensions of political action in Israel and to validate the distinction between mobilized and institutional action. Based on these findings, individuals were divided into the four action types. Profiles of each type were built to provide a graphic demonstration of the social and psychological origins of each repertoire. A final regression analysis served as a useful means of summarizing the major lessons of the chapter.

Validating the Modes of Action

The modes of political action used in any particular study depend on two major factors: the theory being examined and the number of items included in the questionnaire. Verba, Nie, and Kim (1978) concentrated on distinctions between the various types of institutional actions and emphasized the differences between voting, community work, electoral activity, and personal contact; they validated these dimensions in several countries. The Muller (1979) study dealt with the other extreme and was concerned almost exclusively with illegal acts, whereas the authors of *Political Action* distinguished between conventional and unconventional behavior. As can be deduced, the goals of the present study are closest to those of *Political Action* and intentionally blur any distinctions within the category of mobilized and institutional actions.

A factor analysis was carried out to confirm the distinction between mobilized and institutional action.[16] As so few individuals reported carrying out illegal actions, one overall variable was created to represent participation in the various forms of illegal protests. The results of this analysis are presented in Table 3–4.

Table 3–4
Factor Analysis of Israeli Political Action
(Principle Components—Varimax Rotation)

ACTION	FACTOR 1	FACTOR 2
Protest Group	.72	
Demonstration	.71	
Signed Petition	.64	
Illegal Protest	.51	
Join Party		.80
Political Organization Activity		.63
Campaigning		.62
Contact Leader		.53
Community Work		.41
Attend Political Meeting	.52	.57
Eigenvalue	3.19	1.28

The findings illustrated several important points. First, the distinction between mobilized and institutional forms of political action is a legitimate one. The four protest acts and the five institutional acts divide along logical lines.

The findings do not, however, contradict those of Verba, Nie, and Kim (1978), which suggested further divisions within the institutional category. It is clear that the acts of personal contacting and community work have the lowest factor loadings, as would be expected. The fact that membership in a political party is the most important variable among institutional activities is also consistent with previous research. It is indicative of the fact that party membership is a central component of institutional participation, a point which is further explored later.

Finally, the act of attending political meetings loads almost equally on both factors. On reflection, it becomes clear that such meetings are related to both forms of political action.

The general picture of Israeli political action seems, then, to parallel the findings in other countries. A focus on two dimensions of political action is justified, but not exhaustive. The institutional action scale was composed of the responses to campaigning, activity in a political organization, joining a political party, contacting a public official, and community work. The responses concerning legal demonstrations, illegal protests, working for a protest group, and signing a petition were used to build the mobilized action scale. In the case of both signing a petition and contacting a public official, it was decided to define as "acting" only those individuals who reported carrying out such activities more than one time. Although such distinctions are arbitrary, it was hoped that the more conservative definitions would weed out some of the more haphazard types of political behavior. Similarly, although attending political meetings is an important type of political action, the difficulty in fitting it into one of the categories prevented its inclusion in the analysis. Although such a decision somewhat inflates the number of those considered Inactive, the need to distinguish between the different modes of activity was considered paramount in this particular analysis.[17]

Action Type Profiles

The four action types were created from these two scales. Inactives were those who did not participate in either mode of action whereas Conformists had carried out exclusively institutional actions (at least one). Dissidents had limited their political action repertoire to mobilized behavior, whereas Pragmatists had performed at least one act which was taken from each of the two modes of action.[18]

Attitude profiles were built for each of the four action types and the mobilization attitude profiles are presented in Figure 3–5. As before, the national average on each attribute is zero so that any positive scores are above the national mean and negative scores are below that average.[19]

The evaluational profiles offered solid support for the theoretical model. The Inactives and the Conformists both exhibited below average levels of political discontent, mobilization efficacy, and mobilization approval, but the Dissidents and the Pragmatists scored above average on these three components. In addition, the fact that Dissidents scored highest on all three indices and Conformists exhibited the most negative orientation towards mobilized action confirmed the strong correlation between attitudes and behavior.

A similar, although less perfect, result can be found by viewing the institutional attitude profiles which are presented in Figure 3–6.

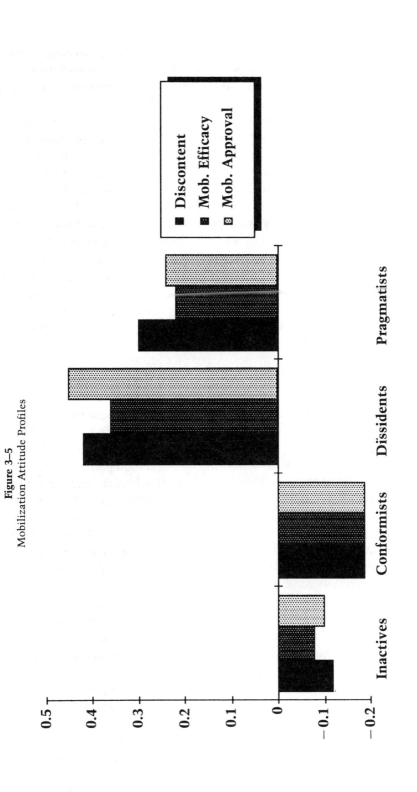

Figure 3–5
Mobilization Attitude Profiles

As expected, the Conformists and the Pragmatists exhibited both the greatest need for political influence and the highest level of institutional efficacy. The Dissidents, however, exhibited an above average need for influence and a level of institutional approval which is slightly higher than the level reached by the Conformists.

The finding about the need for influence is not altogether surprising; it suggested that there is at least some overlap between feelings of political discontent and the neeed to have an impact on the political process. The findings about institutional approval are troublesome, however. Such results lead logically to one of two conclusions: either subjective norms have little to do with the use of institutional modes of action or the operational definition of the concept is faulty. This issue demands further study, but the author's inclination is to believe that the problem lies in method rather than theory.

In general, however, the logic behind the model stands and offers an important lesson about the rational basis of political action. These lessons, in turn, serve as the theoretical springboard for the central thesis of this study. *The politics of provocation occur when a disproportionately large number of citizens are Dissidents who have more positive attitudes towards mobilized action than institutional action.*

To offer a further test of this central hypothesis a *blocked opportunities* scale was created. The scale was designed to measure the extent to which people believed that mobilized action was justified in Israel because other paths of influence were blocked. The three statements used to build this scale were: "The only way to influence the government is to make noise"; "The major reason why people go out and protest is that there is no other way to influence the government"; "It's not nice to carry out an illegal demonstration, but sometimes there's no choice." Dissidents did indeed express significantly more agreement ($\bar{X} = .26$) with this scale then either Inactives ($\bar{X} = 0$), Conformists ($\bar{X} = -.26$) or Pragmatists ($\bar{X} = .04$).

It is assumed in the model that the distinction between the Inactives and the three active types is based on differing levels of political resources and skills. Three indicators were used to build profiles for the four action types. The first two, psychological involvement and internal efficacy have already been explained: the first is seen as the quintessential condition for developing a potential for action, whereas the second offers a subjective measure of political competence. The third measure, organizational membership, was designed to measure the individual's propensity to join formal organizations which were

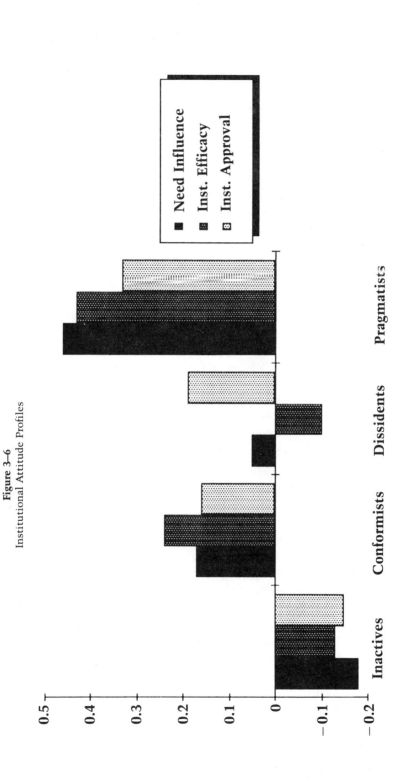

Figure 3–6
Institutional Attitude Profiles

not involved in political activity. The resources and skills associated with such activities also affect the likelihood of political activity.[20] The level of resources and skills associated with each action type is presented in Figure 3–7.

The distribution of scores with respect to psychological involvement and internal efficacy come close to expectations. Israelis with low levels of involvement and internal efficacy are the least likely to participate in any form of political action. It is noteworthy, however, that Conformists exhibited lower scores on these indices than either Dissidents or Pragmatists. Part of the reason for these differences may be related to variations in background. Conformists tend to be older and less educated than the other two active types. Another explanation for these differences has to do with the effects of institutional recruitment, a point soon to be discussed in detail.

Differences with regard to organizational membership are also revealing. Here, it is the Conformists and Pragmatists who exhibit similar tendencies; apparently those who participate in institutional politics have more experience with formal organizations. Dissidents, on the other hand, exhibited an aversion to such long-range commitments, an orientation which parallels their action repertoire.

The evidence supported the thrust of the model, but added some new, unanticipated dimensions. Differences in resources and skills do indeed separate the activists and the Inactives, but some also help distinguish among the three active types. Pragmatists and Dissidents exhibited higher levels of both psychological involvement and internal efficacy, whereas Dissidents exhibited little inclination to join any type of organization. Adding an additional piece of the puzzle helps clarify these points.

Social Background, Institutional Recruitment and Political Action

Who participates in Israeli politics? In the beginning of this essay the fact that some groups might be locked out of the political process due to their lack of psychological involvement was discussed. Israeli women, religious Jews, Jews who were born in either Africa or Asia, and especially those with lower levels of education and income, were less likely to think about politics or develop political opinions.

There is a large gap however, between potential and action: social and structural forces can either hamper or enhance the opportunities for participation. Until now, the obstacles to participation have been emphasized, but the political system is also capable of facilitating political action. Verba, Nie and Kim (1978) made an important

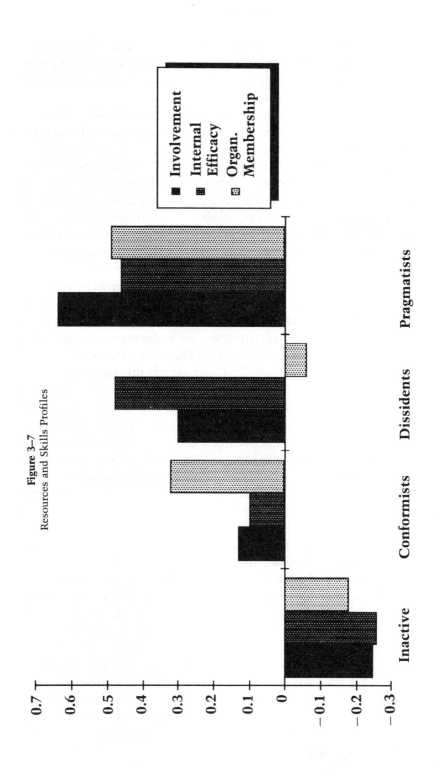

Figure 3–7
Resources and Skills Profiles

distinction between two political cultures. In a dominant institutional system, such as Japan, political organizations (especially parties) have a major impact on the level of participation. Citizens without political affiliation find it difficult to take part in institutional action. In a weak institutional system, such as the United States, organizations have less of an impact and individual potentials are the critical element which determine participation.

Each system has its pluses and minuses. Political organizations in dominant institutional systems often compete for larger constituencies, which leads to fewer class differences within the membership. In a weaker institutional system, on the other hand, people are more likely to particiate as individuals and therefore the political process is likely to be more open and dynamic. In a sense, the choice revolves around the classic dilemma between equality and freedom.[21]

Israel clearly falls into the category of a dominant institutional system. Despite what was said earlier, the parties still have almost total control over institutional access and are active at every political level. Even political competition among students on university campuses is carried out along party lines. The analysis attempts to determine which groups are helped and which are hindered by this monopoly on institutional access. As indicated earlier, those who remain unaffiliated are unlikely to carry out any form of institutional action. The issue concerns the extent to which institutional recruitment serves the interest of political equality.

It is with these points in mind that the profiles of the four action types continue to be built. To explore questions about equality, the extent to which various social groups are represented within each type was examined. Three social groups were selected, each of whom could conceivable be left out of politics: citizens with low education, the young, and women. To determine the extent to which each of these groups was either over- or under-represented within each action type a formula developed by Verba, Nie and Kim (1978) was used. The measure is based on comparing the proportion of a particular social category (e.g., women) found in a particular activist type (e.g., Inactives) to the proportion of that social category found in the population as a whole.[22]

As can be seen in Figure 3–8, education offers clear advantages for political action. Those with less than a high school education are overrepresented among the Inactives and underrepresented among the Pragmatists and especially among the Dissidents. The Conformists once again broke the pattern and the less educated had equal representation in this category.

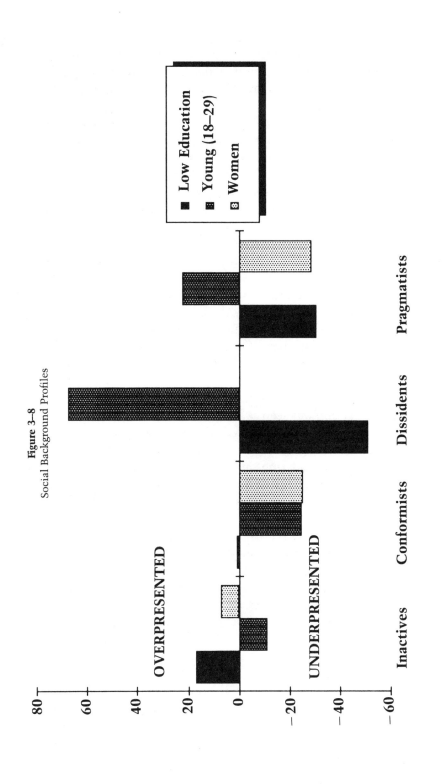

Figure 3–8
Social Background Profiles

A separate analysis revealed that the correlation between education and institutional action is, indeed, quite weak (r = .07). This is especially surprising in light of the strong relationship between education and psychological involvement. The reason for this finding is that political parties in Israel have been quite successful at recruiting the less educated, despite such people's lack of general interest: there is no correlation between education and membership.

The extent to which less educated are underrepresented among Dissidents and Pragmatists illustrates that mobilized politics is in some ways *less egalitarian* than institutional politics. There is a much stronger correlation between education and protest (r = .28). Participation in direct action is more dependent on individual initiative and large political institutions are rarely involved in such activities. A lack of institutional interference means that citizens are more likely to convert their social advantages into political action.

An explanation as to why the Dissidents and Pragmatists exhibited higher levels of psychological involvement and internal efficacy than the conformists may be seen in these findings. Some of the Conformists were assumedly mobilized into action by external institutions.

The results stand traditional theories of protest on their head. Mobilized action was seen as a refuge for the downtrodden and the ignorant; in fact, it is the educated who dominate this mode of action. Their high level of psychological involvement, their positive attitude towards mobilized action, and the lack of institutional restraints leads to a strong preference for protest.[23] The less educated are more likely to be recruited by massive political machines than by protest groups.

The parties have been much less successful at recruiting younger Israelis into their ranks, as mentioned in chapter 1. As can be seen in Figure 3–8, however, young Israelis have more than made up for their lack of affiliation through the use of protest: they are underrepresented among the Inactives and the Conformists, overrepresented among the Pragmatists, and very overrepresented among the Dissidents.

Although it is not shown in Figure 3–8, older Israelis are much more likely to be either Conformists or Inactives. Those over fifty are just as psychologically involved in politics as the younger generation, but they are less likely to convert that involvement into action. Older citizens have fewer options and their limited repertoire forces a choice between either participating in institutional action or staying home.

Given that choice in Israel, many take the latter course of inaction. This evidence supported an earlier claim about the changing political culture: the increasing acceptance of protest has allowed younger Israelis a means to overcome the obstacles which prevented their parents from fully participating. The generation gap in Israel would be even greater were it not for the unusually positive correlation between age and discontent. Given the fact that most young Israelis tend to be more right wing then their elders, even more would probably take part in protests against a Labor government.

It is conceivable that some of the young Dissidents will eventually join a political party. It is not possible to determine the effects of maturity on these trends from the present set of data. What is clear is that the younger Israelis form an important core group for the politics of provocation.

Findings about the level of women's political participation raised more doubts about the scope of party recruitment. The previous discussion on this topic centered around gender differences in the area of psychological involvement and it was found that Israeli women exhibited significantly less interest in politics. It should come as no surprise, therefore, that they tend to be somewhat over-represented among the Inactives in Israel.

Far more intriguing is the fact that when Isareli women are active, they are most likely to be Dissidents. As can be seen in Figure 3–8, this is the one category of activists where women achieve political parity with men. This point should also be made more directly: 56% of Israeli women who carry out some form of political action are Dissidents whereas only 43% of active men fall into this slot. This finding suggested that even those women who do want to participate find it difficult to take part in institutional action.

Two pieces of evidence can be presented to support this claim. First, Israeli women score significantly higher than Israeli men on the blocked opportunities scale. They are much more likely to justify direct action due to cynicism about insitutional means of influence. In addition, even when psychological involvement is controlled, women exhibit significantly less institutional activity than men. The political parties may recruit from a variety of social classes, but it seems that they prefer men. This, combined with the lack of gender differences in mobilized action, leads to the conclusion that Israeli women offer another important constituency for the politics of provocation.[24]

The effects of religiosity and ethnicity on political action (not shown in Figure 3–8) are surprisingly weak. The religious in Israel, it will be remembered, exhibited a low level of psychological involvement and a rather positive attitude towards protest. Neither of these tendencies are reflected in actual behavior.

The level of political action by religious Jews is average. Despite their low level of psychological involvement, they are just as likely as secular citizens to be either Inactives, Conformists, or Pragmatists. This group appears to offer a second, and even better, example of the ways in which institutional recruitment can enhance participation. The religious parties have been more successful in recruiting their constituents than the secular parties. Although 18% of religious Israelis belong to political parties, only 8% of the secular Jews reported such membership.[25] The closer ties of the religious community allow for more effective recruitment, which more than makes up for their lack of individual involvement.

Secular activists are more likely to be dissidents. Although 18% of secular participants fell into this category, only 10% of the religious participants did. This distribution can be attributed to the secular participants' low level of party affiliation and their high level of discontent. Although the religious community has a somewhat more positive attitude towards mobilized action, there is less need for religious protest when so many religious demands are being met by the government. These findings once again offered an important reminder about the ways in which both social and political factors can affect the realization of political potential.

There is also little correlation between ethnicity (or place of birth) and political action. This is a rather important finding and is consistent with earlier results about psychological involvement. Sephardic Jews in Israel have apparently overcome disadvantages in education and income to become just as active as Ashkenazic Israelis. Perhaps the emphasis on ethnic politics in Israel has led to a rather healthy competition for Sephardic members. Whatever the reason, ethnicity in Israel has little to do with either form of political action.

The route to political fulfillment, then, depends on the participants. Israeli political parties have been fairly successful in recruiting some citizens who would otherwise be left out of the political process. The religious and less educated citizens seem to be the primary beneficiaries of this policy. Israeli women, on the other hand, only achieve equality in the realm of direct action. The repertoire of younger Israelis is also dominated by mobilized action, whereas older Israelis limit themselves to institutional behavior. Like all actors, some citizens exceed their potential but others fall short; some are helped by their background, others are hurt. The last major question deals with the flexibility of the script.

Towards a More General Model

What can be learned from these results about the probable configuration of a more comprehensive model of political action? As discussed earlier, there has been a trend among scholars to emphasize the similarities between institutional and mobilized action. From the findings of the present study it can be seen, on the other hand, that there are also qualitative differences between the two roads to political influence. Mobilized action is not just one more type of a political participation; it carries with it a distinctive set of motivations and evaluations. A comprehensive model of political action must be able to specify what the two modes of political action do and do not have in common.

A final analysis offers a useful starting point for building just such a model. Two separate regression analyses were carried out: one for institutional action and one for mobilized action. Such analyses not only tell us about the similarities and differences between the two forms of political behavior, they also offer invaluable information about which factors are the most significant determinants of each separate mode of action. It is important to bring all of the antecedents of political action (background, mobilization, and evaluation) into one model.

In keeping with the model presented at the beginning of this chapter, an overall attitudinal measure was created by combining the responses relating to value of outcome, expectancy of outcome, and social norms. Mobilization attitudes were based on a composite index of the degree of political discontent, mobilization efficacy, and mobilized approval. Institutional attitudes included institutional efficacy and the need for influence.[26] Institutional approval was dropped from the analysis due to a lack of correlation with action, which was discussed earlier. All of the other variables discussed throughout this work were included in the initial analyses, but only those which remained significant (after controlling for the other factors) are presented in Table 3–5.

The most important division between the two modes of action lies in the evaluations associated with each path. A commitment to institutional action is more general and proactive, whereas attitudes associated with protest are specific and reactive. This distinction is also supported by the fact that the attitudinal factors are more central to the statistical explanation of mobilized action. These results reinforce the impression that institutional action is better related to long-term commitment and institutional recruitment, whereas protest is best explained as a matter of circumstance and individual choice.[27]

Table 3–5
Institutional Action and Mobilized Action:
Regression Analyses

Institutional Action		Mobilized Action	
Variable	*Beta*	*Variable*	*Beta*
Institutional Efficacy X Need for Influence	.22	Mobilization Efficacy X Political Discontent X Mobilization Approval	.29
Psychological Involvement	.21	Psychological Involvement	.20
Organization Membership	.19	Internal Efficacy	.12
Ethnicity	.15	Age	.12
ADJUSTED R^2	.21	Organization Membership	.10
		ADJUSTED R^2	.23

As expected, the similarities between the two modes of action lie in the area of individual skills and resources. A psychological involvement in politics appear to be an important component of both modes of political action. The importance of other resources, however, varies between the two paths. Organizational membership is understandably more critical to insitutional action, whereas internal efficacy is only correlated with mobilized action.

It is equally revealing to take note of those variables which did not survive this final selection process. Despite the multitude of social factors introduced into the equations, only two endured this set of statistical controls. Sephardic citizens have a slightly higher level of institutional behavior and the centrality of age to mobilized action remains significant.[28] In general, however, the psychological variables provided a more direct and powerful explanation of political action than did the social determinants.

These results highlighted the importance of individual choice in determining political action repertoires. Citizens' social background do have effects on both their propensity to get involved and the path they take to make demands. But it is the individual, in the final analysis, who decides if political actions are worthwhile, acceptable, and effective. Even the decision to become psychologically involved in politics is, in part, a personal choice. It is heartening to discover that people are not merely born into a mode of behavior; they usually choose it.

In sum, the results offer encouragement to those who believe that any comprehensive model of political action must be based on the notion of rational choice. Citizens tend to choose a repertoire of political action which best fits their own set of needs and expectations.

The model and the results also have taught quite a bit about the nature of political action in Israel. Each repertoire has its own history and its own constituency. The variations within the Israeli polity are just as significant as those which distinguish it from those in other countries. This becomes even clearer when some of its members are encountered.

Chapter 4

BEYOND THE NUMBERS _____

The use of typologies is a dangerous business. Although it is convenient to label people Conformists or Pragmatists, people become involved in politics for hundreds of personal reasons and choose among an equally large number of strategies and repertoires. Although it is not possible to do justice to all of these variations, a more detailed picture of the individual can be offered.

Interviews were carried out with a hundred-and-ten of the original survey respondents. The interviews were more open-ended than the survey and allowed for a deeper understanding of the individual's pattern of beliefs and behavior. Such interviews allowed the researcher a closer look at the subtle differences which lay beyond the numbers. The logic of statistics, which was stressed in the last chapter, must rely on averages and probabilities. Longer interviews with Inactives, Dissidents, Conformists and Pragmatists revealed quite a bit about both the strengths and weaknesses of such classifications. Exceptions to the rule often provided the most food for thought.

The interview transcripts also tell more about the context of participation and protest in Israel. The quantitative material presented in the last chapter was intentionally general in the hope that the analysis would have broader applications. Citizens, on the other hand, are concerned with specific problems and issues and it is important to deal with this perspective as well. The effects of political context are far too powerful to ignore.

The major disadvantage of such interviews is their subjectivity. Accepting such analyses demands no small amount of trust on the part of the reader. It is wise, therefore, to employ such methods only as a compliment to more objective forms of analysis.

The interview schedule (see Methodological Appendix) was designed to accomplish three major goals. The first purpose was to explore the level of *political resources and interests*. How much do the respondents care about politics? How much do they know? Do they express a clear set of opinions and attitudes? The aim of these questions was to gain a richer understanding of the process of mobilization.

The second goal centered on *political evaluations*. Respondents were asked about the extent to which the political leaders "represent the will of the people" and what makes a person a "good citizen." They were also questioned again about the acceptability and the effectiveness of various forms of political participation. To obtain a new perspective on such beliefs, responents were also asked what actions they would take if the city attempted to evacuate them from their homes. These replies offered valuable insights into the limits of acceptable political behavior under conditions of extreme threat.

The final goal of the interviews was to elicit *personal organizing themes* in political thinking. Each citizen has his or her individual logic which binds the various elements of political belief. For some, ideology serves as the organizing principle, whereas others focus on more concrete issues. Appreciating the range of these personal themes leads to a better understanding of the complex set of motivations and beliefs which are associated with varying forms of political action.

A word is in order about the timing of the interviews. Most of them took place almost a year after the original survey, i.e., between February and June of 1983. The major topics of concern at this time were the Lebanese War, the deteriorating economy, and Begin's resignation. The Likud had become especially unpopular due to the bank shares affair in which the general public had lost a considerable amount of money when the government and the banks decided to end their policy of support for these stocks. In Lebanon the casualties continued to mount and the massive demonstration of "400,000" after the Sabra and Shatilla incidents had already taken place.

In the discussion presented below, the interviews were grouped according to action profiles. This allowed a further examination of the validity of the typology. The interviews presented were selected with the aim of giving as balanced a picture as possible. Three respondents were chosen to exemplify each action type. In each case the first interview discussed was felt to be the most representative of that group, the second somewhat less, and the responses of the third subject were used to illustrate some revealing exceptions.

INACTIVES

As in the large sample, the Inactives were the largest group represented. One of the more surprising aspects of this group is its homogeneity, especially in the area of informational resources. Reading over the interviews, their brevity is more striking than anything else. A similar point was made by Neuman (1981) in his study of cognitive integration. Despite being offered the opportunity to talk at length, most of the Inactives chose to confine themselves to one or two sentences for each question. They also tended to be a rather uncommitted lot. When asked about their political views they would either say that they didn't have any or that they were "somewhere in the middle."

Evaluations about political action tended to center on a general lack of efficacy. Most of the Inactives exhibited little motivation towards participation and few felt that it would do any good.

Although there is clearly more variance in the area of personal organizing themes, the number of respondents who have developed a "boy scout" philosophy about politics is striking. Such individuals expressed a desire for "everyone to pull together," and cited the need for patriotism. Many also mentioned concrete personal problems rather than abstract principles.

Respondent 371

The respondent is a housewife in her thirties with a high school education. She was born in Israel and her father was born in Asia. She considers herself secular, places herself somewhat left of center on the political continuum, yet voted for the Likud in the last election.

Her only political activity is voting. The respondent reported an especially low level of psychological involvement. This lack of concern for politics is well reflected in the interview. When asked about the problem that bothers her most, she replied:

> The fact that there aren't any activities for the children here. The children have already finished first grade and I need to be with them all day long . . . They just don't have any framework.

When asked to define her political opinions, the respondent gave a confused answer, indicating that the question had rarely been considered.

I don't think that there's anybody good enough to rule this country, because we have so many problems . . . But I myself don't know what I'd do. You mean economically? Like that suggestion that Aridor [Minister of Finance] made with all those dollars and all that nonsense? I think if they did that it would help a lot. We buy everything by the dollar anyway.

The lack of informational resources leads to an ad hoc response, rather than a more general approach. The respondent was quite open about her lack of involvement, and pointed out that she "doesn't take an interest in such things, maybe because I don't work outside [the home], I'm here all the time."

The feelings she does have about the political system are fairly negative, both in terms of trust and efficacy. She has little faith in politicians and claimed:

They do what they want, without considering what the people want . . . you pick a party because of the opinion they put forth, and after that they don't do it . . . they always change.

When asked about the possibility for political expression, she replied: "I have no say, maybe if a person changes his party or something, but there's no other way."

The respondent failed to display any organizing theme throughout the interview. She has a rather blurred view of the political system, and little faith in either the leaders or the possibility of change. More important this citizen rarely thinks about politics, apart from election time. Burdened by the responsibilities of her children and home, political issues are clearly not on the top of her priority list. Her chances of breaking out of this cycle of apathy seem very low.

Respondent 1036

The respondent is a European woman in her early sixties. She is a survivor of the holocaust and completed a high school education. She exhibited an average level of psychological involvement and declared that she is "in the middle" politically. She did not vote in the last national election.

She has a notable lack of political knowledge and understanding. She claimed to have trouble defining the term democracy and used the word freedom [chofesh] to describe all of the various political terms she was asked about.

When asked if there were any political events or issues that bothered her, she chose to focus on a relatively minor event which had important personal relevance:

> Kohl's [German Chancellor] visit. Why do we have to have him here? They demonstrated against him, but there were also Germans here who met with him.

The political "mess" in Israel also bothered her. The need for more discipline and order is a theme which permeated a good deal of the interview. She expressed exasperation over all of the strikes and disorders, but felt powerless to do anything about it. When asked whether citizens have any way to express their opinions, she replied:

> If he's strong enough but not a private person. I don't think a private person can have influence. Maybe in elections, if there are other votes like mine. But there shouldn't be demonstrations, no shouting, no killing each other.

This theme of order is also reflected in her personal attitudes towards political action. She would never consider any illegal action, even if threatened with evacuation.

The respondent is mostly removed from the world of politics and considers such events as unwelcome intrusions into her life. Although she feels strongly about the need for greater order and discipline in Israel, she feels incapable of doing anything about it.

Respondent 033

The third respondent selected was chosen to represent some of the exceptions to the rule. He is exceptional in that he is college educated and reports a high level of psychological involvement. This involvement was well reflected in his score on the political knowledge test, where he answered all ten questions correctly.

His political beliefs are quite firmly related to past experience. In defining his political opinions he pointed to the fact that he used to belong to a kibbutz and support Mapai but had since moved to both the city and to the ideological camp of the Likud. He was quite adamant about the difference between the two parties.

> One party wants to give up part of the country to those who want to use it so it will be easier to get the rest from us . . . The other believes in the complete Israel and for them the border is not the Jordan River. You [the interviewer] are young, you don't remember what I do. I want to remind

you that in 1917 the Zionist movement presented the League of Nations a plan for the national homeland which would have defensible borders. This was before the British mandate and it included quite a bit of territory past the Jordan River.

The respondent went into a relatively lengthy historical justification for the Israel's rights to the territories. There is little doubt that his own view of history serves as the organizing principle for most of his political beliefs.

He has mixed feelings about political action. He believes that the only way to have an influence is to work through a party, but is quite proud of the fact that he never "sold his soul to a political party." He explained that he dealt with Zionism, not with parties. This contrast between partisan and national interests is very clear to him. He is also intensely opposed to any type of illegal protests, although he admitted that they are sometimes successful.

The respondent is, then, a rather involved voting specialist (Verba, Nie, and Kim, 1978). If it were not for his clear distrust of political parties, his profile would more easily fit that of a Conformist. Israelis of his generation, however, had to choose between the party or nothing and it is this limited number of choices which probably best explains his lack of participation.

Comparing the three Inactives reveals that the first two failed to pass the mobilization stage of political involvement. They exhibited little interest in politics and few political resources. The final subject, on the other hand, passed the stage of mobilization, but his evaluations of political reality inhibited any participation. As anticipated by the model, the respondent had negative attitudes towards institutional and mobilized action. These cases offered useful reminders that the reasons for inaction can be as different as those for action.

CONFORMISTS

The Conformists are in some ways the most problematic of the action profiles. Variations among Conformists appeared more significant because of the diversity of institutional forms of participation. Conformists range from individuals who have been active in political parties for fifty years to people who write a couple of letters to political leaders. A more sophisticated typology would deal with both different forms of institutional behavior as well as the overall level of activism.

In general, however, the Conformist interviews did fit the picture presented by the national sample. They tended to be older, more conservative, and exhibited a distinct preference for istitutional forms of action. Most Conformists also appeared somewhat less psychologically involved in politics than other activists.

The political themes which emerged from the interviews often centered on a more traditional approach to Israeli politics. Nationalism, Zionism, and commitment are concepts which were mentioned more often by this group and many had little patience for the politics of protest. The Conformists are not naive, however: few have complete faith in political leaders. Their beliefs can be summarized by stating that although the party machine may be a little crooked, it is still the only political wheel in town.

Respondent 769

The respondent is a male over sixty-five years old who considers himself himself traditional in his religious beliefs. He is a teacher with a college education and considers himself to be somewhat right of center. He has a slightly above average level of psychological involvement and has participated in political campaigns, political meetings, and written letters to leaders.

He is very proud of his part in building the young state. When asked about how satisfied he is with his life, he tells something of his life:

> I couldn't get work when I first came. Finally I got a job in Holon and did physical labor as well as taking care of youth. As a Pioneer [Chalutz] it was wonderful. I could have worked somewhere else, but I was taking care of my future. I said I'll make less now but I'll get permanent work for the future. I wanted to get a pension, and today I'm living on that pension, and I live pretty well.

The respondent was somewhat cautious about revealing his political opinions, a remnent perhaps of apprehensions about party machines. His major theme was the need for more patriotism. A willingness to sacrifice for the common good, he believes, would bring Israel much closer to solving many of its problems.

He also felt the country would be better off if it had fewer parties. Yet he still views the party as the center for all political activity. When asked about the best way to express political opinions, he replied:

> Almost everyone belongs to a party where they can vote and express what they want and are interested in. The little guy who isn't in a party, that's a bigger problem. He can also go to political meetings. But he must not demonstrate or stop work when he feels like it, stop paying

taxes or not listen to the orders of the government or police. He has to go to the insitutions and talk to them, explain to them and not do things by himself. The biggest problem here is that everyone thinks he's King of Israel and does what he wants without considering that he can hurt the Israeli people.

One might think that such an attitude expresses an unconditional trust in the political leaders. Such is not the case. This Conformist is actually rather skeptical about the degree to which the leaders represent the people:

If the leaders would really work for the people and not for the party, it would be good. But here they work first for the party and only afterwards for the people, despite the fact that we had leaders who said first the people then the party, like Ben Gurion, may he rest in peace. But I regret it's not like that anymore.

This nostalgia for the old Israel is another theme which is heard in many of the Conformist interviews. It is clear to this citizen that the new generation plays the game using a very different set of rules.

A final note is in order about our classic Conformist. Despite his negative opinion about mobilized politics, he, too, would consider using such tactics if the authorities intended to evacuate him from his home. He claimed that in this case he might demonstrate without a license, participate in a sit-in, or even occupy the mayor's office. This is a reminder that in situations of extreme threat even the most conservative of citizens will consider drastic measures.

Respondent 251

The second interviewee represents those Conformists with a more limited activity; her only form of participation is community action. She is in her forties, completed a high school education and reported a relatively low level of psychological involvement. Unlike many of her peers, she has no strong political beliefs:

I don't have many political arguments. I read a lot of newspapers, and I try to understand things, but its difficult for me to know . . . If I had to go today to vote it would be very difficult . . . I think I might be able to vote for a particular personality, but not for a [political] body—it's hard for me to know.

This subject was one of the few interviewees who expressed some type of trust in Israeli political leaders. After discussing her concerns about the economy and the war in Lebanon, she was asked whether she thought there was any chance of solving these problems:

> I think if we're patient I'm sure, well not sure, but I'm convinced that people are trying at least. I don't think people can see what's happening and not care or try . . . I'm convinced that people are making an effort to make things better.

She was much more critical of protesters than of politicians. In reply to a question about what makes a country more democratic, she said that democracy was:

> The possibility for everyone to express his opinion. In our country many things happen, even ugly things recently. If we weren't a democratic country I don't think those things would happen. If there was a government, in an extreme fashion, like in Russia; there it's so powerful that people can't really express their opinion. Here every one, everybody, every party, and every small movement that wants to express his opinion has to make an effort so it doesn't end in violence. But they certainly let them go out into the streets with all of their leaflets and bullhorns, to shout and express their opinions. It's sort of a ritual already.

This notion that there was "too much democracy" in Israel was another theme which was voiced by other Conformists. The respondent continued with this theme throughout the interview and talked about how the demonstrators and worker sanctions really hurt the state. She made it a point to emphasize that she would never think of going to a protest. She also stated though that she has no objection to quiet demonstrations.

Conformists, it will be remembered, exhibited the lowest levels of political resources. One of the reasons for this finding may be related to the inclusion of community activists (such as this respondent) in the group. Despite her lack of involvement, the subject had distinct attitudes towards the two modes of political action which fell squarely into the Conformist approach to political behavior.

Respondent 367

In choosing the person to best represent the exceptional Conformist, it had to be decided whether to select someone with an unusual background (e.g., the college educated young woman who was also conservative) or unusual in terms of their attitudes towards political action. The present respondent fit into the latter category. He is in his fifties, has somewhat more than a high school education, and has the unusual distinction of being a religious leftist. When asked to define his political attitudes, he replied:

> Socialist on the one hand, nationalistic on the other and religious from another perspective. If it is possible to bring those three things together; it's very worthwhile in my opinion.

As might be ascertained, the respondent has a fairly high level of psychological involvement. He was not, however, the most active of the interviewees, although he had participated in a political campaign and contacted political leaders on more than one occasion.

Unlike most Conformists, the respondent has a rather positive attitude towards mobilized action. Although he has never participated in a protest (since the formation of the state) he believes that demonstrating is a legitimate way to express opinions. If threatened with evacuation he'd be willing to take part in an illegal demonstration and, if necessary, block a road. He also stated that he might participate in a sit-in, burn tires, and occupy a mayor's office.

There are also other ways in which the respondent sounds more like a Dissident than a Conformist. He claimed that political violence is justified when people "have no other choice, when they [the government] drive people out of their minds." He went on to explain:

> There are situations where people get carried away. You can understand it, but not justify it. On the other hand when people ask for a license to demonstrate, you have to give it to them. You can't deny them a license and then take action against the demonstrators.

Cynicism, then, can be discovered even among the Conformists. The potential for mobilized action is greater than the level of actual participation. Even the classic Conformist would take to the streets if he had no other choice. What is missing from our static model is the effects of varying levels of discontent and threat.

In general, however, the stereotypes about the Conformists proved to be rather accurate. Their tendency to confine themselves to institutional politics comes from a rejection of protest. Although they may vary in terms of both resources and commitment, Conformists share a firm belief in the need to work within the confines of the formal political system.

DISSIDENTS

The Dissidents represent a very different approach to politics and there is little difficulty learning about these beliefs from their interviews. Most of the protesters expressed strong ideological commitments and a high level of political knowledge. Above all, most have a deep distrust for politicians and political parties. They provided the best examples of the sense of blocked opportunities which leads to the politics of provocation.

Respondent 1013

The classic Dissident is a married university student in his thirties with a relatively high level of psychological involvement. The entire interview reflected this involvement and he exhibited an extremely sophisticated understanding of the political world. An illustration of this knowledge is provided by his description of his political views:

> According to the usual scale I'm more left than right. That's for economics and less for politics. In the rest of the world it's different but in Israel if you're leftist you're more liberal and open with regards to such problems as the territories and the dialogue with the Palestinians.

These ideological beliefs were translated into active work against the war in Lebanon where, among other things, the respondent participated in a vigil against the war outside the Prime Minister's office.

The respondent's attitudes towards the political system are equally well developed. He doesn't believe that appealing to political leaders does any good and one of his major organizing themes was centered on the belief that "power corrupts":

> In general there is a terrible problem because when someone finally gets to a position of power in which he is able to have an influence, he has gone through so many changes and had to get dirty, and dirty others, that he is pretty removed from the will of the people . . . He has to do what the party tells him to do or what people with power tell him to do.

This Dissident is not intimidated by any legal barriers to direct action. His definition of being a good citizen was based more on principles of morality than legality.

A good citizen should follow the law, but not blindly. The laws were made for the average person. If you're beyond that and you see what is for the public good, . . . but it's a very serious problem. What's the public good? But you don't have to go with your eyes closed. You could drive through a green light and run down an old lady and the law is on your side. I mean that the citizen has to be a good person, not just an obedient person, like a robot.

This particular Dissident had formulated a very clear policy for political action. He sees himself as a part of an elite group of people who share not only a right, but an obligation for political participation. He is skeptical about both the legal system and those who are responsible for it. His chosen mode of political action is perfectly suited for just this pattern of beliefs.

Respondent 876

The next Dissident is also college educated and in her thirties but has quite a different set of attitudes and motivations. She is religious and supported the Likud government. In fact her participation in demonstrations and signing petitions does not come from any discontent: she participated in such actions in support of the government's policy in Lebanon.

Despite this support, she is critical of the political leadership. She criticized the government for making impossible laws (such as the restrictions of foreign currency) which "makes all of us law breakers." She also resents the hypocrisy of some of the politicians:

The leaders should set an example. They can't keep saying we have to cut back on everything and then drive around in those fancy minister cars. You can't keep making demands on every citizen; we're just small cogs in the system. You have to oil every cog but first you have to repair the whole system.

She felt that the leaders try to represent the will of the people, but also believed in the need for electoral reform. She offered an articulate analysis of the reasons for political violence in Israel, stating that there would be less turmoil if people could turn to a representative.

In general, however, the respondent has a much lower level of cynicism than the first Dissident. She was firmly against any acts which are illegal or violent:

I'm a moderate person when it comes to my political opinions. I'm in favor of political tolerance and against political violence in any form, even if it's for a good purpose. Politically I identify with Gush Emunim, but not creating settlements by force using illegal methods and all of the other actions which try to convince the public that the ends justify the means.

This theme about the importance of legal barriers appeared throughout the interview. If they came to evacuate her home, she would block the street, lie before the bulldozers, and carry out non-violent physical resistance. She felt that blocking a street is justified, however, if secular citizens try to drive into a religious neighborhood on Shabbat.

The respondent did not express any skepticism about the utility of conventional behavior. Her label of Dissident is probably better related to either the difficulties of a religious woman getting involved in party politics or the convenience of direct action.

The contrast between the first Dissident and the second is, once again, a reminder of the variance within each action type. The distinction between legal and illegal protest is more important for some Dissidents than others.

Respondent 986

The respondent is an atypical Dissident, both in terms of his age (early sixties) and his activity. The only demonstration he participated in was organized by the Engineers Union to fight for workers' interest. He is brought before the reader to break the stereotype which suggested that all protesters are young ideologists taking to the streets for matters of principle. The respondent also represents those Dissidents who are less active and may fall into the category more by chance than design.

The respondent has a college degree and reported an average level of psychological involvement. He placed himself somewhat on the left of the political spectrum and his major political theme revolved around his opposition to religious coercion.

I'm against the situations that the majority of the population is secular but has to be under the thumb of the religious parties. We have to get those parties out of the government so they won't have so much influence.

The subject's interview transcript is rather brief. In general, however, he is rather conservative in his views about political action. When asked about limits to political action, he said:

> One can demonstrate in a legal and organized fashion. He can also have a strike, but not in essential services. Those should be forbidden by law.

When asked about what he would do if threatened with evacuation, the only possibility he would consider would be a sit-in.

He is more typical of other Dissidents in his beliefs about the political leadership. When asked what a citizen could do to express his opinion, he replied:

> Today one has the press, the radio, these are all sorts of possibilities . . . I don't see people who turn to Knesset members though. They [politicians] aren't really interested in what's happening here at home. They're not interested in our problems. Not Knesset members and not the municipality.

This Dissident has no real place to go. He said his only real option is to take part in legal demonstrations. In any case, his rather low level of psychological involvement suggested that he is unlikely to be any more active in the future than he has been in the past.

PRAGMATISTS

The Pragmatist profiles which were presented in the previous chapter painted a portrait of an elite group of involved citizens with high levels of political efficacy. These impressions were reinforced by the in-depth interviews. The transcripts are the longest and the most ideological of all the types. Most of the Pragmatists are quite definite about their place on the ideological continuum, and express ideas which are both organized and intensive. Although many also discuss personal concerns, the general trend is to discuss national topics, such as the war in Lebanon and the withdrawal from Sinai.

The clearest theme to be read in many of these interviews is the importance of personal initiative. Pragmatists see themselves as both willing and capable of making a political impact. Rather than blaming the leaders for everything, they also hold citizens responsible for solving the country's problems. Most of all, the political world is both familiar and important to them.

Respondent 493

The respondent chosen to represent the Pragmatists is a man in his middle fifties who has completed high school. He reported an extremely high level of psychological involvement which was well reflected in his discussion of political issues. The enunciation of his political views revealed an extremely organized and salient set of political interests.

> First, I am against the wars. There's only one solution, and that's on the basis of a mutual recognition of the national rights of the two peoples: the Israeli people and the Palestinian people. I also think one has to show a preference for the workers; but of course that is related to a policy of peace.

The reason a policy of peace is related to sympathy for workers is that the two attitudes are joined by a commitment to the ideology of the political left. This sense of political identification serves as a personal theme which dictates the individual's beliefs and actions.

The respondent had participated in several political campaigns and identified with the more leftists elements of the Labor party. He was also very active against the war in Lebanon through a "Committee against the War," which carried out both protests and lobbying. He is convinced that his work against the war was useful, because "the war is a lot less popular because of groups like ours."

The interviewee expressed somewhat ambivalent feelings about the integrity of the political system. When asked about the extent to which the leaders and parties represented the will of the people, he replied:

> Usually they are not representative. But they can't completely ignore what the people are feeling. You have democratic elections, and people are politically aware, so their basic beliefs are reflected in the policies of the two major parties.

He also believes that most people in Israel have the means for political expression. Although he expressed some concern about the equality of access for Arab Israelis, he claimed that Israel has a very good record when it is compared to other countries.

The attitudes of the respondent towards political action are consistent with these beliefs. He believes that citizens have an obligation to express their political views. He has no objections to any legal forms of mobilized action, but is opposed to those who break the law or carry out violence.

The respondent certainly fits the portrait of the classic Pragmatist. He exhibited an extensive array of political resources and interests, a cautious trust in the political system, and a rich repertoire of political action.

Respondent 866

The respondent is a young soldier who completed high school. Despite his youth he has participated in community work, political meetings, and has worked in a political campaign. He also participated in a demonstration and signed petitions to convince Begin not to resign. These latter acts are again, a reminder that not all political protest comes from the opposition.

He exhibited a fairly high level of psychological involvement, but scored surprisingly low on the political knowledge exam (3 out of 10). He has definite views on both local and national issues and it is clear that these problems concern him. When asked to describe his political opinions, he organized his remarks into three categories— security, economic, and religious. In each he attempted to express how his own personal experience relates to the broader issues. On religion, for example:

> I know the situation here better than anyone, I live in this community which was once secular and has now become religious. In principle I don't care, but all of the secular residents are leaving, people are scared to live here. We had a kid here who had an enlistment party. They [religious activists] came en masse and destroyed the community center; they don't want the center to operate.

His opinions were equally clear on the subject of Lebanon and he felt that Israel should not withdraw until it had accomplished something in that country. He also supported the Likud's position on the territories and had no difficulty enunciating the differences beetween the two major parties.

> The minute this land is called the land of Israel, it is the duty of every citizen to settle where he wants. That's what the Likud platform says . . . the Likud says that we are not willing to give Judaea and Samaria to any other country because that would endanger the state.

The respondent shared with other Pragmatists a belief that citizens have a responsibility to solve their social and political problems. When asked about the issue of political responsibility, he replied:

> I don't think its any particular person's responsibility. We just have to bring the people together and discuss it with careful thought. . . . You can't hold one person responsible, or even a political group which received a majority from the public. The minute it is the responsibility

of the government, then it is the public's responsibility, because they have elected the government.

He felt that petitions, demonstrations, and working through a party are equally effective ways to have an influence. The respondent does not, however, support civil disobedience and violence and if confronted with an evacuation order would limit his action to filing a case in court.

The young Pragmatist has a wide repertoire to choose from when he gets out of the army. Considering his level of involvement, his intense feelings about politics, and his early experience, there is little doubt that he will translate this potential into action.

Respondent 302

The atypical Pragmatist is in his forties. He has a low level of psychological involvement, despite a college education. Unlike most of the other Pragmatists he doesn't belong to a political party and intends to switch his vote in the next election from the smaller more centrist party of *Shinui* to Labor.

The respondent's classification as a Pragmatist is based on two behaviors: working in the community and attending one demonstration which called for a board of inquiry into the massacre at Sabra and Statilla. He is not very involved politically and the issues that concern him are more social than political. When asked what problems bothered him the most, he said:

> Cultural problems for the most part, How people talk to each other, and even how people treat each other physically. . . . There is such aggression between people, in the bus line, at the office, and that puts people under pressure.

He admitted to being somewhat apolitical and his focus is clearly on local community matters. The subject is a social worker who attempts to solve local problems though his work. He does share with other Pragmatists a belief in the need for personal responsibility, but here too it tends to be placed in a nonideological context.

> Its very important to encourage people to take responsibility for their lives, for their environment. Above and beyond politics and economics. We've gotten to be beggars [*schnorrer*] whether it's abroad with our hand always open, or inside of Israel by saying 'I deserve everything'—it's just too simple that way.

Like some of the other Pragmatists he sees both demonstrations and contacting politicians as equally effective ways of exerting an influence. He would be willing, however, to block a street and sit before the bulldozer to prevent being evacuated from his home.

The respondent can be considered a community activist who felt sufficiently concerned to attend one demonstration. Although he has the potential to use both modes of action, most of his efforts will no doubt continue to be devoted to the local arena.

Some Lessons

The interviews provided some color to the outline drawn by the quantitative analysis. The picture is now more complex but probably offers a more accurate reflection of reality. People do not fit easily into the procrustean bed of social science theories. It is hoped that having allowed even a selected few to speak provided at least a partial redress of this injustice.

The variations within each type pointed to new directions of inquiry. A more dynamic typology will need to be focused on differing levels of activism. It is important to differentiate between incidental participants and true activists. Further research should also deal with attitudes about the law. The distinction between legal and illegal acts is likely to prove just as important as the diversions stressed in the present study.

A final lesson relates to the differences which were found among the Inactives. A lack of political participation can stem from apathy, alienation, low efficacy, or a lack of political resources. A better understanding of these variations is dependent on the development of a more detailed theory.

Notwithstanding these gaps, the logic of the model remains intact. Most of the interviews reinforced the conclusions of the previous chapter about the qualitative differences between Inactives, Conformists, Dissidents, and Pragmatists. The attitudes expressed by these Israelis offered vivid support for the advocates of rational choice theory. Political participants adopt a repertoire which is congruent with their level of resources, their political interests, and their evaluations of the political system.

The interviews also offered support for claims which have been made here about the political culture of Israel. A general sense of distrust and antagonism towards the political leadership was found, even among Conformists and Pragmatists. The overriding image was one of political leaders bickering over power and privileges with little concern for public interests.

Many of the respondents also expressed discontent over the emergence of the politics of provocation in Israel. Although most were aware of the changes in political action repertoires, few were pleased with the development. Citizens seemed somewhat perplexed by the contrast between what they have learned about Israeli democracy and what they see in the mass media. Protests, strikes, and violence seem to be the only regular form of political communication.

When taken as a whole, evidence about the political resources, attitudes, and behaviors of individual citizens tells quite a bit about Israeli political culture. Almost all political action, however, is carried out within groups. Political groups mobilize, develop strategy, and act, and the ways in which they carry out these behaviors has a significant impact on the political culture. The discussion turns, then, to the dynamics of collective action.

Chapter 5

EXPLAINING COLLECTIVE ACTION __

The move from individual to collective behavior is fraught with theoretical and methodological pitfalls. Despite the fact that both citizens and groups are political actors, social scientists view each from very different perspecitives. As illustrated in the previous chapters, psychological models of involvement and choice dominate general views of the individual. Those who study groups, on the other hand, emphasize sociological constructs such as social structure, organization, and power.

The methods used in the two approaches are no less divergent. The advantage of survey research is the ability to deal with a large number of variables simultaneously. The study of groups is more complex and cumbersome. The scholar is dependent mainly on secondary records such as books and news articles, which were not written for the purposes of research. Problems of measurement and interpretation abound. Interviews and observations about more current groups can somewhat supplement these data, but gnawing gaps and frustrations remain.

Despite these differences, it is hoped that the theoretical framework presented in chapter 2 allows for some integration. It was argued that very different concepts and variables can be organized under similar categories. Just as an individual actor is born in a certain environment, so are groups; individuals can be distinguished by their level of political resources as can groups. Finally, just as individuals make choices about both the quality and quantity of participation, so political action groups plan strategies of confrontation. These are not identical processes, but they do run along similar paths.

The discussion of collective action is divided into two sections.

The first section is devoted to providing an overview of Israeli collective action. A statistical breakdown of protest groups and actions provides important information about the nature and scope of protest in Israel. In the second section the theoretical framework is adapted to the study of collective action. The explanation of group behavior runs along familiar lines, but employs a rather different set of variables.

A DESCRIPTIVE OVERVIEW

The data for studying protest groups, it will be remembered, was gathered from newspaper articles on all protest actions carried out between 1979 and 1984. The use of the newspaper as a data source has many disadvantages and it is useful to begin by considering them. Newspapers do not report on all protests; they must be selective. The researcher must begin with the assumption that the sample is skewed and that many groups which are not considered newsworthy will be excluded. These groups are likely to have certain characteristics in common. They are likely to be smaller, concerned with more local issues, and less violent. When dealing with the national level of politics, such groups are also not very important to the social scientist. Like the proverbial tree falling where no one can hear, groups which are ignored by the press are not politically important.[1]

An additional problem with using newspapers as a data source concerns the ways in which they cover protest. The news media are concerned with events and provide a great deal of information about collective actions, but much less about groups. An article rarely describes the social origins of a group or its level of resources and almost never gives any indications about group structure. A good deal of this information must be inferred, which presents a great risk for empirical research.[2]

To build the final sample of groups it was critical to establish operational rules of inclusion and exclusion. The definition of an act of political protest was adapted from Taylor and Jodice (1983, 19) and was defined as: " . . . relatively short actions carried out by citizens for the announced purpose of protesting against a regime or government or one or more of its leaders, or against its ideology, policy, intended policy, or lack of policy, or against its previous actions or intended action." It is important to note that under these rules, only strikes which were directed against the government were included in the sample. A protest group was defined as a collection of at least ten individuals engaged in a protest act.

A coding sheet was pretested to determine just how much information could be gathered from the news articles. After several refinements, the final version had a total of twenty-two questions which were divided into three sections: the nature of the group, the nature of the act, and information about the article itself (e.g., size).[3]

The distribution of group traits revealed quite a bit about mobilization in Israel and many of the findings are rather surprising, as can be seen in Table 5–1.

Table 5–1
Israeli Protest Groups: Distribution of Traits

Goals (N = 382)		Permanency (N = 429)		Size (N = 245)	
Economic	51%	New	15%	10–100	26%
Education/ Welfare	25%	Established	85%	101–1000	37%
				1001–	36%
Political	21%				
Religious	3%				

Scope (N = 409)		Number of Acts (N = 454)		Intensity (N = 454)	
Neighborhood	12%	1	66%	All Legal	67%
City-Wide	41%	2	17%	Illegal	20%
Area	12%	3	5%	Violent	13%
National	35%	4–5	5%		
		6–10	5%		
		11–	2%		

Starting with group goals, most groups, it is found, are concerned with material issues, not ideology. Seventy-six percent of all the groups made demands which were related to either the economy, education, or welfare, whereas only 24% of the protest groups had political or religious demands. It will be remembered that Maslow's (1954) need hierarchy suggested that people only seek achievements in the ideological sphere when they have met their more material needs. If "postmaterialism" (Inkelhart, 1979) is the major theme of protest in the Western world, it is not found in Israel.

The permanency, size, and scope of Israeli protest groups also revealed something about mobilization patterns. Most of the groups who are active in Israel have achieved a substantial level of organization and resources. The majority have permanent structures and an impressive number of members. A large proportion of the groups are organized at either the municipal or the national level, which reflects the two centers of power in the country. This predominance of organized groups can be seen as the first piece of evidence about the relationship between structure, resources, and action.

The most surprising result is related to the small number of acts carried out by each group. The fact that 83% of the groups carried out two acts or less is a finding that demands further attention. One possible reason for this result is, no doubt, the large number of economic groups represented in the sample. A strike, even if it lasts for several days, is still considered one act.

Two other explanations should also be considered. One explanation suggests that the difficulties of mobilizing are much greater than usually thought. Even organized groups may find it difficult to carry out more than one act. A second explanation is that protests in Israel are so successful that one act is sufficient to achieve most goals. In each of these claims it is assumed that one of the two sides in a political conflict is easily defeated. Although no definitive answer can be given to any of these suggestions, some light is shed on this issue by the evidence presented below.

The proportion of groups which breaks the law is similar to figures presented earlier. The fact that a third of all protest groups breaks the law is even more remarkable in light of the general level of organization and resources. Even organized groups in Israel apparently feel the need to resort to provocative politics.

Impressions about the level of organization and resources of Israeli protest groups is reinforced by the distribution of collective actions (Table 5–2). Over 60% of all protest acts consist of either strikes or workers' sanctions, acts which can almost only be carried out by organized groups. Most acts of protest include at least one hundred people and over a third exceed the 500 mark. Very few ad hoc groups are capable of executing such a mobilization.

The breakdown by type of action suggested that there is very little innovation in Israeli protest; few groups go beyond the standard fare of strikes, demonstrations, and sanctions. Even the less conventional acts are somewhat ritualized and street blocking and stone throwing are clearly the most popular forms of disorder and violence. The repertoire of Israeli protest appears rather narrow. The majority of acts are also short; few last for more than a few hours.

The final distribution, concerning geographic spread, also provided some food for thought. Although the political center of Jerusalem is the most popular single place for such acts, the percentage carried out in other locations is quite high. Indeed, 26% of all protest acts fall into the "other" category which is composed mostly of small towns.

Table 5–2
Israeli Protest Acts: Distribution of Traits

Type (N = 978)		Size (N = 408)		Duration (N = 741)	
Strikes	46.3%	–100	35%	Hours	74%
Demonstrations	24.8%	101–500	27%	Day	11%
Sanctions	12.3%	501–1000	26%	Days - Week	12%
Protest Vigils	5.5%	1001–	12%	More Than	
Sit-ins	1.8%			Week	3%
Meetings	1.3%				
Other	7.8%				

Disorder/Violence[a] (N = 1010)		Location (N = 741)	
Throwing Stones	15%	National	18%
		Jerusalem	26%
Blocking Streets	14%	Tel Aviv	13%
Trespassing	9%	Haifa	5%
Damage Property	5%	Occupied Territories	13%
Burning Tires	5%		
		Other	26%
Blows	3%		

a. Some acts may fall into more than one category. Percentages are based on proportion of total acts which fall into each category.

The picture of Israeli collective action is now a bit clearer. It is dominated by fairly large groups carrying out very few acts of short duration. Most groups tend to adhere to a narrow set of options, but disorder and violence are surprisingly frequent. Most of the demands are material rather than ideological and the scope of mobilization is usually municipal or national.

It is worthwhile to consider these acts as forms of political communication. If, as claimed, many Israeli groups find it difficult to make demands through formal channels, then the avenue of protest offers a convenient substitute. The messages need not be long nor complicated, merely public. Ironically, this process leads to the *institutionalization of protest*, where each side plays out a well-known script.

Once again, however, an emphasis on trends and averages can be misleading. The important question about political protest is which groups carry out what types of actions. Having described the "what" of collective action, the "why" must now be explained.

THE MODEL

The model of collective action to be used in this chapter is presented in Figure 5–1. As in the past, the model begins by considering the effects of background factors on the potential for action. This potential is determined by the degree of successful mobilization. Group leaders then attempt to develop a strategy and a repertoire which is congruent with their organization and resources, the needs of their particular group, and beliefs about the efficacy and risks of various alternatives. An additional part of the model, not considered in previous formulations, is related to the outcomes of this behavior. It is detached from the rest of the model and is dealt with in a separate chapter.

The model is not meant to be comprehensive. Rather, it is an attempt to demonstrate how the basic logic of political action remains consistent. In addition, the model is limited to including those major variables which are conducive to farily direct empirical measurement. Despite this intention, the variables set in parentheses are, again, those which proved impossible to measure, although some can be inferred from the overall pattern of results.

Background and Mobilization: Developing a Potential for Action

The most important determinant of collective action is the level of group organization.[4] It will be remembered that Tilly (1978, 53) defined organization as " ... the extent of common identity and underlying structure among individuals in a population." In keeping with this notion, the discussion begins with an attempt to understand the effects of internal ties on the crystallization of interests and the mobilization of resources.

The first variable is the degree of *group structure*, which is clearly one of the most important factors affecting the potential for action. Such factors as a clear division of labor, a central leadership, and

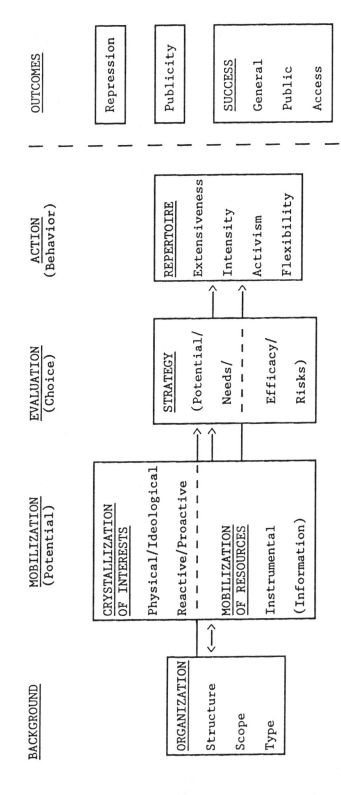

Figure 5-1
Explaining Collective Political Action

an existent bureaucracy enable a population to both accumulate and exercise collective control over *resources*. As Gamson (1975) put it, these are the best indicators of a group's "combat readiness."

Structure also affects the crystallization of *interests*. In creating a group structure leaders must define these interests and communicate them to the membership. During mobilization, a more sophisticated structure allows for both a clearer definition of group interests and a more efficient process of socialization. A labor union, for example, will formulate an explicit list of demands and publicize their aims to the membership. Ad hoc groups, on the other hand, will be less formalistic about such goals and the crystallization of interests is likely to be more ambiguous.

Consideration must be given to the reverse process: how the crystallization of group interests affects group structure. Eighty-seven percent of all economic groups in the sample have permanent structures whereas only 31% of educational and welfare groups are organized. It could also be said, however, that people only develop professional organizations because they work together. It is best, therefore, to think of a cycle of mutual influence between structure and interests.[5]

The *scope* of group ties also affects the process of mobilization. The range of internal ties influences both the crystallization of interest and the mobilization of resources. Seventy-six percent of all local protest goups in Israel have demands which relate to either education or welfare, whereas only 13% of all national groups deals with these issues. National mobilizations, on the other hand, are much more likely to deal with either economic (60%) or ideological (28%) issues.

The scope of the group also affects its ability to mobilize resources. Local groups have more limited means, due to their size. They may compensate for this flaw through an unusual sense of identity, but this is the exception rather than the rule. A neighborhood group trying to get a new traffic light installed can almost never hope to mobilize many outsiders to their cause.

The final variable concerned with group ties uses the ambigious term *type* and is meant to convey the importance of understanding the nature of the bonds. It is useful to know whether the group is based on such principles as professional relations, religious affiliation, or ethnic identification to better deal with the degree of collective identity. The relationship between the nature of the ties and interests often borders on the obvious, (religious ties lead to religious interests) but the categories should be kept analytically distinct.

In Israel, for example, 70% of all Arab groups mobilized for explicitly political purposes. In other countries such groups might be more likely to make either economic or educational demands, but minority ties in the Jewish state are inherently political. The number of "type" distinctions is almost limitless, but it should be possible to identify the modal classifications for a given culture.

The effects of group background on the process of collective mobilization are, in many ways, similar to those which were discussed in reference to individual political actors. The effects of organization, for example, resemble those of education. There are also, however, important differences between the two levels of analysis. The relationship between group background and mobilization is more complex. This is because the division between the two stages is more distinct for individual actors than for groups. The relationship between group organization and resources is so close that researchers often find it difficult to empirically distinguish between the two variables (Tilly 1978, 78–79). Is the existence of a group office, for example, indicative of a higher level of organization or of more resources?

The relationship is also more complicated because of the aforementioned cycle of mutual effects. Individual interests and resources rarely affect a person's background, but the same can not be said about groups. It is important to keep this complex relationship in mind when attempting to explain actual behavior.

Patterns of Mobilization and Collective Action

Having dealt with the relationship between background and mobilization, the effects of varying patterns of mobilization on collective strategy and actions must be considered (See Figure 5–1).

At the stage of *mobilization*, the population becomes a coherent group, i.e., crystallizes in terms of both form and content. The form of the group is determined by its level of physical and personal resources. A distinction is made between instrumental resources, which must be constantly replenished, and informational resources, which tend to be more cumulative.

There is a relationship between the two types of resources. Political knowledge and experience allow leaders to better mobilize and exploit instrumental resources such as money and membership; instrumental resources such as an office staff allow a group to gain experience and knowledge.

Both types of resources not only establish the potential for action but also have an effect on the crystallization of interests. The range and quality of interests are clearly influenced by the number of staff, membership, and amount of knowledge of the political world. Bureaucracies tend to perpetuate themselves.

The type of *shared interests* provides the content for group mobilization. Two types of distinctions are considered here, ideological versus physical interests and reactive versus proactive interests. Physical interests include collective motivations which offer concrete benefits to the population, such as housing, money, or workers' benefits. Ideological interests are more related to symbolic gratification and include such needs as political change, religious observance, and the preservation of culture.

The degree to which an interest is reactive or proactive refers to the source of conflict. Reactive interests are formed on the basis of some type of action by another party, such as the political authorities. A synonym for such interests is threats and in such cases the group is usually attempting to maintain the status quo. Examples would include plans to evacuate a community or threats to prevent certain religious practices. When proactive interests crystallize, it is the group which seeks to change the status quo. Such interests would include workers' struggles for better working conditions and campaigns designed to influence public opinion.

The pattern of mobilization is critical to the development of group *strategy*. Group leaders must take into account the group's level of organization and resources and collective goals, as well as the relative risks and benefits of alternative actions. They then choose a political action repertoire which reflects these differences. To simulate such choices, a model of mobilization is needed in which the complex interactions of these variables are considered.

Patterns of Mobilization: A Typology

A starting point is provided by Oberschall's (1973) theory of collective action. The author distinguished between two types of group links: those within the "collectivity" and those between "collectivities." Oberschall described the importance of internal links in terms which should now sound familiar:

> For sustained resistance or protest an organizational base and continuity of leadership are necessary. The organizational base can be rooted in two different types of social structure. The collectivity might be integrated and organized along viable traditional lines based on kinship, village, ethnic or tribal organization, or other forms of

community. . . . On the other hand the collectivity might have a dense network of secondary groups based on occupational, religious, civic, economic, and other special interests and . . . associational ties. (119)

Oberschall went on to distinguish between three types of links: weak, associational, and communal. Collectivities with weak ties rarely mobilize, but communal and associational ties both lead to a "sentiment of solidarity that can be activated for the pursuit of collective goals." (119)

Turning to the subject of external links, Oberschall emphasized the importance of the population's integration into the general society. He argued that *segmented societies* provided an especially fertile breeding ground for group mobilization.

On the vertical dimension as we move from a vertically integrated to a segmented social structure, social control over the collectivity from outside weakens and shared sentiments of collective oppression and common objects of hostility are likely to increase among members of the collectivity with grievances. Thus, the minimum conditions for collective protest are more likely to be present as the group or collectivity becomes increasingly cut off from other strata in the society. (121)

When the three dimensions of internal links are combined with the two categories of external links it provides a convincing six-group typology. What is lacking from the Oberschall model is the effects of differing types of shared interests. Just as the motivations of individuals have a direct effect on their choice of strategies, so collective interests influence group choices. The model used in the present study overcomes this problem and is presented in Figure 5–2.

Figure 5–2

Patterns of Mobilization: A Typology

| | | Internal Ties | | |
		Weak	Communal	Associational
Shared Interests	Physical	AD HOC	COMMUNITY ACTION GROUP	UNION
	Ideological	AD HOC	SECT	MOVEMENT

The model maintains the Oberschall distinction with regard to internal links but substitutes the distinction between physical and ideological interests for the previous division concerning group segregation. Later the effects of reactive versus proactive interests are also considered. Although the notion of external links is an important one, the present approach should offer a more appropriate tool for explaining the political action repertoires in more integrated Western societies. Many of Oberschall's principles can still be incorporated into the present formulaticn.

The purpose of the model is to offer a way of summarizing the effects of background, resources, and interest on patterns of mobilization. Five ideal group types are presented, each representing a different *process of mobilization*. The logic of the analysis is based on the assumption that groups develop strategies and actions which are appropriate for their particular set of needs. These needs, in turn, are best understood by examining the organizational base of the group and the nature of shared interests.

Ad Hoc protest groups have little or no organizational structure and very few collective resources. They are usually formed in reaction to a specific event and are often based on either friendship networks or loose geographic ties. A typical example for Israel is offered by groups of unemployed workers who are organized from time to time. They are almost always local groups and are rarely able to carry out more than a demonstration or two against the government. Ad hoc groups can also have ideological interests such as the secular groups which sometimes spring up in reaction to religious protests.

Four ideal types are used to distinguished among the many organized collectivities: Communal Action Groups, Sects, Unions, and Movements. All these groups establish at least a minimal level of common identity and bureaucratic structure.

The organizational structure of *Community Action Groups* is usually based on elected councils of either neighborhoods or towns. Although such councils usually exploit more formal channels of influence, they too are often stymied by government intransigence. Local leaders in Israel find it useful to mobilize community residents into a protest group to publicize their demands. This scenario is especially common when local councils run out of funds and hope to embarrass the central authorities. Also included in this category are the organized agricultural settlements in Israel which have become quite adept in the use of mobilized action.

A very different type of communal mobilization is organized around *Sects*. Here the shared interests are ideological, a fact which both segregates the community from the rest of society and strength-cns the members' sense of common identity. Two of the clearest examples in Israel are the ultra-religious Charedim (the fearful) and Israeli Arabs. Although both Arabs and Charedim are also joined by associational ties, their most common form of mobilization is communal and ideological.

The internal ties of such groups are not merely geographic; they encompass religion, language, law, and even dress. Sect membership establishes rules for an entire way of life. Although Sects also share physical interests, most conflicts with the outside world center on a clash between cultures.

Associational ties are less encompassing than communal bonds. The internal ties are more artificial and more diffuse. Association members must make a point of coming together to act: they live separately.

Associations which were formed for the pursuit of material interests are labelled *Unions*. This is the most common form of mobilization in Israel and it includes all professional groups and workers' unions. They resemble Community Action Groups in the sense that many of their demands are made in private. Unions also find it useful to turn to protest periodically and, due to the centralized nature of the Israeli economy, a good deal of this protest is against the government.

The final ideal group type is a *Movement*, which is defined as an association with ideological interests. Technically, this would also include political parties, but the discussion is explicitly concerned with extra-parliamentary forms of mobilization. It is important (but not always easy) to distinguish between an ad hoc ideological group (e.g., Elections Now) and an organized Movement. Movements are distinguished by a commitment to longterm social or political change and a viable organizational structure. As mentioned, the two best known movements in Israel are Peace Now and Gush Emunim.

As with the previous typology, these classifications tend to gloss over important differences within categories. The distinciton being made between organized and unorganized groups, for example, is rather crude and in a more developed theory a wider range of resources could be considered.

The typology is also not all inclusive. Lobbies, for example, were purposely left out of the model because of the emphasis within this study on extraparliamentary types of mobilizations. The typology does, however, offer a convenient summary of the most common interactions between organization and interests.

Political Action Repertoires

The research hypotheses will attempt to explain how each group type is associated with a different repertoire of political actions. Collective repertoires are defined in the present study by looking at four dimensions of group activity: *extensiveness* (number of participants), *intensity* (level of disorder and violence), *activism* (number of acts), and *flexibility* (degree of innovation). The hypotheses are based on understanding the ways in which internal ties and shared interests affect group strategy.

When internal ties are weak, the type of interest being pursued is irrelevant. The lack of resources of Ad Hoc groups puts a severe limit on group options. Turner (1970), for example, distinguished between expressive and strategic acts. He argued that unorganized groups tend to employ expressive acts in which insecure leaders use the maximum force to coalesce their following. Recognized leaders from more substantial groups, he argued, can address themselves to the strategic problems at hand rather than group maintenance.

Oberschall's (1973) hypothesis about such groups ran along similar lines:

> If a collectivity is disorganized or unorganized along traditional communal lines and not yet organized along associational lines, collective protest is possible when members share common sentiments of oppression and targets for hostility. . . . Such protest will, however, tend to be more short-lived and more violent than movements based on communal or associational organization.

The lack of resources leaves few options for such groups and, when forced to act, they turn to the only real weapon available. Thus, it is reasonable to hypothesize that the repertoire of Ad Hoc groups will be short and violent.

The effects of communal ties and associational ties on political action can be related to a similar dilemma: choosing between a strategy of intensity and a strategy of extensiveness. An intensive strategy relies on the use of force to make an impact, whereas the extensive approach relies on large scale numbers. The choice between the two paths is determined, it is claimed, by the nature of group organization.

There are also a number of reasons to argue that communal ties lead to a more intensive strategy. First, communal groups find it easier to execute the type of rapid mobilization associated with political violence. People living together are quickly assembled. Associational mobilization, on the other hand, must be planned longer in advance so members can be gathered at a particular time and place. This may offer one explanation as to why many modern forms of disorder—blocking streets, rioting, and throwing stones—are inherently territorial. Although violent demonstrations may also take place at work or even on neutral ground, protesters probably feel more secure carrying out such acts when they are closer to home.

In addition, as alluded to earlier, groups which share a strong communal identity often share other social or ethnic identities which tend to segregate them from the rest of society. In keeping with Oberschall's (1973) theory, this sense of segregation leads to more intensive forms of protest.[6] In Israel, for example, the very term neighborhoods (schunot) is used as a shorthand for improvised communities, especially in reference to protests. Strong communal ties are rarely based on geography alone.

A third rationale for the link between communal ties and violence is related to the scope of communal ties. The intimacy of communal ties works as a two-edge sword. On the one hand, the strong network allows for a very comprehensive mobilization, i.e., a good proportion of the population are likely to take part. The relatively small size of that population, however, limits the scope of potential recruitment. Unlike associations, communal groups have a fairly well-defined limit to the extensiveness of their protests. Similar to the point made about resources, violence may serve as a convenient substitute for size.

If true, this explanation suggests that *associational ties lead to a repertoire which is more extensive and less violent* than that carried out by communal groups. Associations can rarely achieve the type of solidarity which characterize communal groups. They and their members tend to be more integrated into the general society. Associations are engaged in a process of constantly recruiting new members whom they hope will be available when needed. This need for widespread recruitment inhibits the use of violence because extreme measures tend to alienate the general public.

A strategy of extensiveness is based on the scope of the act rather than its drama. An extensive act is one which either affects a large number of people (e.g., a massive demonstration) or has a significant impact on society (e.g., a strike in essential services). It is no mere coincidence that these two alternatives also help define the concept of newsworthiness. In a sense, all conflict groups must pay the dues of admission to the political arena in one of these two currencies.

The type of shared interests is also likely to have an effect on the level of intensity. There are at least two reasons to suspect that *ideological interests are related to the use of violence.* First, a group with ideological goals may justify a variety of tactical means to achieve a morally important end. Early works by Simmel (1955) and Coser (1956) also put forth this view.

> The parties' consciousness of being mere representatives of super-individual claims, of fighting not for themselves but only for a cause, can give the conflict a radicalism and mercilessness which find their analogy in the general behavior of certain very selfless and very idealistically inclined person . . . and to the consciousness of the individual that he fights not only for himself, and often not for himself at all, but for a great super-personal aim (Simmel 1955, 39–40).

This process of moral justification should be especially prevalent in religious groups (Lofland 1985; McCarthy and Zald 1979) who have individual definitions of moral authority.

A second reason why ideological groups should prove to be more volatile is related to their level of bargaining power. Unless they have a massive amount of public support, most ideological groups enter the political arena with very few concrete weapons. Unlike many organized groups making material demands, ideological goups are unable to carry out strikes. The use of violence is one of the few ways in which such groups can achieve both public attention and the possibility of gaining new recruits. Although such tactics may often prove counterproductive, there may be few alternatives in the modern age of mass media. Once again, violence is seen as a substitute for real power.

Ideological interests should also lead to a more activist repertoire. This expectation concerning the number of acts is explained by the fact that groups seeking ideological goals must mobilize for a long-term struggle; political change is an extremely slow process. In addition, such groups may have to be continually active to convince the membership that the group is still viable. Assuming (as the author does) that such groups also have a sufficient level of organization, they will try to carry out as many acts as possible.

Physical interests are usually more ephemeral. When citizens make demands about such issues as wages, schools, or street safety, they can only be mobilized for public action for a limited amount of time. Such issues tend to be resolved one way or another and do not involve long-term commitments. Some associations (such as unions) are permanently organized, but prefer to use more private means, which are less costly, of making demands. Groups with physical interests should have less activist repertoires.

It is useful to test these initial hypotheses before continuing. It is argued that a strategy of intensity is associated with groups which have less organization and resources, more communal ties, and ideological interests. Groups with higher levels of organization and resources and wider scope should, on the other hand, be more likely to carry out repertoires based on extensiveness.[7]

Scales of intensity, extensiveness, and activism were developed on the basis of group actions. The intensity of a given act was measured by assigning one point if the act was coded as illegal, two points if it was a non-violent disorder (e.g., blocking streets), and three points if it included some act of violence (e.g., throwing stones). The extensiveness of an act was determined by the number of participants. Group scores for these two variables were based on the amount of violence and extensiveness which was exhibited in all of the acts carried out by the group.[8] The number of acts carried out by the group was the measure of activism. The results of the analysis are presented in Table 5–3.

Table 5–3
Mobilization and Political Action: First Cut[a]

	Intensity	Extensiveness	Activism
Permanency[b]	− .34	.31	.08
sig.	(.001)	(.001)	(.05)
N	419	305	419
Scope[c]	− .23	.35	.08
sig.	(.001)	(.001)	(.05)
N	408	302	419
Ideological Interests[d]	.24	− .01	− .22
sig.	(.001)	(n.s.)	(.001)
N	382	293	382

a. The correlations are Pearson coefficients. The results using non parametric measures are very similar.

b. There were two categories: 1. New   2. Established.

c. Groups were ranked in the folowing manner: 1. Neighborhood   2. City Wide   3. Regional   4. National.

d. Groups were ranked in the following manner: 1. Economic   2. Education/ Welfare   3. Political   4. Religious.

All the hypotheses are supported by the data. There seems to be a clear distinction between a strategy of intensity and a strategy of extensiveness. Communal groups, groups without a permanent structure, and ideological groups are the actors who are most prone to violence. Groups with greater levels of organization and scope, on the other hand, are more likely to carry out large, peaceful acts. Finally, the most active groups are, indeed, those who have long-range, ideological interest. Patterns of mobilization clearly have significant effect on political action repertoires.

Armed with this knowledge, it is now possible to anticipate the political action repertoires associated with each of the five patterns of mobilization. These expectations are based on understanding the interaction of organization and interests.

A pattern of mobilization can be either consistent or inconsistent. A consistent mobilization occurs when a group's organizational background and interests both point towards the same type of strategy. Sects, for example, combine communal ties with ideological interests and both of these traits lead to a strategy of violence. The mobilization of movements, on the other hand, is inconsistent. Although associational ties are correlated with an extensive strategy, the ideological interests of a movement tend to drive group leaders towards a policy of intensity. It would be expected that such groups have a rather mixed type of repertoire. *An inconsistent pattern of mobilization should lead to a higher level of flexibility.*

This interactive model should provide a much richer explanation of collective action, as illustrated in Figure 5–3.

Ad Hoc groups lack the organizational structure and the resources necessary for sustained protest. This lack of viable alternatives leads many such groups towards violence. Other, less desperate groups may disband after one or two protests. The repertoire of Ad Hoc groups is likely to be short and unruly, and is summarized by the label Inactive/Dissident.

Community Action Groups are labelled Short-Term Pragmatists. Their level of activism will probably be low due to the temporal nature of the issues which concern such groups. Community Action Groups are labelled Short-Term Pragmatists. Their level of activism will probably be low due to the temporal nature of the issues which concern such groups. Community Action Groups will also be unlikely to carry out an extensive strategy; the size of their constituency and their lack of ideological fervor should also inhibit the use of full-scale violence. This is the rationale for hypothesizing a high level of Pragmatism: the cross-pressures associated with communal ties and physical interests should lead to a greater degree of innovation.

Sects represent the Dissidents in this typology and their consistent pattern of mobilization should, as indicated, produce the highest level of violence. Strong, communal ties and ideological interests point to a repertoire which is both active and intensive. Sects usually have ongoing conflicts with the political authorities and legal restrictions are often viewed with contempt.

Figure 5–3

Mobilization and Political Action Repertoires: Hypotheses

Group Name	Description	Repertoire	Action Type
Ad Hoc	Ties: Weak Interests: Mixed	Activism: Low Intensity: High Extensiveness: Low Flexibility: Low	Inactive/Dissident
Community Action	Ties: Communal Interests: Physical	Activism: Low Intensity: Medium Extensiveness: Low Flexibility: High	Short-Term Pragmatists
Sect	Ties: Communal Interests: Ideol.	Activism: High Intensity: High Extensiveness: Low Flexibility: Low	Dissidents
Union	Ties: Assoc. Interests: Physical	Activism: Low Intensity: Low Extensiveness: High Flexibility: Low	Conformists
Movements	Ties: Assoc. Interests: Ideol.	Activism: High Intensity: Medium Extensiveness: High Flexibility: High	Long-Term Pragmatists

Unions have a completely opposite set of strategic needs and represent the Conformist approach to political action. These associations attempt to mobilize the maximum amount of resources and, given a sufficiently strong organizational base, have a little need for either violence or innovation.

Movements, on the other hand, must find a balance between the need to maintain an effective association and the desire to sustain their ideological integrity. Attempting to achieve both of these aims leads quite logically to a Pragmatist approach to collective action. It is a repertoire which has a strong component of activism, extensiveness, and flexibility. Movements cannot, however, completely avoid the benefits of drama and they should exhibit a medium level of intensity.

The concepts of Inactive, Conformists, Dissident, and Pragmatist take on a somewhat different meaning than before. As all the groups are involved in some form of protest, the labels refer to the extent to which a group relies on legal or illegal means of action.

Despite these differences, the underlying logic of the analysis remains the same for both individual and group actors. The repertoire of the Inactives is, once again, determined more by a lack of resources than by strategy. Conformists are the most fully integrated of the actors and Dissidents are the most alienated. Finally, it is the Pragmatists who find themselves straddling the two modes of action.

To test the model, all the protest groups had to be classified into one of the five ideal categories. They were divided according to the following rules. All new groups were automatically coded as Ad Hoc. For established groups, the most difficult issue was whether to consider a group to have communal or associational ties. Groups with communal ties included all those whose name contained a geographic reference, all non-Jewish ethnic groups, ultra-orthodox groups living in the same community, and all groups organized around a primary or secondary school.[9] Associations included all on-going regional and national organizations, workers' committees, and college and university student groups. Group interests were simpler to classify and any groups with either economic, educational or welfare goals were considered to have physical interests and any groups with either political or religious goals were considered to have ideological interests.[10] Using these decision rules, all the gorups were classified as either Ad Hoc (N = 55), Community Action Groups (N = 88), Sects (N = 44), Unions (N = 215), or Movements (N = 14).[11]

The first analysis refers to differences in intensity, extensiveness, and activism. Action profiles were created for each of the five ideal types and are presented in Figure 5–4. Once again the population means on each of the variables are set to zero to illustrate which groups are above and below the population average.[12]

The model received a good deal of support. The term of Inactive/ Dissident was clearly an appropriate one for Ad Hoc groups. They scored low on activism and extensiveness and high on intensity. Their repertoire is, indeed, both short and brutish.

The results concerning the Community Action Groups were the only ones which were not completely in line with expectations. In fact, it is almost impossible to distinguish between these groups and the Ad Hoc groups. It was assumed that the cross-pressures associated with this particular mobilization would lead to an average level of intensity, but they were second only to Sects in this category. As

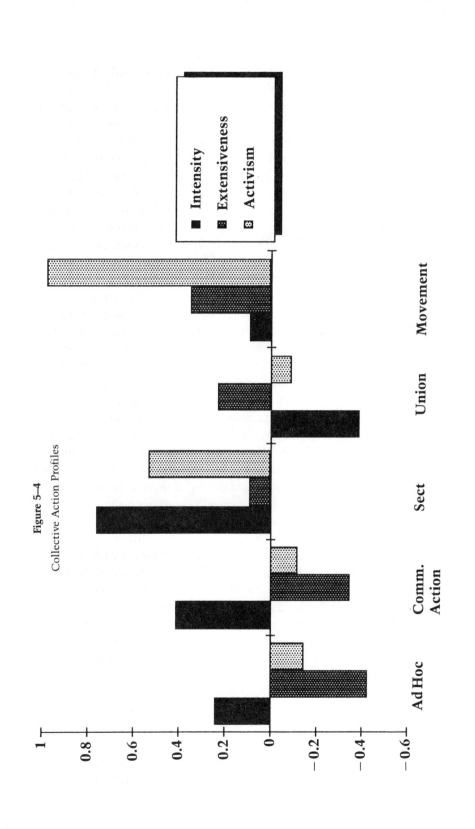

Figure 5-4
Collective Action Profiles

Intensity
Extensiveness
Activism

Movement

Union

Sect

Comm.
Action

Ad Hoc

predicted, however, they exhibited a low degree of activism and extensiveness.

The reason for this finding may have been related to a sense of blocked opportunities. Although community councils *should* be able to use peaceful means of protest, many may feel skeptical about the use of such tactics in Israel. Feeling blocked, such groups are acting more like Dissidents than Pragmatists. If true, this would certainly help explain why the overall level of uncivil disobedience is so high in Israel. This idea would also be consistent with an earlier idea about the institutionalization of protest in Israel. Although only cross-cultural data could offer convincing evidence on this point, there is reason to believe that civil disobedience has become more of the norm than the exception for such groups.[13]

The two groups with consistent patterns of mobilization (Sects and Unions) have political action repertoires which could serve as two points on the intensive-extensive continuum. Sects have an extremely high level of violence and activism and, despite their strong ties, have only an average level of extensiveness. Although in the model an even lower number of participants was anticipated, the fact that these groups are more segregated than Community Action groups may allow for a more comprehensive recruitment.

The Conformist Unions also behaved as expected. They have the lowest degree of intensity, a low degree of activism, and the second highest level of extensiveness. This last figure is somewhat of an underestimation of the power of such groups. If the duration of their acts is looked at, they are the only group with an above average score, due to the use of strikes and sanctions. Unions are able to have an impact without the use of violence.

Movements reflected the dilemmas already discussed. They have an extremely high level of activism, a high rate of participation, and an average level of intensity. The fact that they exhibited medium levels of violence also lends support to the notion of competing needs. It is also noteworthy that only the two ideological groups (Sects and Movements) have above average levels of activism.

The model offers, then, a useful way of summarizing the effects of different mobilizations on these three elements of collective action. It is, however, a static model: it offers no account of how these repertoires would change under varying political circumstances. A further distinction about group interests offered a useful example of such effects.

A *reactive* mobilization will be quite different from a *proactive* mobilization. A group threatened with harm or damage is like a cornered animal with few strategic options. Pressured by time and emotional intensity, the level of violence is likely to be proportional to the degree of threat. The greater the threat, the more dissident and active a group will become.

All groups will take on repertoires which are more intense and more active. Even a conservative Union faced with the possibility of real losses will move in that direction. A group of workers faced with massive lay-offs will become Pragmatist, combining violence with their more conventional types of responses. Movements and Community Action groups facing repression or evacuation are likely to give up peaceful protest and turn to exclusively violent behaviors. Sects and Ad hoc groups will also become more violent. In short, although each group will retain something of its former character, each will move in the direction of dissidence.

Wherever possible, protest acts were coded as to whether they concerned "new issues raised by the group" or "a reaction to some other group." The hypothesis linking reactive protests to violence was supported by the empirical evidence. Reactive protests were more likely to be illegal ($r = .29$, $p. < .001$) and more likely to be violent ($r = .22$, $p. < .001$). This is yet another way in which the nature of group interests affects action.[14]

The remaining variable, flexibility, is the most difficult to operationalize. Ideally a group's repertoire would be looked at over time and an attempt made to determine the level of variability. Unfortunately, the fact that most groups carry out only one or two acts makes this approach unfeasible.

The alternative developed was to examine the deviation from normal protest behavior. As indicated, most collective action in Israel centers around three major formats: demonstrations, strikes, and sanctions. The measure of flexibility was based on the extent to which a group carried out alternative kinds of acts, as can be seen in Table 5–4.

The key column to note is the one labelled "other." It was hypothesized that Movements and Community Action groups would exhibit the greatest level of innovation, due to the cross-pressures created by their internal ties and interests. It was expected that the other three groups would show little flexibility because of the consistency of their collective needs.

The hypothesis is mostly supported, but not perfectly. Movements did indeed, exhibit the highest level of innovation and a remarkable 47% of their acts fall outside of the modal types of collective behavior. This finding fit in well with the image of Movements constantly trying to find new ways to attract interest and recruits.

In addition, both Unions and Sects proved to be conservative in their approach to political action. Considering the proven effectiveness of strikes and sanctions, there is nothing surprising about the first outcome, but the inflexibility of Sects is less obvious. Despite their high level of violence and activity, Sects confined themselves to the same basic script of demonstration after demonstration. The ritual of taking to the street seems to have become especially institutionalized among such groups.

Table 5–4
Mobilization Type and Flexibility

Group Type	N^a	Type of Act		
		Strikes/ Sanctions	Demonstrations	Other
Ad Hoc	88	4.5%	65.9%	29.5%
Community Action	154	12.3%	66.2%	21.4%
Sect	205	7.8%	79.5%	12.7%
Union	406	73.2%	16.5%	10.3%
Movement	93	2.2%	50.5%	47.3%

a. The N refers to the number of *acts*, not the number of groups.

Contrary to expectations, however, Ad Hoc groups showed an even greater degree of flexibility than Community Action groups. It was suggested that lack of experience and resources would limit the creativity of new groups. Perhaps the lack of resources actually has an opposite effect. It might be argued that truly weak groups do not have sufficient resources to mount a demonstration and must, therefore, find other, possibly more violent alternatives.

In general, however, the model proved to be a powerful tool for predicting political action repertoires. Although it was not possible to actually observe the development of group strategy, the logic of strategic needs appears to be sound. Patterns of mobilization have a clear and predictable effect on political action repertoires. The case studies presented in the next chapter allowed for a closer look at this relationship.

Chapter 6

BEYOND THE COLLECTIVE NUMBERS _____

This chapter is devoted to three purposes. First, it is meant to provide a deeper look into the central variables which were introduced in the last chapter. The quantitative analysis was general in its description of organization, resources, and interests. As before, the use of interviews offered a much greater degree of detail and a richer understanding of the dynamics of political action.

The second purpose is to explore those elements of the model which were neglected in previous analyses. The most important of these variables is related to group strategy, which serves as a link between mobilization and action. Interviews with group leaders revealed quite a bit about the ways in which they attempt to choose the best path for achieving group goals. The interviews also shed light on the effects of some of the other actors involved in the conflict, such as the press, the authorities, and other groups. Although the information is biased by the perspective of the interviewees, it offers a starting point for understanding these interactions.

The final goal of the chapter is to deal with several useful exceptions to the model. As in the past, it is important to deal with such deviations to avoid simplistic generalizations and to point to directions for a more complete theory.

The cases chosen were not picked in a random manner. Some of the groups were selected because they protested over the same issue, which provided a useful basis for comparison. Others were selected to illustrate the dynamics of a particular kind of protest, such as that mounted by Community Action Groups and Sects. The sample of cases is not meant to be representative: It is intended to elucidate specifics rather than explain general laws.

In keeping with this approach, the interviews were extremely open-ended. The core questions centered on three areas of interest: organization and mobilization, strategy and repertoires, and interactions with other actors. The bulk of the interviews were based on following up ideas suggested by the leaders' responses to the more general queries. Although the general framework of the interviews was determined by the theoretical model, the sessions were also devoted to exploring new perspectives.

The discussion is divided into four parts. The first section deals with three groups who were active during the Israeli withdrawal from the town of Yamit.[1] The second part deals with a total of four groups who organized to protest against the Lebanese War. In the third segment the case history of a Community Action Group is looked at, whereas the final discussion is devoted to exploring the protest politics of a particularly important Israeli Sect: the ultra-orthodox Charedim of Jerusalem. Within each case study group variations are highlighted with respect to the three interview sections: organization and mobilization, strategies and repertoires, and interactions with other actors.

PROTEST IN YAMIT

Organization and Mobilization

The Camp David accords, whereby Israel agreed to evacuate the Sinai in exchange for peace with Egypt, were signed in September of 1978. Protests against that decision were carried out from that same month until the last day of withdrawal in the spring of 1982.

There were three major groups active against the government: the farmers, the businessmen, and the Movement to Stop the Retreat from Sinai. The farmers from the agricultural settlements surrounding Yamit were the first to become organized and active. Although some of their initial protests were against the withdrawal itself, they reluctantly accepted the inevitable and most of their actions were designed to persuade the government to grant them the maximum amount of compensation for evacuation and resettlement.

The businessmen's protests were also centered on the compensation issue but began at a much later time. This was the smallest of the three groups (about sixty members) and claimed to represent the owners of the independent enterprises who were especially concerned about the costs of starting new businesses after the evacuation.

The third group, and by far the largest, was the Movement to Stop the Withdrawal from Sinai. It was a coalition between religious Jews who believed that Yamit was part of the historical, holy land of Israel and secular Israelis who were opposed to giving up Sinai for security reasons. The movement was distinguished from the other two groups not only by its ideological focus, but also by the fact that its members came almost exclusively from outside of the Yamit area.

The businessmen were the best example of an Ad Hoc group. No formal organization had been set up before the governmental decision to evacuate the town. The group had been organized much later than the others and the sense of common identity was based on an intensive bitterness about how the evacuation was being handled by the government. The group had no office, no common treasury, no formal division of responsibility, and no experience to guide them. The leadership was never formally elected and many of the early meetings were devoted to power struggles about who would represent the group to the authorities.

The setting for the interview with the leader of the businessmen's group was revealing. It was held in his back yard, sitting on lounge chairs, and there were no interruptions. This was rather surprising because the group had just returned from a major news conference in Jerusalem in which he attacked the rather large amount of compensation the government had agreed to pay the farmers.

This scene contrasted markedly with the one which was observed during the interview with the farmers' group leader. It was held in his office and although his secretary attempted to protect him from too many phone calls, the interview took about three times as long as planned. The phone calls were from both representatives of the mass media and fellow organizers. The mimeograph machine in the outer office was, at the same time, running off the latest press release.

The Farmer's group falls somewhere in between the ideal types of Community Action Group and a Union. Most of the farms represented were located in a fairly small area. The formal organization was an association whose executive committee was comprised of representatives from each community. The agricultural settlements surrounding the town of Yamit were both *kibbutzim*, which are completely collective exterprises, and *moshavim*, where there is more private ownership of land and production. All the settlements had an elected and recognized leadership, a history of collective decision making, and an ongoing collective treasury.

These factors offered tremendous advantages in the mobilization

tion of resources. One of the first acts of the farmers' organization was to choose a leader who would work full time on the issue of compensation. Other members of the communities were often given the job of attending protests: members had no need to miss work in order to participate. The leaders also had a wealth of political experience and contacts which had been gained from years of negotiating with the government about agricultural policies. This means of access was especially important because the Ministry of Agriculture was put in charge of their evacuation.

The Movement to Stop the Withdrawal from Sinai also had many organizational advantages. Despite the fact that it was created after the signing of the Camp David Accords, the largest nucleus of members came from Gush Emunim settlers living on the West Bank. All the movement leadership moved to Yamit and brought with them a good part of the political and organizational infrastructure. One of the leaders talked about the difference between Gush Emunim and Peace Now in terms which should sound familiar.

> Peace Now doesn't have our resources; they do a demonstration here and a demonstration there. If we didn't have established settlements, we could never have brought the people to Yamit. Organization means communication, water, food, and generators. Only a movement that has a base can accomplish something.

The Movement to Stop the Withdrawal from Sinai was a coalition of groups, both religious and secular. It did not, therefore, have the same sense of common identity as the core group of Gush Emunim. The driving force of the parent movement was a major reason for the group's successful mobilization: the membership list numbered in the thousands.

Strategy and Repertoires

For the most part the strategies and repertoires of the three groups in Yamit were consistent with their respective patterns of mobilization, i.e., the Ad Hoc Businessmen, the Union of Farmers, and the Movement to Stop the Withdrawal from Sinai. All the groups, however, were understandably more activist and more intensive than the ideal types: they all experienced reactive mobilizations. The evacuation of Sinai was not only an especially traumatic type of threat, but also had a specific date of execution. It is rather exceptional for a protest group to know exactly when it will be forced to disband.

The businessmen's strategy was one of brinksmanship. They had no resources to bargain with and their only hope was to provoke the government with threats and acts of violence. They burned several abandoned houses and then proceeded to close the town, with the cooperation of most of the Yamit residents.[2] Neither people nor vehicles were allowed to enter or leave the town and the barbed wire gates were guarded twenty-four hours a day. The leaders threatened to violently resist any attempts by the army to open the town. Politicians were hanged in effigy on a daily basis.

The strategy was one of desperation. The businessmen were hoping to force the government to the negotiating table. Their only real weapon was the publicity they had generated. Some were also prepared to forcibly resist the army but they were clearly in the minority. Most hoped that their cry of need would settle the issue once and for all.

The government did in fact send a representative to meet with the businessmen, but as the issue faded from the news, the negotiations began to drag. The second time the group closed the town they were better organized and turned all their attention to exploiting mass media coverage. Children filling sandbags were readily provided for photo opportunities, houseburnings were coordinated to ensure television coverage, and a bulldozer dug a few small channels at the entrance to the town which were labelled "anti-tank bunkers." As long as the press was willing to treat such stunts as news, real violence seemed unnecessary.

The strategy of brinksmanship, however, is a dangerous game. The risks of real violence are always present and pseudo-violence has a natural time limit associated with it. The businessmen came to face the inevitable dilemma of either turning to real violence or giving up the cause. Threats were no longer newsworthy.

In addition, although the first closing had created public sympathy, the second caused a severe backlash within the Israeli public. The businessmen were protrayed as a small group of unrepresentative "extortionists" in newspaper editorials, government statements, and even comedy shows on radio and television.

The risks of continued action proved too great. After receiving a symbolic gesture from the government, the businessmen gave up their public struggle. Two of the leaders threatened suicide during the last days before the evacuation, but they were barely heard above the protests of the other, more organized groups.

The strategy and repertoire of the farmers' group offered a sharp contrast to those of the buinessmen. The Farmers began their struggle immediately after the treaty signing at Camp David. They hired one of the most prestigious law firms in the country and withheld their produce shipment to the northern part of the country, which depends on the fruits and vegetables during the winter months. Only an organized group with resources can use such tactics.

They also carried out a number of public protests, including a demonstration with tractors in front of the Knesset. For the most part, however, their protests were relatively minor acts of disobedience designed to bring pressure on the government at certain critical junctures in the negotiations. One reporter summed up a conclusion shared by many observers of Yamit:

> The businessmen waited till the last minute and then went overboard. The farmers were much more restrained but they got what they wanted. . . . During the negotiations with the government you couldn't get a word out of them, but if the negotiations were not going the way they liked, they'd close the road to Egypt for a few hours and almost always got exactly what they wanted.

The farmers' level of organization and resources allowed them a much wider choice of options. They carried out their struggle against the government on a variety of fronts and exhibited a good deal of innovation. In this sense they were an exception to the theoretical model in which it is claimed that Unions are always the most conservative actors. The extent of the threat forced the farmers to use more intense tactics. Such actions are consistent with the claim that Unions behave more like Pragmatists under such circumstances.

The farmers signed a rather generous agreement with the government not long after the businessmen began their protests. The agreement was eventually nullified by a special act of the Knesset, but few would question the ultimate success of the farmers' protest.

The strategy of the Movement to Stop the Withdrawal from Sinai changed during the course of the struggle. Initially, the leaders hoped to bring a massive number of supporters to live in Yamit. If the tens of thousands who had signed petitions had moved to Yamit, it would indeed have created a very large problem for the government. Although several thousand people did come to Yamit, even those who might have made the sacrifice were deterred when the government closed Yamit and declared it a military area.

To attract new recruits, the leaders adopted a strategy which was based on choosing actions which were exciting enough to gain media coverage, but peaceful enough to avoid alienating the general public.

The acts included setting up new, illegal settlements, breaking into abandoned homes, and physically obstructing all attempts to dismantle equipment and structures.

One of the leaders explained the rationale for this strategy of peaceful resistance.

> It's always a problem with any popular movement, and certainly a protest movement. On the one hand you want publicity, on the other, you don't want to create scandals—it's just not our way, and in any case it's not effective from a public relations point of view.

As the date of the evacuation grew near, the strategy turned in two directions. The first theme was one of martyrdom, when many of the members threatened to commit ritual suicide if the land was given up. Such a strategy offered a convenient option for those who feel ideologically opposed to actual aggression. Threats or acts of martyrdom provided the drama of other forms of violence without the risks of either public backlash or official repression. No one, however, actually committed suicide in Yamit.

The second strategy was based on making the final evacuation of Yamit as traumatic as possible. Although the leadership stressed the concept of non-violent resistance, many of the more radical elements were quite vocal in their threats. Televised news carried daily scenes of settlers building fortifications on their roofs and preparing rocks, cans of nails, and other home-made weapons of resistance. Although few expected to actually prevent the evacuation, it was hoped that the trauma would prevent any similar scene later taking place on the West Bank.

The final roof top battle was indeed dramatic, although any collective lessons which emerged from the event remain controversial.[3] Despite all the threats and preparations, both the army and the protesters exercised a great deal of restraint. There were no major injuries. One of the leaders explained the executive's decision to limit the level of violence:

> We decided that Yamit was lost and there was no point continuing the violence. Don't get me wrong—it wasn't out of the beauty of our souls. It's just that we saw that there were other battles, and it wasn't worth the price in terms of our image without the benefit of saving Yamit.

It was the long-term interests of Gush Emunim, therefore, which helped determine the final level of intensity. Although ideological fervor pushed many followers to consider more extreme acts, the leadership understood the importance of a wider perspective. The development of a strategy by the Movement to Stop the Withdrawal from Sinai offers a perfect illustration of the pressures associated with a Pragmatist approach to political action.

Other Actors

It is useful to consider at least some of the interactions which all three groups had with other actors during the conflict. These effects are mostly ignored in the theoretical model and it is worthwhile to consider some of the ways in which other actors can affect political action repertoires.

One is struck first by the degree of competition between the groups over the resource of publicity. The businessmen were unable to get any coverage for their demands until they closed the town. One reporter described the process:

> For months they ran around begging to get more coverage of their demands. The government was basically ignoring them and using the time [before the evacuation] to reduce their claims. As soon as they closed the city and burned those houses, they were surrounded by reporters and cameras from all over the world. Now the press was running after them.

Problems of competition were especially acute for the leaders of The Movement to Stop the Withdrawal from Sinai. The issue of money and greed was easier to package for the news than ideology. It became especially difficult after the businessmen became active. As one leader put it:

> We had a real problem when we wanted to transfer the public's attention from the compensation issue to the withdrawal. It was almost impossible. . . . They [the businessmen] were threatening and getting coverage and we were creating settlements and being ignored.

This was one of the major reasons the Movement to Stop the Withdrawal from Sinai decided to use more dramatic tactics.

There was also a good deal of competition between the businessmen and the farmers. It was the businessmen who publicized the farmer's agreement with the government, in an attempt to embarrass both sides. The farmers, however, pretty much ignored the businessmen and saw them as amateurs.

The mass media were another set of actors which had a significant effect on protest. The relationship between reporters and protest leaders can be described as a "competitive symbiosis" (Wolfsfeld, 1984b). The symbiotic part of the relationship was based on the fact that both protest leaders and reporters have a mutual interest in publicity. Many of the reporters in Yamit had high hopes for the effect the story would have on their careers. The reporters were eager partners in the creation of media events.

Despite this cooperation, protest leaders and reporters also had conflicting interests. The rules of the news industry demand that the story be dramatic, which often means scandalous. All the groups had to adapt their action repertoires to meet the demands of the mass media. Few were pleased about the way in which the media presented the story.

The businessmen and farmers were enraged when depicted as extortionists, whereas the leaders of the Movement to Stop the Withdrawal from Sinai complained that the news always emphasized the weird and unusual elements in the movement. The leaders learned that obtaining media attention is not the same as media control. Although the exchange of publicity for information was usually carried out smoothly, each side attempted to insure an optimal level of profit.

A final note is in order about the relationship with the government. The experience at Yamit was quite illustrative of the government's ability to raise and lower the cost of political action, a process with a clear effect on political action repertoires. The Likud government was in some ways embarrassed by its agreement to dismantle Jewish settlements. This helps explain its extremely high level of tolerance and even encouragement of protests in Yamit. There were a few arrests and several fines were paid, but for the most part none of those involved in civil disobedience at Yamit were ever punished.

Indeed there are many who argued that the government had a direct interest in facilitating the activities of the groups, especially those of the Movement to Stop the Withdrawal from Sinai. The government was fully aware, for example, of the ways in which the movement was smuggling people into Yamit for the final confrontation. The political leaders had their own reason for favoring a traumatic end to the Yamit story. Several days before the evacuation, government representatives took reporters on a tour of the area, emphasizing the sacrifice Israel was making for peace. This theme was emphasized by the pictures of the resistance which were broadcast around the world.

The activities of Yamit offered an important example of Israeli political action. They showed the relationship between organization, mobilization, and action, as well as the ways in which group leaders attempted to meet group needs through the formulation of a coherent strategy. Yamit also showed some of the inadequacies of the model. Moving from ideal types to concrete cases, the theoretical gaps become more manifest. There is a great deal to learn from these gaps, as further illustrated below.

PROTESTING AGAINST THE WAR IN LEBANON

Organization and Mobilization

On June 6, 1982, Israel invaded Lebanon in an attempt to solve security problems on its Northern border. As in Yamit, the move was controversial, especially when it became apparent that the government had no intention of carrying out a limited operation. This time however, the ideological protest came from the left rather than the right. A large number of groups were formed to oppose the war and other protests were organized by existing organizations.

Extensive interviews were conducted with leaders from three Ad Hoc groups and one Movement. The three Ad Hoc groups were Women Against the War, Soldiers Against Silence, and Parents Against Silence; the Movement was Peace Now. One leader was interviewed from each group. Despite the fact that all three groups were attempting to achieve the same aim, their backgrounds and patterns of mobilization set the stage for very different types of strategies and repertoires.

The least organized group was Women Against the War. It was one of the first groups to mobilize and was formed by a number of individuals who had been active in the feminist movement in Israel. At first glance it might seem that this base would offer an important focal point for organization. The group was unable to exploit this resource, however, apart from obtaining access to the mailing list.

Almost all the ties between the group were personal ones and the telephone was the primary means of internal communication. The group had no collective funds, no office, and no organizing structure. The leaders had full time jobs and little time to devote to the cause. Despite the fact that almost all the members identified with the left in Israel, many of the early sessions were devoted to debates about ideological positions towards the war. The members were fully in agreement about women's issues, but the attempt to transfer this sense of common identity to a new agenda totally failed.

Soldiers Against Silence was also an Ad Hoc group, but with a very different pattern of mobilization. The group illustrates that not

all Ad Hoc groups are either weak or doomed to failure. It was organized by soldiers from elite units who returned home from reserve
duty after the initial stages of the war. The soldiers felt betrayed by the
government and wanted to bring their version of the war to the general
public.

The group had a number of advantages over the women's group.
Their sense of common identity was very strong, as many of the men
had served in combat together and the sense of resentment over the
dead and wounded provided a strong emotional bind. Many of the
leaders were students and this allowed them more time for group
work when they were released from reserve duty in the summer.

The group did not, however, have either an office, an initial pool
of money, or a formal division of responsibilities. There was a distinction between those who worked in the public domain and those who
lobbied members of the Knesset, but no chairman was ever elected
and the meetings resembled informal get-togethers among friends.
Based on the previous discussion, much success would not have been
anticipated from such an ad hoc organizational structure.

Soldiers Against Silence had, however, a number of hidden resources which more than made up for both its small size (about thirty
individuals) and its lack of bureaucratic structure. The organization of
the group's first press conference is illustrative in this respect. One of
the early members was Avraham Burg, the son of a cabinet minister
from the National Religious Party. The celebrity status of Burg assured
a large turnout of the press. The group also had some coaching from a
media expert borrowed from Peace Now. The novice soldiers were
taught how to best prepare their message for media consumption:

> A person from Peace Now came and coached us on just how to run the
> news conference. Who should say what, when, etc. . . . That made a big
> difference, because he knew just what they would want to quote. There
> were only fifteen of us then, but we looked much more important
> because of the media coverage.

An even greater resource for the soldiers was the information
they were gathering from the front. It was much more difficult for the
press to gain access to combat units and in any case many soldiers
were reluctant to talk to reporters. Once Soldiers Against Silence had
been formed, however, it served as a convenient address for those who
felt disturbed about the war. As detailed below, this information
proved invaluable in persuading political leaders about the true story
in Lebanon.

Unlike most protest groups, the leadership had no intention of expanding the membership. They were extremely careful about accepting new members.

> We knew that the group had to stay small because of the kind of information we were holding. We could not let just anyone in, it would be a danger to the state. And there were people who wanted to use the group as a springboard for politics and we had to get rid of those people right away. So we were called elitist—which was true.

Soldiers Against Silence was an unusual type of protest group: small, elite, and resourceful. It proved to be a very efficient combination.

The third Ad Hoc group, Parents Against Silence, falls somewhere in between the other two in terms of organization and resources. Although some of the leaders were active during the early stages of the war, the formal group came into existence through a letter to a newspaper by a mother asking other mothers to join her in a group which would parallel Soldiers Against Silence.

Like the other groups, the internal ties of the initial group were based on friendship and there was no formal division of responsibility. One of the members ran the treasury and another was in charge of contacts with the press. The leaders only opened a bank account when the group became a national organization. Revealingly, the leader who was interviewed viewed this informal framework as an advantage.

> That was our strength. We really had no idea the whole thing would last so long. The minute you become institutionalized, you get into all of the power struggles and fighting. . . . We didn't have any of that, there was no President or anything; whoever was active made the decisions.

As with the soldiers, this emphasis on being small and compact was an essential element of the group's mobilization pattern. The leaders had no aspirations to become a massive organization. They also resembled the soldiers' group in that their concerns about their children in danger provided an intensive sense of both purpose and common identity.

The final group to be considered is the Movement of Peace Now. Peace Now was founded in 1978 by a group of soldiers who were not convinced that the government was doing enough to bring about peace with Egypt (Bar-on 1985). The movement grew over the years and is now perceived as the leftist counterweight to Gush Emunim. Its major interest is to contribute to the peace process by opposing what it sees as obstacles to reconciliation (e.g., West Bank settlements). The mobilization of Peace Now during the war offers an important contrast to those of the Ad Hoc groups.

Peace Now has a main office in Jerusalem, and branches (without offices) in Tel Aviv, Haifa, and Beer Sheva. Its treasury is funded from both Israel and abroad. All its workers are volunteers, apart from a fund raiser who works with supporting groups who have been established in the United States. There are several official positions such as spokesperson and treasurer, but no formal chairman. There are regular meetings of the executive, which is made up of those members willing to devote the time. As with many Movements, Peace Now attempts to strike a balance between the need to maintain an informal atmosphere and the necessity of building a formal organizational structure.

Although there is a clear sense of common identity within the peace movement in Israel, the need to maintain a large association takes its toll on solidarity. Leaders find themselves attempting to chart a middle ground between a wide spectrum of political ideologies. The executive member described the group's constant battle against factionalism:

> One example is in the West Bank. Many of the people in Peace Now would not accept the kinds of things that the left in the movement would like to do, either with the P.L.O. or with the Palestinians, so the whole trick is to know what the limits are, you don't want to lose them. These are discussions that go on constantly. It's a very difficult task, and the job of the leadership is to remember what the overall goal is and to avoid becoming a peripheral left wing movement which would wipe us off the map.

The organization and mobilization of Peace Now offers a second illustration of the dilemmas which every Movement must confront.

Strategy and Repertoires

The strategy and repertoires of the four protest groups all reflect something about their organizational base. In contrast to Yamit, however, the relationship between organization and action is more subtle and complex. Whereas the case of Yamit highlighted the strengths of the model, the protest groups in Lebanon also pointed to some of its inadequacies.

The least organized group, Women Against the War, did behave as expected. The group was able to carry out only three small acts: a demonstration of about two hundred in Jerusalem, a smaller gathering in Tel Aviv, and a day of street theater in Jerusalem. Only the demonstration in Jerusalem was covered by the press. The leader of the group was quite lucid about the reasons for failure.

> First of all we organized too early. The public did not really know what was going on in Lebanon, and was certainly not ready for any opposition to the war. The second problem was all of the fighting between the different factions in the group. There were too many disagreements about just how extreme a position to take. After the first demonstration a different group organized a hunger strike and most of the leadership took part. There wasn't much strength after that. There were many groups becoming active and we didn't have anything special to offer. We tried to organize a women's conference on the war, but that never got off the ground because of all the ideological differences.

The point about timing is an interesting one and comes up again. More central to the present argument, however, is the leader's points about the lack of a common identity and the failure to successfully compete with other groups. These basic flaws sealed the fate of this Ad Hoc mobilization. The leadership came to the decision that there were many groups dealing with the war, but only one which was interested in women's issues. This realization supported one of the basic tenets of the research: a successful mobilization is dependent on having a genuine focal point for identification.

Soldiers Against Silence had a much more elaborate strategy. They hoped to use an initial burst of publicity to gain access to the political leadership and then combine private lobbying with public protests. This plan of action proved successful.

First, the very notion of soldiers protesting was, in and of itself, newsworthy. The mass media found this angle extremely appealing and the soldiers had extended coverage for even the smallest demonstrations. Especially helpful, argued the protest leader, were the counter-demonstrations which guaranteed more publicity. The novelty of soldiers demonstrating both for and against a war was clearly news.

Once the media had made them celebrities, the soldiers had complete access to the highest level of government. The government ministers grew to be dependent on the soldiers to find out what was really happening in Lebanon. One minister gave his home phone number to the group and told them to call any time, day or night. The leader described the high point of their influence.

> The height was on August 8, when we let the ministers know that Sharon [the Minister of Defence] was ordering a group to reserve duty and he was forced to release them. There was a decision to go into Beirut and Sharon and Begin believed they could get away with it. We let the other ministers know what was going on in the field, and a really tough cabinet meeting began. Reagan called in the middle to ask if Israel was going into Beirut; Begin said no. Then the other Ministers began to ask really tough questions, because they knew what was going on. Our tactics were very clear: if we go into Beirut, let no one say he didn't know. And when Begin was pressed he changed his mind and canceled the invasion. Sharon got very upset that the ministers knew so much.

The story about the reserve unit which was "called up and not called up" became a major news story in Israel. After that, the leader bragged "they [the other ministers] didn't make a move without us."

There is a good deal of evidence that Soldiers Against Silence had a real impact on the course of the war. The group disbanded after larger forces (Peace Now and the Labor Party) began to lead the opposition. As the school year began in the fall, the leadership decided to disband the group in the same ad hoc manner in which it was formed.

> Everything began with emotions, and ended with emotions. We felt that we had to express what we did. We participated in the demonstration of 400,000 [against the Sabra and Shatilla massacre] and we felt that this was as well as we could do and there was never a meeting again. There was one decision to transfer all the funds to Peace Now—together with the leaders that went over with them. We felt there was no more point to it, the lies had all come out, we had said what we had to say.

The success of Soldiers Against Silence had less to do with organization than their unique set of resources. The initial publicity allowed them through the front doors of power, where they could then exchange information for influence. Few other Ad Hoc groups could expect to achieve so much with so little. The group offered, therefore, an important exception to the rule about Ad Hoc groups.

Parents Against Silence offers a second exception. It followed a similar strategy to the soldiers and although it certainly never achieved the extent of influence exhibited by that group, it did have an impact. Their major strategy was one of diligence. The group carried out some type of action almost every week, sometimes with only a handful of people. A vigil outside of Begin's house (which they had taken over from some medical students) became the focal point of their activities.

If it were necessary to point to a single factor which contributed to the group's survival, it would be necessary to point to their successful mobilization of the mass media. Parents Against Silence received a great deal of coverage and almost all of it was sympathetic. Some of the other group leaders openly expressed admiration for the way the group handled the press. Revealingly, the leader in charge of press relations was, by profession, an image consultant. As she put it, she certainly knew how to speak in front of a microphone. Unlike the feminist group, Parents Against Silence were pictured as mainstream Israel: mothers worrying about their sons in combat. To oppose the group politically was equivalent to insulting motherhood and the army at the same time. As with the soldiers, the parents used their celebrity as a springboard for lobbying efforts. They were extremely fortunate in the amount of publicity they obtained and fit perfectly into one of the central media "frames" (Gitlin 1980) about the war constructed by the Israel press.

Parents Against Silence never considered using illegal tactics and due to the power of the press had no need for such stunts:

> Our group was a test of democracy. The police always tried to help us out and there was no problem getting to see any of the leaders. There was no reason for any more drastic measures because all of the doors were open. We also knew that if we ever broke the law it would boomerang and we'd get a real blow in return.

Unlike the businessmen in Yamit, the mothers who organized the group were able to gain media attention without resorting to civil disobedience. They illustrated the fact that some groups can be novel without using violence. Nevertheless, leaders found themselves always trying to innovate for both internal and external reasons.

> We were always trying to find new ways to protest. Not only for the press but for the members of the group as well. If you don't try new things it's no longer exciting and people aren't going to come.

A continual format of small protests, vigils, and lobbying characterized the group's activities throughout the war. Although neither the amount nor the level of political contacts approached that of the soldiers, Parents Against Silence became an important political reference point for the political elite and the mass media. The group finally disbanned when a new government in Israel made a formal decision to withdraw from Lebanon.

Parents Against Silence illustrated how a group which is adopted by the mass media can achieve a level of importance which would otherwise be impossible. It also showed that some Ad Hoc groups not only survive, but do so without resorting to violence.

The strategy of Peace Now offers a useful comparison to those exhibited by the Ad Hoc groups. The best way to summarize these differences is to distinguish between a short-term and a long-term perspective. One of the leaders of Peace Now described their overall strategy:

> One of the most important things we learned is that you cannot *create* a process. Even if we want peace in Israel, we don't have the power to do that; what we can do is take an existing mood and channel it. If there is no mood there is very little we can do. And that's extremely frustrating—that's the most frustrating thing there is . . . but that's a given, that's the way it is. [Question: Is it a problem because there's only so many times you can call your people out?] Absolutely, when I call out my friends to come to something, they won't come. The art of the game is to know when the public mood exists and not to call them too much or too little, and when you have it not to move it too far, so people won't come back. You have a mandate, and it has limits . . . The trick is to know when . . . The strength of the movement is in numbers and masses. Our limits are the public mood and the fact that we are a voluntary movement. But even if we pay somebody to make a hundred phone calls, they won't come if they are not angry. You can't call them too many times.

During the War in Lebanon many criticized Peace Now for waiting so long to hold its first demonstration. The decision was based on resistance by supporters fighting at the front who objected to any protests while they were in combat. When the movement finally did mobilize it had 150,000 people at the event. The timing of an event is an important strategic decision.

The Lebanese War was seen by the leadership as one event in an ongoing struggle for public opinion. Part of the overall strategy of Peace Now is to avoid breaking the law. When asked about this tendency, the leader's comments were revealingly similar to those expressed by the leaders of Gush Emunim.

> The guiding principle is that we want to be effective, and thus we have to obey the law—the Israeli public won't tolerate it. People often argue for more forceful actions. The summer of '82 was the time I best remember, when those arguments came up the most. When Milson [civilian administrator of the West Bank] was in office, people asked for acts of civil disobedience or violence—let's say you ask for a license in one place but carry out the act in another. But I think the major

consideration is that if we do violate them, we won't get another one. Our relations with the police and the army are very important, and we can very easily be boxed in by legal means; I think that's what guides us. There's always a temptation to block the streets, its a great way to get attention, but in the long-term if we are seen as a bunch of militants we won't have the kind of power we want.

Strategic calculations about the use of unconventional tactics seemed to be based more on questions of practicality than morality. It should not be assumed, however, that this basic commitment to peaceful means is immutable. Given a sufficient threat, even the most moderate members would be willing to break the law.

There's an expression in Peace Now: "Where is your red line?" Annexation is a red line for everyone. If there would be a law for annexation of the West Bank, I wouldn't even try to control the people, although I often try to calm people down. After a certain point no one would care about bad publicity.

This is a good illustration of the effects of threat on group strategy and action. Leaders are not as equiped to either plan strategy or exercise control during a crisis. The only illegal demonstration against the Lebanese War by Peace Now occurred immediately after news reports came in about the massacre in Sabra and Shatilla.

Saturday night, during Rosh Ha'shana (New Year) the news about Sabra and Shatilla came out, and I told them not to demonstrate during the holiday: 'I'll leave the movement, you'll ruin us in the eyes of the public, can't you wait just one more day?' People went to Begin's house and went a little crazy—yelling things they shouldn't have like 'Begin is a murderer,' 'Arik (Sharon) is a murderer.' Then the police came with tear gas. In this case the members had a sense, and they were right, that the public would tolerate an illegal demonstration, because of Sabra and Shatilla. They felt that the event was so bad and the mood so heavy, that it would work, and they were right.

As suggested earlier, a movement must adopt a strategy which is both extensive and activist. This description certainly applies to the activities of Peace Now during the war. The height of its activities came during the protests which demanded a national board of inquiry into the Sabra and Shatilla massacres. Several political parties joined the movement in a demonstration which brought an estimated 400,000 Israelis into the streets against the government. Although the number of protesters never returned to those levels, Peace Now was able to carry out scores of demonstrations throughout the war.

It also attempted a fair amount of innovation. Although demonstrations were its main method, these protests were supplemented by vigils, petition drives, lobbying, and press conferences.

The strategy and repertoires of Peace Now were quite in keeping, then with the ideal type. Attempting to achieve a long-term ideological goal, the Movement adopted a strategy of extensiveness, moderation, and innovation.

Other Actors

One of the interesting things about the protest against the war was the degree of cooperation among the various groups. Apart from Women Against the War, which was damaged by competition, all the other groups coordinated their efforts. The anecdote about Peace Now giving media advice to Soldiers Against Silence is only one example of this phenomenon. The Peace Now leader was asked about the extent to which the presence of other groups was functional or dysfunctional to their own efforts against the war.

> Functional. I think that each one had a different role. Besides many were members of Peace Now who wanted to do something a bit different. Parents Against Silence were absolutely Peace Now people, I mean I know they were. But they found a way to function when Peace Now was tired, or oversaturated. They had a special angle, although there were people who thought that angle was wrong. Parents Against Silence didn't care if they had twenty or fifty, because that's what they were—a small group of parents. At the time of Lebanon we thought the more the better; now there's so little room for anybody.

Leaders from the other two groups expressed similar attitudes about the lack of competition. The leader of Soldiers Against Silence was asked about a second, more radical group, which encouraged soldiers to go to jail rather than serve in Lebanon. He did not see this group as a rival.

> We knew that we couldn't give a clear message—to say one has to both oppose the war and yet fight it. It's a complicated message, which clearly can't be used to mobilize masses of people. They had it easier and had a simple message—this is the limit and that's it. It had a much greater potential as an extra-parliamentary group than we did—because its messages were so simple.

The fact that Soldiers Against Silence transferred its funds and leaders to Peace Now was mentioned earlier. The coordination of small group and large group strategy probably maximized the effects of protests against the war. Competition among conflict groups is not, therefore, inevitable.

A dependency on the mass media is unavoidable. All three groups directed their efforts at public opinion and publicity was an essential part of each of their strategies. The road to political contacts leads through the press. Even Peace Now must constantly renew its level of publicity to maintain stature. When the Peace Now leader was asked about the accessibility of political leaders, she replied:

> It depends on the stocks of Peace Now at the time—in other words what would stop him [the political leader] would be the thought that there would be an article in the newspaper that he refused to see us. That won't matter if nobody cares about us, so we don't always have access. If we're in good shape, then we do.

Although Unions can sometimes avoid the media, neither Ad Hoc organizations nor Movements have that option.

A final note is again in order about the role of the Israeli government. Due to the fact that the majority of protests were peaceful, there was no direct repression of these groups. The government did attempt, however, to delegitimize the protests by publicly questioning the loyalty of the demonstrators. Some argued that this inflamed atmosphere encouraged private citizens to carry out their own reprisals, including throwing a grenade which killed a Peace Now activist and wounded several others. Although few would claim that the government expected reprisals to go so far, the authorities did have a clear interest in raising the risks of protest.

Although there were many other groups protesting about the Lebanese War, the four described here give a certain feeling for the significant variations in both potential and action. The cases pointed to important lessons for the study of collective action, which are dealt with below.

COMMUNITY ACTION: KFAR SHALEM

Organization and Mobilization

Community Action groups represent a more traditional type of collective action. Citizens mobilize to achieve interests which are a natural outcome of their physical proximity. As stated earlier, the extent of solidarity and common identity is a function of the degree of segregation from the rest of society.

Kfar Shalem is a good example of a segregated community. Although formally a part of Tel Aviv, the housing and landscape of Kfar Shalem clearly separates it from the rest of the city. Rather than the normal multi-level apartment houses, the village has a combination of extremely old houses and shacks made of tin. Most of the roads are unpaved and the community has very few services to offer its inhabitants.

The most important factor bringing the people of Kfar Shalem together is the threat of evacuation. In 1962 the government of Israel decided to tear down Kfar Shalem and promised to build a better community in its place. Many of the original settlers left, but were reportedly very disappointed with the transition to a less communal lifestyle and the amount of compensation they were awarded for their homes. Five hundred families remained in Kfar Shalem and refused to move. Unlike Yamit, there is no international deadline which insures an end to the conflict in Kfar Shalem.

The level of common identity is also reinforced by the relatively homogeneous ethnic make-up of the population. The majority of residents are of Moroccan origin (i.e., either they or their parents were born in that country) and most observe at least some religious customs. Tel Aviv as a whole, on the other hand, has a majority of secular, Ashkenazic Jews. Despite the fact that most of the protests revolve around the issue of evacuation and compensation, the leader makes a point of telling of the deeper conflict involved.

> The bitterness is deeper than the physical problems. You see the rich guy in Tel Aviv, and your boss is Ashkenazic, and you were put in *mabarot* [tent camps for the early immigrants] and you have a whole store of bitterness against the system. They brought you here without decent living conditions and they screwed you . . . they make it clear that they're running the show. You go to Tel Aviv and they have a machine for cleaning the streets; they even have a guy that his whole job is to pick up the leaves that drop—really. Then someone thinks— why don't I have that, what, don't I pay taxes? There's something black about me?

Common feelings of discrimination provide a powerful set of internal bonds.

The community council has a formal structure with a chairman, a treasurer, and a spokesperson. Although there is a small amount of money for community projects, the most important collective resource is the citizens themselves. As might be presumed, it is extremely easy to mobilize the citizens to come to protests. The time and place of demonstrations are often announced at the synagogues during Friday night religious services. The initiation of demonstrations, however, rarely comes directly from the council itself. The leader explained the normal process of mobilization in terms similar to those used by the leader of Peace Now.

> The committee doesn't say that tomorrow there will be an activity. It's like with the Histadrut [the national Labor union]. The people are getting upset and it's up to the leadership to direct that anger. When there is anger from below we direct it. The committee decides about the timing of the event and the place, it doesn't initiate it, but it plans it.

Strategy and Repertoires

Protests in Kfar Shalem have ranged from quiet picketing, through the blocking of streets to complete riots. In terms of strategy, the committee has to decide how extreme an action to carry out. The group is divided between the moderates and the militants. The leader who was interviewed is considered a moderate. He opposes the use of violence and clearly prefers to work out some type of compromise with the authorities. His opposition to violence is a question of principle rather than efficacy. He argued that as a citizen he cannot accept everyone living by the "law of the jungle." His faith in the system, however, is rather limited, as illustrated by the following anecdote.

> There was a time when we couldn't get regular bus service to Kfar Shalem. We wrote letters to every public official there was, and as usual the thing dragged on for years. Finally, someone said that we were wasting our time; the only way to get a bus to Kfar Shalem is to burn one. So a bunch of people took a bus and burned it. The next day we had a regular bus coming in. I'm sorry it works that way, but it does.

This is one of the best examples of the effects of blocked opportunities. Everyone, he said, has their own "red lines." If the authorities break the rules of the game then he, too, would become more militant.

> It doesn't matter that you represent the system and I don't, you can't break all of the agreements. You can't simply accept whatever the authorities decide. . . . You could get to an absurd situation where they decide to hang you and you agree to give them the rope. Every man has his limit which he is willing to tolerate and after that he becomes militant. For others that threshold is very low, with me it is in the middle.

The militants of Kfar Shalem are the classic Dissidents and apparently have few qualms about the use of violence. During one period of unrest, they invited the television cameras to photograph a store of Molotov cocktails, threatening all-out war if the authorities tore any more buildings down. The more moderate leader claimed that they had a large cache of weapons taken from the army which served as a powerful deterrent for the authorities. It was no coincidence, he related, that the police avoided these houses and chose safer targets.

The residents of Kfar Shalem tended to vacillate between the strategies of dissidence and pragmatism. The choice is more a matter of circumstance than planning and is better explained in reference to the behavior of the other actors.

Other Actors

It was suggested earlier that protest repertoires evolve out of a process of interactions between group leaders and other actors. Leaders attempt to assess their own potential, the level of threat, and the efficacy and risks associated with alternative paths of action. The local council in Kfar Shalem has an ongoing relationship with three such agents: municipal officials, the police, and the press. Each relationship has its own set of unwritten rules and understandings in which a framework for interactions is established.

The relationship with municipal officials alternates between one of competition and cooperation. The cooperative aspects of the relationship are most obvious when the committee serves as mediator between the residents and the authorities. There is an unwritten agreement, for example, that residents are allowed to build extensions on their homes if they are within their own yards. If someone puts up an additional structure, the community council will not intervene when the city comes to destroy it and will discourage the residents from protesting.

Similar types of understandings define the relationship between the police and leaders. When asked whether or not any members ever went to jail or paid fines for protest violence, the leader explained the rules of the legal game.

> Look, you have to understand how its works. Let's say we decide to block a street. Well, it costs the police a lot of money. They have to bring extra men, give them special equipment, it costs them a lot. Now if they arrest fifteen people, we will make a bigger demonstration, and it

will cost them even more money and time—they have other things to do. So we say to them, 'Look, let them out or we will bring 500 people and that will tie you up but good.' So they say, 'Look, we want to stay home [on our day off]' and they release the people and everything is done honorably. We have sort of an understanding.

The leadership agrees to play the game of protest at a particular level of intensity if he feels the system is playing fair.

Once again, however, it is the mass media which is seen as the key element in success.

Unless you make noise the government doesn't pay any attention to you. When a person is in the dark, you can't see him, that's all there is to it. That's the way the game works. If you have a demonstration and you break things up or you burn something and the television doesn't come, it won't have any effect at all. [Question: Did that ever happen?] No, and that's good, that's democracy, that's the game of democracy. The small guy can express himself by using the mass media. A dictatorship can do whatever it wants, it doesn't have to worry about the press. In Russia you can burn the whole capital down, and there won't be any reaction because it won't be in the press.

He went on to explain that they have learned through experience what the press wants: new things, bigger things, and events which can be photographed. The press is the only way to get results; any other tactic allows the authorities to drag out the conflict in a war of attrition. The latest government plan, for example, calls for the residents to build their own homes on the land with government loans. It was "suddenly" unveiled when the two sides met in a televised confrontation.

The relationship with the press is partially a function of the relations with the authorities. During periods of tension the press is clearly an important ally in raising the issue on the public agenda. During negotiations, however, both the leadership and the authorities have a mutual interest in keeping the press at bay. Publicity about compensation offers can ruin any chances for a negotiated settlement.

In a sense then, the community of Kfar Shalem is an example of the institutionalization of protest politics. It also illustrates the advantages and disadvantages of local mobilizations. The most important advantages are a sense of group solidarity and an organizational structure which is recognized as a legitimate spokesman by both the residents and the authorities. The disadvantages are the natural limits in size which create an unhealthy dependency on the mass media. A more open government bureaucracy might very well change the rules of this rather dangerous game.

A SECT: THE CHAREDIM

Organization and Mobilization

The Charedi Sect [*Ha'Aida Ha'Charedit*] is actually an umbrella organization representing a wide variety of ultra-religious groups, each with its own leaders (usually Rabbis), organizational structures, strategies, and repertoires. Indeed, the variance among Charedi groups closely resembles the distinctions made more generally: it is a veritable microcosm of secular society. This particular discussion centers on the Charedi groups in Jerusalem.

It is useful to talk of two ends of the protest spectrum within the Charedi community. At the conservative end of the political spectrum is *Agudat Yisrael* (the Society of Israel), which has evolved from its historical Anti-Zionist position to one of reconciliation with the mostly secular Jewish state. The Agudah political party has been a coalition partner in all of the recent governments. At the radical end of the scale, is found the militant *Neturai Karta* (the City Guardians) group which continues to oppose the existence of the state and forbids any official contact with the Israeli government. This continuum gives a fairly good representation of both the size of the group (the smallest being Neturai Karta) and the intensity of political actions. All the groups, however, have been involved in forms of civil disobedience and violence in their struggle for a more religious state.

Two in-depth interviews were carried out. The first respondent was not a protest leader, but a reporter for the major Charedi newspaper who has covered religious protests for many years. He belongs to Agudat Yisrael and tends to stress the differences among the groups. The second interview was with one of the better known radicals. Although he has no formal position, the fact that his grandfather is an important official in the Charedi Sect grants him a considerable amount of influence. He finds himself moving from issue to issue trying to mobilize both ad hoc and established groups to his cause.

The entire community is extremely structured and disciplined. There is an overall council which sets general policy for the Sect and groups with disputes are required to bring them to the court. The court also hears petitions about the need to be involved in religious issues and when it gives formal consent, the orders are given throughout the hierarchy and every member is required to participate.

Most mobilizations, however, begin with a particular Rabbi making a proclamation which expresses his concern with a particular religious issue. The more influential the Rabbi, the more likely the cause is to attract followers from other groups. The reporter described the usual chain of events.

> The Rabbi simply turns to his people and tells them that something bothers him and he thinks that public protest can solve the problem. Now, the Charedi community is very disciplined, and structured. It's a hierarchy, the leadership tells the Gabai [Caretaker of the synagogue] what he heard and he passes it on to his people, by telephone, in the streets, whatever. And it's considered an order, if the Rabbi says it, that's it—the Gabai just passes it along, he has no authority. [Question: They leave for the demonstration from the synagogue?] Yes, yes. But that's only good for the Sabbath. During the rest of the week they announce the time and place at morning prayers when they have the biggest congregation of people.

A third pattern of mobilization is organized by smaller groups, some of whom spend all of their time on one issue. There is a small office in the community which is explicitly concerned with combating Christian missionaries, for example. Although they rarely organize a large following, their protests against the building of a Morman center in Jerusalem eventually received an official endorsement which set the stage for massive demonstrations against the municipality.

Finally, there are what appear to be totally spontaneous demonstrations. The reporter described one such event.

> It happens when there is something that really shocks the Charedi community, like the issue of autopsies from a few years ago. That's a matter of faith, if the body doesn't come complete to the cemetery [it can not be buried]—you won't convince him with any other arguments—the sanctity of the body is a central value for him. And when they performed autopsies on Charedim then there were spontaneous outbursts of fury all over the country. They were spontaneous demonstrations, really spontaneous. Not the Rabbi, not anyone else organized it. The family and their friends demonstrated by the doctor's house, by the hospital—whatever, about their pain. That is a pain you can't explain—they go to bury their dead and the cemetery committee tells them, 'You have a problem—there are pieces missing from the body, he can't be buried.' That is something that would inflame any family—and those are spontaneous demonstrations.

A whole range of organizational levels and scope is found within the Charedi community. The Charedi executive and the Rabbis are selective in choosing topics which are of more general concern. They leave room for mobilizations which are more specific in both scope and content.

Strategy and Repertoires

These differences among groups illustrate once again the distinction between extensive and intensive strategies. In fact the newspaper reporter began the interview by stating one of the central findings of this study.

> We can start with an axiom. The smaller the group the more aggressive it is because in a large organized structure, like a party, there is a careful decision-making process. A small group can organize within a few hours with signs and shouting, in (what is called) a spontaneous protest.

He went on to explain that the more influential Rabbis are quite vocal about their objections to violence and often include such warnings in their initial proclamations about protests. Any use of violence would be considered a personal insult. Traditions, however, vary from group to group:

> Most of those leaders are bound by the examples of the past Rabbis, like: 'What did Avraham Blau do in these circumstances, he worked day and night?' People remember how Blau broke into a movie which was half-pornographic and was beaten and even though all the younger people ran away he stayed and fought. You must carry out the commandment [mitzvah] of being present till the end—even if it means your life. The next rabbis can't be more moderate than he was—they must show that they are just as brave, there is a symbol they must imitate.

This sense of sacrifice is an important theme which will be returned to later on in the discussion.

The radical agreed with the distinction between the small violent mobilizations and the larger more orderly protests, but suggested that the discipline is not always completely effective.

> When the council decides on a protest there are exceptions. During the protests against the City of David [archeological excavations] members of the council themselves came and there was still trouble. [Question: People didn't know that there would be violence?] Well the leaders don't know, but we know, those that come to stir up things. The council is always against violence and tries to stop it. But it also depends on how the police act, during the archeological digs the police were very provocative—so violence was more likely.

He also pointed out that the court will sometimes send representatives to the demonstration and can bring violators before the religious court.

Despite these distinctions there are several factors which lead religious protest in Israel to be especially violent. The first is the fervor of a true believer. The reporter attempted to offer an explanation for Charedi violence.

> It happens because he [the Charedi protester] comes to change the world and he doesn't know where to stop. He was taught to give everything he had, he doesn't understand about limits. That's why he uses all of his force—when he demonstrates he gives all his heart. [Question: Do you think it would be different if it were about more general issues, such as housing?] Undoubtedly. He won't demonstrate on cosmopolitan issues. Our population fights for the walls of religion—that's what interests the Charedi people—when you come to a wall you must find some way to overcome it.

This helps explain the value which is put on personal sacrifice. It is necessary to be willing to give up anything in defence of the *Torah* (Law of Moses). The young radical leader talked proudly of those who are willing to take police blows and those who sit in prison the longest: these, he said, are the signs of true commitment. These comments should offer pause to those in the secular community who call for a more aggressive policy towards religious violence. The definition of costs and benefits are in the eyes of the recipient.

The radical also offered a more familiar explanation for his aggressive strategy: it works.

> Take the example of Yam Suf road [a road the religious people want closed to traffic during the Sabbath]. There were demonstrations over two years ago to try to get the street closed, and they [the municipality] promised that if we kept it quiet, they would close the street. And they did nothing—and I said it won't work. We have to have more demonstrations. If you look at all of the streets they closed in Mea Shearim [the central religious neighborhood in Jerusalem] . . . none were ever closed because the Rabbis sat and talked to city hall—only through demonstrations. [What about quiet demonstrations?] Who cares about them? You can have a quiet demonstration every day—and then go home, because no one will hear about it.

Interestingly, however, the leader was not completely comfortable with the term "violence." He tried to explain that the Charedi definition might be somewhat different than that used by the rest of society.

It also depends on what you define as violence—when you close a street, a lot of people will call that violence. With us, that's not violence. On the other hand none of our people will go and kill somebody. Nobody really wants to come to blows with others. [What about throwing rocks?] It's like a tradition. Done from generation to generation. People used to say its forbidden to throw rocks on the Sabbath, but whatever is prepared before the Sabbath can be used—so I guess there must be somebody who prepares the rocks.

Although the statement is somewhat dubious, it does illustrate that there are limits to the level of permissable violence among the Charedim. As the more conservative reporter pointed out, none of the Charedim serve in the army and few have any knowledge or experience in the use of weapons. Again what is striking is the small number of injuries which occur in all of the violent demonstrations. Both interviewees suggested that Jewish law not only motivated the protesters, but also set certain boundaries to their behavior.

Other Actors

One of the interesting questions concerned the extent to which there is cooperation and competition between the various Charedi groups. The picture which emerged from the interviews is surprisingly similar to that which emerged in reference to protests against the war in Lebanon. The large groups and the small groups serve different functions and the ability to mobilize in a variety of frameworks works to the benefit of the overall cause.

The larger organization is again reluctant to overuse the huge political machine it has at its disposal. The reporter described some of the ways in which the work is divided.

Let us take an important authority—like the Rabbi of Gur, who is a dominant personality in the Charedi community. If he says that people should come out and demonstrate against the Ramot pool [a pool in a mixed neighborhood which religious residents want closed], thousands will come and from many groups—even those who don't support him, but he would not do that. [Question: Why not?] Because he makes a clear distinction between local matters and those that demand national attention. Thus, the El Al issue [in which the religious demanded that the airline not fly on the Sabbath] was important because it is the symbol of the country. Same with the issue of abortions—he feels that this is a national issue and one with important implications for the whole community. Local issues can often be solved through negotiations.

The radical also referred to this division of labor by suggesting that people know not to bother the council with small issues.

There is also, however, an element of competition and even conflict between the groups. Both of the interviewees talked about groups trying to pull people in different directions. Conflicts between groups can become quite violent and almost always center around ideological disputes. The young leader explained the process of conflict resolution.

> When things get hot, there is no problem in the Charedi Sect. There is the court—and it decides. Everything it says, every word, is law. The other groups, *Toldot Aaron*, *Satmar*, [two of the more militant groups] they won't do anything; if they do go against the court then the entire community will go out and make sure they obey. They can't do anything against the Sect; they can do lots of things that the Sect doesn't favor, but nothing against the Sect. They don't have the power.

The relations with the police are based on a set of understandings, similar to those found in Kfar Shalem. After violent demonstrations, some people are arrested. Few are brought to trial, however, as they become bargaining chips which the police use to keep peace in the community.[4] Indeed, the younger respondent argued that the most violent demonstrations occurred when people are arrested.

> If there are people arrested then it is always hotter. [Question: Why?] Because if there are people under arrest, we want to free them. That's reality. [Question: Are you saying that without violence you can't free them?] It's a fact. Usually it's the police that come and recommend a "package deal." If you stop the demonstrations we will free your people. It's not just once or twice that the police came to the head of the council and offered him a deal. And you'll almost never find any Charedim that sat for more than a few days, or went through a trial. All the police really care about is quiet.

Breaking protest laws in Jerusalem is hardly a risky adventure. The long-term effectiveness of this policy might be questioned, but the dilemma for the police is not a simple one. A larger amount of repression might lead to even more violence, but no enforcement at all has broader implications. A contempt for the law is a theme which is heard far too often in all these interviews.

Finally, relations with the press must be considered. The role of the mass media is more complicated when it comes to the Charedi Sect. First, many have no contact with the secular press and are only interested in the Charedi media. Secondly, the more observant refuse to be photographed and none have televisions. In addition, those who attempt to exploit the mass media are often accused of cheapening the struggle.

The mass media, however, are too powerful to ignore. Many of the struggles for religious issues combine street demonstrations with political maneuvering in the Knesset. The need to keep the issue on the public agenda demands dealing with the press.

Revealingly, the more militant respondent is a fervent advocate of working with the press. He admitted to having arguments with his peers about the issue, but claimed that only media coverage insures widespread mobilization. He suggested that publicity is one of the best ways to get the Charedi establishment to take notice.

Another use of the mass media among the Charedim is to send messages to supporters who live abroad. Some argued that much of the violence in Jerusalem is intended to help fund raising there. The reporter agreed with this claim:

> The claim is proven by the fact that there are photographers that arrive at these demonstrations who the police didn't invite, and they are not part of the Charedi community, so how did they get there? Who told them about the time and place of the demonstration? [Question: Are you talking about the Charedi press?] No, if you want to go for long term planning you have to go for all of the media, and to bring out your own materials which tell the world that the police are "repressing" you, that it is the Jewish State which is lying and cheating and breaking religious laws. . . . Not that any secular paper has ever reported positively on these protests, especially the violent ones, so these papers are less useful for those purposes . . . the fact that the secular newspapers will see you as the enemy and condemn what you have done will not be very helpful.[5]

No protest group then can be totally segregated in modern society. All must interact with other groups, the government, and the press. The interactions of the Charedim revealed quite a bit about the conflicting pressures of isolation and integration.

It is appropriate that this part of the analysis is concluded with the case of the Charedim. They illustrate both the similarity and differences among collective actors. In contrast to the image often presented to the public, the Charedi groups face the same dilemmas about resources, strategy, and action as any other protest group. Their leadership structure and their collective definition of costs and benefits may be different, but the major themes remain the same.

SOME LESSONS

The question of similarities and differences among protest groups brings the discussion full circle. The first goal of this chapter was to achieve a more detailed understanding of group organization, resources, and interests. The cases brought out some intriguing variations with regard to all three of these constructs.

A strong sense of common identity, for example, appeared to be a more important determinant of a good organization than the existence of a formal bureaucratic structure. Indeed, for Soldiers Against Silence and Parents Against Silence there was a conscious attempt to keep the groups small and informal.

These two cases also illustrated how difficult it is to operationalize the concept of collective resources. The use of political information by the soldiers and media contacts by the parents suggested that it is rather presumptuous to limit the focus to the conventional indicators such as group size and funding.

Understanding of the construct of interests was also enriched by the case studies. Although the distinction between ideological and material interests proved to be generally useful, it was less applicable to the case of Kfar Shalem. The primary grievance in that community was material, but there was a deeper, cultural resentment which also fueled the flames of conflict.

Differences between reactive and proactive mobilizations also became clearer in the course of the interviews. All the groups in Yamit, for example, were facing immediate evacuation and this explained why even the most organized group (the farmers) used illegal tactics. Protests against the war in Lebanon, on the other hand, are more difficult to classify. Was the struggle to get the troops out of Lebanon a reactive or a proactive mobilization? If it was reactive, then why were most of the protests so peaceful and orderly? These concepts need to be refined.

A second goal of the study was to explore variables which had been excluded from the previous analyses, specifically the role of strategy and other actors. Strategy is seen as a series of choices in which group leaders attempt to meet group needs with a minimum of risk and cost. The notion of rational choice was certainly reinforced by the interviews. Perhaps the best example of this fact is offered by the repeated references to "red lines" of resistance. All the group leaders were quite capable of describing alternative scenarios of protest and how they would react to varying circumstances. Notions of costs and benefits were not merely academic abstractions but integral parts of group discussions.

One of the most important choices is whether or not to stay within the confines of the law. A number of factors were shown to influence this decision: alternative resources, perceptions about efficacy, as well as normative beliefs. The rationale for most decisions about breaking the law were based on beliefs about the utility of violence. Although both the Movement to Stop the Withdrawal from Sinai and Peace Now saw violence as counter-productive to their ultimate aims, the Charedi rebel and many from Kfar Shalem felt it was the only way to have an effect.

Other leaders, however, exhibited less utilitarian formulations. The moderate leader from Kfar Shalem and the Charedi reporter both suggested that social norms did have an effect on the level of violence. A dynamic model of collective strategy should offer a fuller explanation for the ways in which potential benefits of violence are weighed against both subjective and objective costs. What this study has shown is that the pattern of mobilization has a significant impact on that calculation.

Yet another collective choice is concerned with the distinction between short-range and long-range strategy. Groups such as Gush Emunim, Peace Now, the Charedim, and even Kfar Shalem must weigh immediate benefits against later costs. Leaders from all of these groups find themselves constantly deciding about collective priorities, a process which determines how collective resources are spent. Those with more immediate goals, such as the businessmen in Yamit, or the spontaneous demonstrators in the Charedi community, are more likely to expend all they have in one burst of collective energy, with little thought to the future. Perhaps the most important distinction is between those who deal with tactics and those who plan strategy.

The evidence which emerged about other actors was also important. The variety of different cases allowed examples of both cooperation and competition between protest groups to be seen. In Yamit the groups competed for both publicity and compensation money, whereas the groups protesting against the war in Lebanon had more of a symbiotic relationship. The example of the Charedim provided illustrations of both kinds of forces. The dynamics of cooperation and competition among protest groups offers yet another important area for further research.

The cases also showed the ways in which the government and the police can affect the course of protest. The government tried to lower the costs during the struggle over Yamit and raise the costs of protest against the Lebanese War. Protest leaders always consider the reactions of the police, but few are intimidated. Deals were usually worked out and the picture of the police which emerged is of an authority more concerned with short-term peace than long-term deterrence.

The press was the one constant in all of these cases. All the groups strived for publicity, although some more enthusiastically than others. Sometimes the press served to augment other strategies whereas, in other cases, it was the only means of communication. It helped to spawn some groups and merely reported on the activities of others. The role of the press must also be included in any truly comprehensive model of protest.

The third, and final, goal of these case studies was to exemplify some exceptions to the rules offered by the model. In a sense, the entire chapter was dedicated to this aim. All the groups helped illustrate the wealth of variation within each type. The differences among the Ad Hoc groups protesting against Lebanon and the range of groups found within the Charedi community offered us a glimpse of the trees in place of the forest.

Notwithstanding these exceptions, the model remains intact. Background, resources, and interests have a predictable influence on political action strategies and repertoires. The collective needs of each type are quite distinct and an understanding of these variations leads to a better explanation of political behavior.

The interviews with the protest leaders also reinforced conclusions about the politics of provocation. Discussions about protest strategy inevitably revolved around the rules of the game. The rules of Israeli protest center on the nuisance factor. Protest groups must make a sufficient amount of noise in the mass media to become celebrities. Having achieved that status, it is often cheaper for the authorities to offer concessions than to escalate the confrontation.

The fact that so many groups choose this route attests to its perceived effectiveness. It is with these points in mind that attention is turned to the outcomes of collective action.

Chapter 7

OUTCOMES OF COLLECTIVE
ACTION _____

It is impossible to tell the tale of collective action without saying something about how the story ends. Although the majority of
this study has been devoted to explaining the roots of protest, the
political significance of collective action depends on the final outcome. The theoretical importance of this analysis can be best understood by reviewing several themes which have been emphasized
throughout this work.

All the themes center around the notion of alternative paths to
political influence. The first theme claims that the popularity of direct action in Israel can be related to its relative efficacy. Whereas the
institutional road is seen as virtually impassable, the route of direct
action is viewed as more open, convenient, and effective. It is important to measure the extent of successful protest in Israel to test this assumption.

The protest road has a fork in it, however, and a good deal of the
previous analysis was devoted to explaining which protest groups
take which paths. One of the major routes is usually taken by the powerful. It is a wide, well-paved avenue befitting the wealthy travelers
who use it. The groups which take this road own large organizational
vehicles whose reliability has been proven through many years of
travel.

An alternative course is used by weaker groups. It is open to all,
but the path is a treacherous one permeated with pitfalls and dangers.
Weak challengers must build their vehicles from scratch and usually
produce rather rickety machines which are unlikely to survive more

than one trip. Their only chance of success is to take a short-cut through the mass media. This is a toll road, however, and protest groups who choose this road must be willing to pay the price of pasage.

The nature of the journey towards political influence is also affected by the specific destination. Groups with physical interests, it was argued, spend much less time on the road. Ideological groups, on the other hand, must be prepared for a long haul. Genuine social and political change can rarely be seen over the horizon and ideological groups may have to take a variety of paths to influence.

The study of outcomes completes this map. What are the best roads to political influence? What are the advantages and disadvantages of alternative routes? What are the relative chances for a successful trip? Group leaders make a series of choices about probable outcomes and it is important to test these premises.

Three outcomes are examined in this study: repression, publicity, and success. The first outcome reflects some of the risks and costs of protest whereas the latter two variables indicate the level of short-term and long-term benefits.

The three outcomes being considered are set in order of their most likely occurrence during the journey towards political influence. Acts of repression usually occur at the time of the protest and take the form of either dispersal, arrests, and even physical attack. Publicity, on the other hand, comes from television and newspaper reports which are prepared and disseminated after the act is over. The most final outcome is the degree of success, which can only be determined by the reaction of the public and the authorities long after the final protester has returned home.

The measures of group outcomes were taken from two sources. Data about the extent of repression and publicity come from the newspaper articles whereas information about success is based on telephone interviews which are carried out with leaders from sixty-nine protest groups. The sample was constructed by contacting leaders who were mentioned in the newspaper articles.[1] The interviews also included questions about group resources and several general questions which are discussed below.

REPRESSION

The use of repression by political authorities increases the costs of collective action. The risks of arrest, injury, or even death stand as a strong deterrent to protest. The use of repression in democratic countries is tempered by public opinion. Acts of government repression which are seen as either exaggerated or unjustified are likely to be much more costly to the authorities than to the protesters. Like protest leaders, political decision-makers must anticipate the risks and benefits of the use of force.

It has been suggested that part of the reason for so much protest in Israel is related to just this calculation. Political leaders and police usually find it easier to offer compromises than carry out arrests. Empirical evidence was presented in the first chapter which showed that protest groups in Israel have a better than even chance of breaking the law with impunity.

The system of sanctions in not, however, random. A repression index was calculated on the basis of police reactions to protest events. One point was added to the index for each of the following events: dispersion, dispersion by force, arrests, use of tear gas or clubs, and injuries. There is a strong correlation between levels of group intensity and government repression ($r = .63$, $p. < .001$). Any achievements obtained by violence must be weighed against these costs.

A more interesting question is whether some groups incur a disproportionate level of repression. Organized ideological groups (Movements and Sects) often question the very legitimacy of the political authorities and represent the greatest threat. Sects should be especially prone to repression due to their segregation from the rest of society. Public opinion should be more tolerant of police violence when carried out against outsiders. This logic suggests that the lowest level of repression should be experienced by Unions and Community Action Groups who have the closest ties with the authorities and that ad hoc groups should fall somewhere in the middle.

An analysis of variance was performed to test this hypothesis, using repression as the dependent variable, group type as the independent variable, and controlling for the level of protest intensity.[2] The highest costs were, indeed, incurred by Sects (.24) and Movements (.16) and the lowest by Unions ($-.13$) and Community Action Groups ($-.10$). Also as expected, Ad Hoc groups experienced a level of repression which fell in between the other extremes (.04) ($F = 9.44$, $p. < .001$). A strategy of intensity is especially expensive then for those who depend on it most.[3] This becomes even clearer as the benefits side of the equation is examined.

PUBLICITY

The second outcome, publicity, can also be related to differences in mobilization. As Lipsky (1970) pointed out, mass media coverage is especially important for poorer groups who depend on the media to mobilize the public to their cause. It is again the same groups that need publicity who find it the most difficult to obtain. Less organized groups have neither the experience, the skills, nor the resources needed to manipulate the media (Wolfsfeld 1984a, 1984b). As suggested earlier, the only recourse for such groups is the use of violence to attract attention.

There are at least three well-known paths to publicity: extensiveness, activism, and intensity.[4] It is important to consider which of the two criteria of newsworthiness takes precedence: the drama produced by violence or the social significance offered by established groups carrying out larger, more peaceful protests. Can those who adopt a strategy of intensity successfully compete for the public agenda with those who can mobilize the masses?

To answer this question two separate indicators of publicity were developed. One was based on the page number of the article (the closer to page one, the higher the level of publicity) whereas the second was based on size.[5] The use of more than one indicator proved propitious, as can be seen in Table 7–1.

Table 7–1
The Correlates of Publicity

	Page Number[a]	Article Size
Extensiveness	.32	.16
Sig	(.001)	(.05)
N	324	140
Intensity	.03	.24
Sig	(n.s.)	(.001)
N	440	217
Activism	.24	.22
Sig	(.001)	(.001)
N	440	217

a. Page numbers have been reversed so that pages closest to the front have highest values.

The extensiveness of the groups' actions appears to have a stronger correlation with page number whereas intensity has a stronger relationship with the size of the article. The level of activism, on the other hand, is equally correlated with both indicators of publicity.

This distribution of results tells quite a bit about the way in which the news media cover protest. The political significance of an event is probably best reflected by the page number of the article; the number of people mobilized seems the best way to communicate political significance. An intensive strategy also brings publicity, but in the form of more, rather than better, exposure. Protest violence is often regulated to the human interest part of the paper, where stories are often longer and more personal. It is questionable, however, whether such coverage can be considered the equivalent of being on or near the front page.

One of the more intriguing correlations is the relationship between the total number of acts and the amount of publicity. Activism is related to both types of coverage, a fact which illustrates the dependency of the mass media on celebrities (Gitlin 1980). Once protest groups have been defined as significant, everything they do will be covered. Social movements tend to be especially dependent on such self-fulfilling prophesies. Famous protest groups offer a convenient peg for editors trying to provide a context for the news.

It is also useful to consider how patterns of mobilization affect the generation of publicity. It is again important to consider the interaction of organization and interests. Organized ideological groups (Sects and Movements) should generate the greatest level of publicity, for they are the only groups which have both the need for coverage and the resources to achieve it. Unions should fall somewhere in the middle, as they have the potential for extensive action, but rarely have the need to use it. The ability of Community Action Groups and Ad Hoc groups should be low as they depend more heavily on violence. Their more limited scope and resources will make it difficult for them to compete for public attention.

Calculating the mean publicity scores (based on page number) for the five ideal types it was found that the highest score was obtained by Sects (.36) who have a repertoire which combines high activism with intensity. The second and third highest levels were achieved by Movements (.12) and Unions (.09); the former stresses activism whereas the latter emphasizes extensiveness. As expected, Ad Hoc groups $(-.28)$ and Community Action Groups $(-.25)$($F=4.59$, p.<.001) had the lowest levels of publicity.

Due to the effects of violence, however, there were no significant differences with regard to article size. The conclusion, then, is a mixed one. Groups who rely solely on violence can successfully compete with more established groups in terms of the amount of coverage, but not in the quality of coverage. The difference with regard to effects on public opinion remains an open question, but the risks involved in carrying out a repertoire of violence further tip the scales against such a strategy.

SUCCESS

The final outcome, success, is both the most important construct to understand and the most difficult. It is the most important because it serves as the final link in the causal chain of collective action. It is the most difficult of the outcomes to explain because of the multitude of definitions associated with the concept (Gurr 1980, 1983).

In his seminal study on the American protest groups, Gamson (1975) used two definitions of success: recognition by government authorities and the achievement of new "advantages." O'Keefe and Schumaker (1983) developed a 6-point coding scale with which to attempt an analysis of the cost/benefits ratio of collective actions. Shin (1983) examined actual changes in government policy in Korea.

As a partial solution to this problem, the interviews with protest leaders contained three separate questions about success. In the first question, leaders were asked about the extent to which they thought their actions had generally succeeded; in the second, they were asked about the degree to which they had succeeded in mobilizing public support for their cause. A final indicator of success was based on first asking if there was a particular public official (or office) they wanted to influence. Those that said "Yes" were then asked if they were able to make contact with that person. Thus, the responses to these questions offered information about general success, public success, and success at achieving access to the authorities.

The use of subjective measures of success is clearly problematic. It offers the possibility, however, of comparing the rates of success for very different groups. Although leaders may all have a need to exaggerate their level of success, there is no reason to believe that interpretations based on second- or third-hand reports would be any more accurate.

The discussion about group success is divided into two sections. In the first part descriptive evidence is offered about the level of success among all the groups who were interviewed. The second section explores some of the correlates of group success. The conclusions from these analyses are more tentative than in the past due to the relatively small number (n = 69) of group leaders who were interviewed.

Despite this drawback, the results provided important insights about the dynamics of group success.

The Success of Protest in Israel

The general level of success for Israeli protests is very high, as can be seen in Table 7-2. The majority of groups reported general success, success in persuading the public, and success at meeting with public officials. The popularity of direct action in Israel is quite understandable in light of these findings. Protest does, indeed, serve as a communication channel which is both convenient and effective. Although some of these positive reports may be attributed to the need to avoid dissonance, the fact that three-quarters of the protest groups met with public officials presents an optimistic side to Israeli politics.

Table 7–2
The Distribution of Success

Success	General Success	Public
	(N = 69)	(N = 69)
Great Deal of Success	46%	54%
Partial Success	41%	38%
Failure	9%	8%
Complete Failure	4%	0

	Met with Public Official (N = 57)	
	Yes	74%
	No	26%

Leaders, however, also expressed other, less optimistic views about the political system. Seventy-five percent of the leaders expressed the opinion that "the only way for a group to achieve something is to make a lot of noise." The question was included as yet another indicator of the sense of blocked opportunities. In addition, despite their success, only 48% felt the authorities had treated them fairly.

All these results lent support to the central theme of this study. Israeli protest serves as an alternative means of making demands on an otherwise unresponsive political leadership. This path of influence runs directly through the mass media and it is revealing that 95% of those interviewed claimed that the press was a help to their cause. It seems that the politics of provocation represents a quite rational approach to political action in Israel.

THE CORRELATES OF SUCCESS

Mobilization and Power

The results of previous studies suggested some of the most probable correlates of group success. The notion that organization and resources leads to success is implicit in the resource mobilization approach to conflict. Gamsón (1975) found that such factors as bureaucracy, centralized leadership, and a lack of factionalism were all correlated with success. The results of Shin's (1983) study of Korean protest also supported this thesis. O'Keéfe and Schumaker (1983), on the other hand, reported mixed findings on the topic.

The working hypothesis of the present study is the claim that organization and resources increase the probability of success. A powerful protest group is one which can successfully make demands on the political system. Although a strong organization cannot guarantee victory, it greatly increases the potential for sustained political action and presents a more serious challenge to the authorities.

In addition to the previous measures of organization and resources, the interview schedule included questions about the size of the membership, the existence of an office, and whether or not the group had a common treasury. The correlation between organization, resources, and success is detailed in Table 7–3. The results provided support for the resource mobilization approach, but they also offered some welcome detail.

New groups, for example, are indeed less likely to compete for either general success or access to public officials, but do just as well as established organizations in the mobilization of public support. Although a degree of caution is in order due to the subjective nature of these reports, there is some appeal to the notion that new groups find it easier to compete for public support (or at least attention) than for concrete goods.

The relationship between organizational scope and success was also revealing. Although groups with a national scope are more likely to achieve general success, they are less likely to gain access to officials. It is no doubt easier to meet with local officials than with national ones.

Although the measurement of group resources was admittedly primitive, it too pointed in some meaningful directions. Membership size and the existence of a common treasury appear to be better indicators of collective power than the existence of an office. In addition, an increase in group resources increases the probability of all kinds of success.

Table 7–3
Organization, Resources, and Success

	General Success	Public Success	Contacted Official
Structure	.24	−.05	.24
Sig	(.03)	(n.s.)	(.08)
N	67	61	46
Scope	.22	.05	−.22
Sig	(.03)	(n.s.)	(.05)
N	67	61	50
Membership Size	.18	.18	.24
Sig	(.08)	(.09)	(.05)
N	63	57	48
Office	.13	.13	.10
Sig	(n.s.)	(n.s.)	(n.s.)
N	67	51	50
Treasury	.19	.25	.21
Sig	(.06)	(.02)	(.07)
N	64	58	50

Any attempt to talk of only one type of success seems misguided. The distinction between the various types of success also helps clarify the relationship between interests and success. This is because the focus on collective interests brings up the notion of group needs. The most important need for protest groups with physical demands is to meet with officials who can solve their problems. For ideological groups, on the other hand, the most important goal is to mobilize public opinion to bring about political change.

Each group, it turns out, gets what it wants. Ideological groups are more likely to achieve public success $(r = .24)$ and physical groups are more likely to meet with public officials $(r = .26)$.[6] There were no significant differences with regard to the level of general success.

Returning to the previous analogy, both the nature of the organizational vehicle and the destination have affects on the journey's outcome. The concept of outcome, however, is more complicated than first believed. Rather than speak of either a successful or an unsuccessful trip towards political influence, different types of success must be considered.

This lesson helped explain the success rates of the different group types. The small number of cases impared the analysis but it was possible to detect certain tendencies, as can be seen in Table 7–4.

Table 7–4
Mobilization Type and Success

Mobilization Type	N	General Success	Public Success	Contact Officials
Ad Hoc	8	75%	75%	50%
Community Action	13	77%	92%	70%
Sect	6	50%	100%	40%
Union	36	97%	93%	86%

There were only two movements in the sample so they were excluded from the analysis. As might be expected from previous discussions, Unions are the most powerful of the ideal types. They achieved a high level of success on all three dimensions. They have the least trouble meeting with public officials, they have almost a perfect record of general success, and 93% of the Unions surveyed claimed to have also succeeded in mobilizing public support.

Even unorganized protest groups in Israel have a good chance of success, but their probability of victory is consistently lower. Only 50% of the Ad Hoc groups obtained access to public officials, whereas 75% of these groups reported general success and public success.

Although little difference was found between Ad Hoc Groups and Community Action Groups in terms of political action repertoires, there are differences with regard to success rates. Although the probabilities of general success are almost equal, Community Action Groups are more likely to meet with public officials and also seem more capable of mobilizing public opinion.

The six Sects which were included in the sample offered a timely reminder about the importance of understanding the interaction of interests with organization. Despite their high level of solidarity, Sects are the weakest of the four action types. As outsiders, they are the least likely to meet with public officials and only half of the groups reported success. The fact that all the groups reported public success is somewhat surprising due to their segregation from the rest of society. It is conceivable that the replies to this question referred to the degree of support among their own constituencies, which is consistent with other findings which were presented.

Although the picture is hardly complete, a somewhat better understanding of the relationship between mobilization and success has been established. Although organization and resources certainly increase the potential for success, the ability to translate this potential into victory depends on the interest being pursued. The less threatening the goal, the easier it is to convert resources into victory. This theme returns as some other correlates of success are examined.

Repertoires and Success

The relationship between repertoires and success is even more complex. The success of a given act depends on a number of different variables. A massive demonstration against a war may fail, but an equally large protest for higher wages may succeed. Although it is impossible to deal with all such contingencies, it is possible to point in some useful directions.

One central question which concerns researchers is whether there is power in numbers. A strategy of extensiveness is based on the belief that the degree of political pressure is proportionate to the number of supporters which can be mobilized. Groups which carry out a large number of acts adopt a similar approach to political influence. The nature of group interests also affects this process, however, as can be seen in Table 7–5.

A strategy of extensiveness is especially effective for groups making material demands. It increases the probability of both general success and public success. For ideological groups, on the other hand, the relationship is reversed; the more extensive the protest, the less likely the success. A similar pattern emerged with regard to activism, although the trend is less extreme.[7]

The concept of threat seems to again offer a useful explanation for these seemingly contradictory results. Small ideological mobilizations offer no threat to the regime, but large ones must be resisted and even (as seen) repressed. It is also conceivable that groups who carry out less extensive mobilizations are usually making more minor demands. A meager protest about a major issue can be counter-productive.

The route to success for groups with physical interests appears more straight forward. The larger the act, the more likely success. The logic of politics suggests that leaders should resist strong ideological groups but give in to massive protests on more marginal issues.

A second issue concerns the nature of the relationship between intensity and success and it has proven to be a point of controversy among scholars in the field. In a section entitled "The Success of the Unruly," Gamsón (1975) came to the conclusion that the use of force is often an effective way to make demands. Protest groups which used some form of sanctions were more successful than those who did not.

Table 7–5
Extensiveness, Activism, and Success:
Controlling for Interests

		General Success	Public Success	Contacting Officials
Physical Interests	Extensiveness	.22[a]	.27	.01
	N	(35)	(29)	(26)
	Activism	.12	.08	.04
	N	(41)	(35)	(30)
Ideological Interests	Extensiveness	−.26	−.23	.15
	N	(18)	(19)	(14)
	Activism	−.34	−.20	.18
	N	(18)	(19)	(14)

a. Due to small number of cases statistical significance is not listed. Results should be seen as suggestive.

In a secondary analysis of the Gamson data, Goldstone (1980) contested this conclusion by arguing that the relationship was a spurious one which disappeared after applying certain statistical controls.[8] Studies by Schumaker (1975) and O'Keefe and Schumaker (1983) also ran counter to Gamson's conclusions and these researchers suggested that the effectiveness of constraints depends on the political context in which they are used.[9]

It may be possible to partially reconcile these differences. First, it is important to define what is meant by constraints. As Gamson (1968) put it in an earlier work the emphasis should be on the ability of the group to coerce the authorities into meeting their demands. Non-violent means of constraint such as strikes and sanctions allow a group to exert an enormous amount of pressure with little risk and few could argue about the effectiveness of such measures.

The more intriguing question asks about the effectiveness of disorderly constraints. The answer to this questions may lie in the approach taken by many protest leaders (Wolfsfeld 1984a), which suggests a curve of diminishing rewards. For those with few alternatives, the optimal strategy may be to use a medium level of intensity: a completely peaceful protest will probably be ignored whereas too much violence is likely to be counter-productive.

If this is true, the key to success is to find a point at which the most attention could be gained with the least amount of group costs. Costs in these cases would involve a loss of public support, arrests, and injuries. In more technical language, it is claimed in this hypothesis that there is a curvilinear relationship between intensity and success for groups without alternative resources.

The data collected for this study allows at least an exploration of this notion. When all the groups are looked at as a whole, a strategy of intensity leads directly to failure. Most groups which use violent tactics are likely to fail.[10]

When workers' groups were removed from the analysis, a rather different picture emerged. The remaining protest groups were divided into three groups: those who carried out peaceful acts, those who carried out non-violent acts of disorder, and those who carried out at least one act of violence. Although the extremely small number of cases can only be suggestive, the trends presented in Table 7–6 certainly supported the research hypothesis.

Table 7–6
Disorder and Success[a]

Level of Disorder	N	General Success	Public Success	Contact Officials
Legal	13	62%	83%	50%
Disorder	8	88%	100%	67%
Violent	6	67%	83%	50%

a. All Unions were removed from the analysis.

Those which carry out non-violent disorders reported the highest level of general success, public success, and success in gaining access to public officials. The fact that violent groups had the highest level of failure supported the rule of diminishing returns. There does seem to be a curvilinear relationship between intensity and success for these groups.

Some Lessons

The map of the journey towards political influence is now a bit more detailed. The journey's outcome will depend on the strength of the vehicle (organization), and final destination (interests), and how it takes to the road (repertoire).

Organized groups seeking material aims uaually have the easiest trip. The ability to adapt a strategy of extensiveness enables these groups to achieve both publicity and ultimate success without any of the costs of repression. Such groups also have the least need for protest due to their integration into the political system. When organized groups do turn to direct action, they have a very high rate of victory.

Organized ideological groups, on the other hand, have a much more difficult journey. They pose a threat to the authorities and their tendency to use violent tactics makes them an easy target for repression. A strategy of extensiveness only increases this sense of threat and is also unlikely to lead to success. Organized ideological groups do achieve a good deal of publicity and they must rely on the hope that through sheer endurance they will eventually succeed.

The prognosis for weak protest groups is mixed. Although many do achieve success, the road to victory is a difficult one. Those which resort to violence may achieve some publicity, but very few are able to successfully compete for the public agenda. Their only alternative is to stay home. If a handbook of strategy was composed for such groups, it would probably recommend a policy of carrying out just enough disorder to be noticed, but too little to get hurt.

Perhaps most important, the study of outcomes has offered a finishing touch to the description of Israeli political culture. A much better understanding of the attractiveness of direct action has been established. Although the journey is more difficult for some groups than others, there is no better route to political influence in Israel.

CONCLUSION _____

This study was devoted to two goals. The first purpose was to better understand the political culture of Israel and the second aim was to contribute to the development of a comprehensive model of political action. The conclusion is accordingly divided into two sections and in each the attempt is to both summarize the major findings and to suggest some implications of this research for social scientists and policy makers.

THE POLITICAL CULTURE OF ISRAEL

The Politics of Provocation

A good deal of evidence, gathered from a variety of sources, offered strong support for the major thesis of this work. The attitudes of ordinary citizens, the testimony of protest leaders, and the actions of both, pointed to a political culture in which protest is the first course of political action. The findings also suggested that one reason for the politics of provocation is that many Israelis feel locked out of institutional paths of influence and find mobilized action an alternative which is both safe, convenient, and effective.

The objective evidence offered support for these beliefs. Most groups carry out a few, short protest acts and a surprisingly high percentage apparently achieve success. Despite the fact that a significant number of these groups carry out acts which are illegal or violent, few suffer any consequences. The authorities have contributed to the spread of cynicism by making "deals" with protest leaders to ensure peace.

It is important to also note some of the more positive aspects of this process. The fact that so many protest groups reported success means that the Israeli political system does have a way of dealing with public demands. As discussed, most of the incidents of disorder and violence tend to be rather controlled, designed more to impress than to injure. Such acts may serve as a safety valve for venting political frustrations which might otherwise find expression in more dangerous forms of political action.

As a form of political communication, however, the politics of provocation leave a good deal to be desired. At least three reasons can be offered for this conclusion. First, the threat of disorder and violence is always present during protests, especially when groups are so dependent on the mass media. Secondly, the use of mobilized tactics, especially illegal ones, is likely to lead to a more general contempt for the law within the society. The final disadvantage of this form of political communication is related to the nature of protests. As discussed, mobilized action tends to be more specific, more negative, and more reactive than institutional action. Protests therefore can never really serve as a substitute for more traditional kinds of participation in which the citizen can participate in the decision-making process in an ongoing fashion.

It is difficult to make any predictions about the future. There has been a definite rise in the number of protests (both legal and illegal) but no rise in their level of intensity. The youth of Israel are the most enthusiastic proponents of protest politics, but this could change with maturity. They show no inclination to participate in institutional politics, however, and they are less disturbed than their parents about legal boundaries. The political action repertoires of future generations will depend on the political system they must confront.

Israel has developed a participatory democracy, but the modes of participation leave something to be desired. The not-so-hidden agenda of this study is centered on the need for electoral reform. The Israeli public believes that the reason for so much protest is rooted in a lack of alternatives. If the political leaders of Israel were to be held personally responsible for their decisions, it would make insitutional modes of action much more attractive. If the major problem has to do with blocked opportunities, the solution is to remove those obstacles.

A change in the political system could also have an effect on social norms about civil disobedience. Those who break the law would find less sympathy from the public and those who are responsible for enforcing the law might receive more support. An increase in arrests and repression without a similar change in representation, on the other hand, might prove counterproductive.

Electoral reform is not, however, a panacea for dealing with provocative politics. Old habits are hard to break and that principle applies to both citizens and politicians. Direct action would still be very popular and it would offer an important means of access for those unable to lobby. Nevertheless, the establishment of authentic representation in Israel could bring about a major change in patterns of political communication.

Questions of Political Equality

An additional area of concern is centered on the degree of equality which characterized political participation in Israel. Here the picture was somewhat more encouraging: the individuals and groups who participate come from a wide variety of social and ethnic backgrounds. Social gaps still remain, however, and the research findings have shed some light on these difference.

The relationship between social background and psychological involvement in politics was similar to that found in other cultures. The poor, the less educated, women, and the religious in Israel were all less likely to think about politics and to form political attitudes. People born in such environments have less of a potential for political participation and these inherent disadvantages cannot be ignored.

The dominant role of the Israeli political parties, however, helped many citizens overcome such disadvantages. The political parties have been rather successful at attracting members from both working class and middle class homes and there is virtually no relationship between education, income, and institutional action. In addition, Sephardic Jews are just as likely to participate in politics as Ashkenazic Jews. Indeed, the lack of ethnic differences was an important discovery which surfaced throughout the study. Religious Jews also profited from their high level of institutional affiliation. Despite their generally low level of psychological involvement, observant Jews were just as likely to participate as secular Jews.

Israeli women, on the other hand, do not achieve political equality. Women who want to be politically involved are less likely than men to choose the institutional route to influence. They are much more cynical about such modes of action and the lack of recruitment by political parties no doubt contributes to this skepticism. Israeli women only achieve equality among protesters.

The world of protest, however, is also not open to all. It is a mode of action mainly exploited by the young and the educated. It might be argued that such tendencies are merely matters of choice, but the outcome is the same. If direct action is the only effective way to make demands in Israel, then a significant proportion of the population remains frustrated spectators.

Impressions about the inequality of political protest in Israel are bolstered by the evidence about the groups who are involved in such actions. Most protest is carried out by organizations with a permanent structure. The use of direct action by such groups merely augments an already rich repertoire of political choices. In addition, those with resources can carry out a strategy based on extensive actions with little risk and a very good chance of success. Resources bring power.

Poorer, less organized groups have fewer options. The alternative strategy of civil disobedience and violence is more likely to lead to repression and less likely to lead to success. Such groups are totally dependent on the mass media, but even here they find it difficult to compete with more established groups. Groups react to blocked opportunities in the same way as individuals. Those who feel left out of the political process attempt to force their way in through the use of expressive tactics and often use the press as their battering ram.

The findings about political equality in Israel also point to the need for electoral reform. An electoral system based on regional representation would produce more independent candidates and this might also encourage more women to participate in insitutional politics. It would also greatly increase the power of local groups,who could then attempt to lobby regional representatives rather than protest against a faceless government.

The results of this study also pointed to a need for a less centralized political system which could encourage more wide spread participation. Individuals and groups with less political resources would find it easier to influence local authorities and pressure groups would have less need to use media stunts to attract national attention. The key term is access and any attempts to increase the level of political equality in Israel must strive for the development of a less intimidating political structure.

The political culture of Israel is still in transition. Political parties continue to serve as the major power brokers of the state but new and important avenues of influence are gradually emerging. The syndrome known as the politics of provocation is neither inevitable nor incurable. The vitality of democracy in Israel will depend on the ability of the political leadership to develop a more open means of communicating with a public eager to be heard.

TOWARDS A COMPREHENSIVE THEORY OF POLITICAL ACTION

It was stated in the introduction to this work that the study was designed to add to, rather than replace, the considerale store of knowledge about political action which already exists. The discussion in this section is an attempt to offer a summary of both the findings which tend to reinforce previous trends in the literature and those which point in new directions.

This synopsis is divided into three segments. The first is an outline what has been learned about individual participation, the second deals with the subject of collective action, and the final section provides some final comments about the similarities and differences between the two levels of analysis.

Individual Participation

The results of this study offered support first and foremost for those theorists who are attempting to build a rational choice model of political participation. The findings also offered important insights about ways in which such theories should be modified. The contributions in this area can be described by referring to two principal themes which have been given considerable empirical support in this study.

The first thesis states that individuals develop a strategy of political participation which is based on perceptions about the value, efficacy, and legitimacy of various forms of political action. The use of the term strategy emphasizes the need for a change in theoretical focus. Although most previous research on political participation has concentrated on the individual's general orientation towards the political system (e.g., political trust and efficacy), the present effort has stressed the importance of studying much more specific attitudes towards political behavior which better reflect the notion of choice.

The second thesis is that mobilized action is a qualitatively different form of political participation. As discussed earlier, there has been a growing trend among researchers to emphasize the affinity between the two modes of action. Although this study has also pointed to some of the similarities between the two types of action (e.g., the need for psychological involvement) a good deal of evidence has been provided which shows that the decision to take part in protests is based on a relatively unique set of motivations and beliefs. Mobilized action is not merely one more type of particpation.

The significance of these two theses can best be illustrated by returning to the distinction between mobilization attitudes and institutional attitudes. The interaction of these attitudes towards the two modes of action provided fairly accurate predictions about political action repertoires. Yet each set of attitudes was rooted in very different types of soil. Whereas attitudes towards institutional action are rooted in such nonpartisan factors as the level of psychological involvement, attitudes towards protest are better explained by a person's social and political background. Those who hope to build a comprehensive model of political action would be well advised to keep both of these findings in mind.

These shifts in focus also have implications for the more general study of political culture. As amply illustrated by the case of Israel, citizens do not always participate in politics out of a sense of trust or good will. A negative orientation towards the political system can also lead to political action. An appreciation of this point should lead to a broader typology of political cultures and a better understanding about the ways in which the system can have an effect on political attitudes and behavior.

The results of this study also pointed to a more dynamic notion of political action repertoires. The distinction between Inactives, Conformists, Dissidents, and Pragmatists was shown to be a useful way to describe at least some of the ways in which citizens make choices about how to make demands on the political system. As illustrated by the qualitative interviews, however, a political action repertoire should not be seen as a rigid routine. A strategy of action is based on a particular set of individual attitudes and political circumstances. When those attitudes and circumstances change, so do political action repertoires. This more flexible view of the notion of repertoire may offer at least a partial solution to the inconsistencies discovered by those attempting to understand the ways in which such repertoires change over time (Kaase 1983).

The findings about political action in Israel may also have provided some alternative explanations for a puzzle originally described in Verba, Nie, and Kim's book *Participation and Political Equality* (1978). The authors were intrigued by the fact that the correlation between socioenomic status and psychological involvement in politics was in many countries much stronger than the correlation between status and political participation. Why, they asked, were so many people unable to translate their potential for participation into actual behavior?

The explanation offered in that work was centered on the previously discussed notion of institutional recruitment. The importance of this factor was also confirmed in Israel. This study also offered, however, an additional solution to the puzzle. In keeping with the major theme of the book, citizens may find alternative ways of expressing their psychological involvement in politics. Verba, Kim, and Nie did not, unfortunately, include protest among the types of political participation and this study has shown how these modes of action offer an additional means of realizing the potential for participation.

The distinction between potential and behavior brings up one final lesson about individual political participation which can be gained from the results of this study. It is extremely important for researchers to avoid using measures which are focused exclusively on intentions. Although it is understandably difficult to collect data about mobilized behavior, the evidence provided about the gap between potential and action suggests that it is vitally important to make the effort.

COLLECTIVE ACTION

The findings about collective action in Israel have offered strong support for the resource mobilization approach to the subject. The level of group organization and resources was shown to have a powerful effect on both the extensiveness and the effectiveness of protest. The study also formulated and tested a number of original hypotheses about collective action which pointed in some new directions for such research.

The most important innovation centered around the notion of strategic needs. Whereas most previous studies of collective action have been focused almost exclusively on the ways in which organization and resources affected collective behavior, the results of the present study pointed to the importance of also considering the role of group interests. The interaction between group ties and interests has provided a useful guideline to understanding choices about collective action.

The distinction between a strategy of extensiveness and a strategy of intensity offered a good illustration of this point. Several pieces of evidence were provided to illustrate that both group ties and interests have an effect on decisions about collective action repertoires. The thesis about the effects of group ties was best exemplified by the tendency of Ad Hoc groups to turn to violence. Group interests, however, were also shown to have an effect on decisions about political action: groups with ideological interests were much more likely to choose a strategy of intensity than groups with physical interests. It is important then to take both of these factors into account when attempting to predict collective behavior.

The study also developed a more detailed formulation of the notion of reportoire. Although the elements of extensiveness, intensity, activism and flexibility do not constitute an exhaustive list of possible repertoire dimensions, they do provide a logical starting point for research on the subject. Once again repertoires are seen as being changeable and it is important to study and explain these transformations in collective behavior.

Some relatively new ideas were also suggested by the various case studies of protest groups. Those who wave the theoretical banner of resource mobilization tend to emphasize the degree of competition among groups over assumedly scarce resources. Although the different groups who were active in Yamit did indeed exhibit a high degree of competition, those protesting about the war in Lebanon exhibited the opposite type of behavior. It is important, therefore, to also investigate areas of cooperation among groups.

The findings from the case studies also pointed to the importance of studying the role of the media in political conflicts. This topic has been sorely neglected in the past and although it was difficult to come to any firm conclusions about specific effects, the media served as a central focus for all of the protest groups who were examined. Any comprehensive model in which an explanation of the dynamics of collective action is sought will have to deal with the ways in which the media affect group strategy and behavior.

The findings about group success offer yet another example in which the study both confirms previous theories but also suggests new directions for research. Thus, in keeping with resource mobilization theory, organization and resources were shown to be important antecedents of success. The distinction among the various forms of success, however, demonstrated the need to develop a more dynamic approach to the topic. Smaller groups, for example, were better able to make contact with public officials. Researchers studying this question should attempt to explain which types of variables explain what types of success.

The Study of Individuals and Groups

The theoretical plan of this study was based on a four-stage model of political action which was designed to highlight the similarities between individual participation and collective action. The empirical evidence which was gathered about the relationship between background, mobilization, evaluation, and behavior offered sound support for this notion, but also pointed to some differences between the two levels of analysis.

Evidence about the effects of background and mobilization offered the first illustration of this point. The potential for both individual and collective action was clearly affected by the interaction between social background, the crystallization of interests, and the mobilization of resources. Patterns of mobilization were shown to have analogous effects on both the quantity and quality of political action.

Despite these similarities, the effects of background appeared to be more pivotal in explaining group behavior. The level of group organization proved to be the most important determinant of variations in collective action. Individuals, on the other hand, found it easier to break the bonds of social constraint. The effects of social background proved to be much less important than individual motivations and evaluations. It is also true that it is easier to measure the attitudes and orientations of individuals than of groups. Considering the evidence about institutional recruitment, however, it is difficult to believe that the differences between the two levels of analysis are merely methodological artifacts.

The findings about rational choice offered the strongest evidence about the need for a more unified theory. Potential actors all try to find a strategy which reflects both their own particular mobilization and the demands of political reality. Group leaders make decisions which are very similar to those made by individuals and they, too, must find a match between their level or resources, their interests, and the costs and benefits associated with alternative forms of action. The interviews with these leaders revealed a decision-making process which was both cautious and realistic. Those who chose to engage in acts of disorder or violence appeared to be fully aware of both the purpose and the consequences of such tactics.

The formation of group strategy is not, however, identical to the process associated with individuals. Leaders must consider problems of group maintenance and just keeping the organization alive often becomes a major goal. In addition, the group dynamics associated with collective decision-making are quite different from the ways in which individuals make decisions. The attempt to emphasize the similarity between the two levels of analysis should not obscure the need to understand these differences.

Where to?

The need to develop a more interactive model of political action has been emphasized throughout this work. The results of this study offered some insights about possible directions for future research.

The analyses attempted to illustrate the ways in which outside agents influence strategies and repertoires. Beliefs about the relative risks and efficacy of various modes of action are based on both observations and experience. The effects of interaction are especially likely to have an impact on group repertoires as leaders attempt to find the optimal path to influence.

The distinction between a proactive and reactive mobilization was offered as one way to examine this issue more systematically. Actors under threat behave quite differently from those who are attempting to change the status quo. A more sophisticated model of political action must provide a fuller explanation about the ways in which moves and countermoves between groups and authorities affect both the nature and outcomes of conflict.

Future researchers might also attempt to take a closer look at the crystallization of political interests. Although the present research stressed the effects of internal factors, a more comprehensive model could also be used to try to explain how external forces affect the mobilization process. There is also a great need to offer a more sophisticated classification of interests and their relationship to strategic needs.

It would also be useful to further examine the dimensions of mobilized action. Although Verba and Nie (1972) have developed a powerful typology with regard to institutional behavior, no parallel study exists on the subject of protest. In the present study the concern was more with the distinction between institutional and mobilized action but there are surely qualitative differences within each set of behaviors. Until now most researchers have been satisfied with the rather direct division between legal and illegal acts. The results of the present study, however, suggested the need for a more sophisticated continuum. It might be useful, for example, to distinguish between strategies of persuasion, provocation, and coercion.

The greatest challenge is to build a comprehensive theory which also explains the relationship between the individual and the group. What is the process by which individual interests are crystallized into collective goals? How do individual social attributes of the membership affect collective mobilization and action? Is the development of group strategy more dependent on collective needs or the personality of particular leaders? These are all difficult, but important questions.

The potential for answering these questions depends on the ability of researchers from a variety of disciplines to develop a common language of discourse. Students of political participation and collective action appear to be moving in similar directions. There is a growing agreement about the importance of better understanding such factors as the dynamics of resource mobilization and the roots of rational choice. These scholars may disagree on the specific components of a unified model of political action but there does seem to be a growing consensus about its general shape. It is hoped that this study has contributed to the dialogue.

METHODOLOGICAL APPENDIX _____

The appendix is divided by chapters. It is designed to offer supplementary information about the specific procedures which were used to collect data for this study. Some of these procedures are described in the text and footnotes and are not repeated here.

Most of the data which is used in this section was collected in a representative national survey of the adult Jewish population which was conducted in December of 1984 by the Israel Institute of Applied Social Science Research. There were 631 respondents. The Institute uses a cluster sampling procedure based on dividing the country into geographic areas.

The major goal of this survey was to offer a data set which could be compared to the questions which were asked in *Political Action* (Barnes and Kaase, 1979). It was essential that an identical question format be used to allow for comparison. Questions about psychological involvement and institutional action were considered to be one scale (conventional action) in the original work. The question format was presented as follows: "There are people who are quite involved in politics while others don't find the time, or maybe the interest to participate in political activities. I'm going to give you a list of such activities. Please tell me how much you do each one."

The list of activities were: read about politics in the newspaper, talk to people about political subjects, work with other people in your community to try to solve local problems, try to convince others to vote as you do, attend political gatherings or meetings, contact a public official or a politician, invest time working for a political party or candidate. Possible responses included very often, sometimes, seldom, almost never. It is important to note that the measures of psychological involvement and institutional action used in chapter 3 are different, as they were not designed for cross-cultural comparisons.

The statements which were used to measure the relative level of institutional efficacy were taken from the three questions used in *Political Action* for measuring government responsiveness and are described in the text. Note that a different measure of insititutional efficacy was used in chapter 3 where no comparison was intended.

Measurements of mobilized action were also taken from the list of unconventional activities in *Political Action*. The format of the question was: "I will now present you with a list of actions which are carried out by people in order to protest against something or just to express their opinion. Please respond to each one using the following choices: 1) I have done this in the last ten years. 2) I would participate in this if it were important to me. 3) I might do this under certain circumstances." 4) I would not do this under any circumstance." The list of activities can be found in Table 1–4.

The general methods used to collect data about protest groups are detailed in reference to chapter 5. There is, however, one difference between the two analyses of collective action. In chapter 1 the discussion about the amount of illegal and violent protest and the likelihood of arrest refers to Arab and Jewish citizens of Israel. This description of Israeli political culture excludes Arab protest groups from the occupied territories.

CHAPTER 3: WHO, WHAT, AND WHY: EXPLAINING INDIVIDUAL PARTICIPATION

The data for this chapter came from a national survey carried out for the author by Modin Ezrachi, a national polling organization. The survey was carried out in April of 1982 and included a total of 1046 respondents. A cluster sampling procedure was used among the adult Jewish population.

The format of the demographic question was similar to those used in most national surveys in Israel. The measure of ethnicity asked about the place of birth for the respondent and the respondent's father. The seven categories can be found in Table 3–1. Respondents were also asked: "How would you define yourself in religious terms?" Three choices were given: religious, traditional, and secular.

The education categories were elementary or less, partial high school (or technical school), finished high school, some studies after high school, or a university degree.

Respondents were asked about their monthly income, using four levels of income which were appropriate at the time of the survey.

The measure of psychological involvement was based on three questions. The first asked: "To what extent do you take an interest in politics?" The choices were "not at all, somewhat, quite a bit, very much." The second asked: "How many times a week do you tend to read the newspaper?" The choices were: "Almost every day, a few times a week, seldom, almost never." The final question asked: "To what extent do you tend to have discussions on political subjects." The choices were: "To a very great extent, to a great extent, to a certain extent, seldom, almost never."

A political knowledge test was given to the smaller sample (which is described later). It contains ten questions about Israeli politics and respondents were given a score on the basis of the number of correct answers. The questions were: 1) Name the chairman of the Knesset Finance committee. 2) Who is the Speaker of the Knesset? 3) Who is the Minister of Tourism? 4) Who is the Israeli ambassador to the U.S.? 5) What was Moshe Arens' position before he became Defense Minister? 6) Who is the Legal Advisor to the government? 7) How many members are there in the Knesset? 8) Who is the leader of the Druses in Lebanon? 9) Who is the Assistant Foreign Minister? 10) Who is the Minister of Trade and Commerce?

The level of informational resources was also measured by asking about the respondents' understanding of the concepts of left and right in politics. The question format was taken from Klingemann (1979): "In politics the terms right and left are used a lot. What do you think the concept 'right' means?" and "What do you think the concept 'left' means?" The original coding followed the guidelines laid down by Klingemann, but were then coded into the categories of correct and incorrect.

The concept of internal efficacy was considered to be a self-report of political competence. Two statements were taken from the traditional efficacy scale: 1) "Sometimes politics and government seem so complicated that a person like me can't understand what's happening." 2) "People like me have nothing to say about what the government does." The second item is not considered a measure of internal efficacy in the United States. In the item analysis performed in Israel, however, these two questions were found to have the highest correlation $(r = .25)$ with one another and to be most correlated with similar types of measures.

The crystallization of political interests, which is listed above, is based on the question about how much the respondents attempted to convince others how to vote.

An index about the extent of opinion formation (evaluations) was based on simply counting the number of times the respondent offered no opinion with regard to questions about political environment, insititutional and mobilization efficacy, and insititutional and mobilization approval.

The political discontent scale was created by combining a variety of different indicators. Four statements were taken from Muller's (1979) measure of diffuse support: 1) I and my friends think we are well represented in the political system. 2) I have a great deal of respect and admiration for the political institutions of Israel. 3) I am very worried about the gap between the values which are important to me in life and what is happening in the political system. 4) When it comes down to it, the Israeli police deserve a lot of respect. Respondents were given the choices of "Definitely Agree, Agree, Not Sure, Disagree, Definitely Disagree."

The format of the other questions measuring political discontent were taken from the continuing survey of the Israel Institute for Social Science Research. The first asked: "What is your opinion about the way the government is dealing with the present situation?" There were four possible choices for this question: "It's dealing with it very well, It's dealing with it well, It's not dealing with it very well, It's dealing with it very poorly." The second asked: "What is your opinion about how the government is dealing with the security problems of the country?" And the third asked: "What is your opinion about how the government is dealing with the economic problems?" There were five possible answers to these questions: "Very Well, Well, Not Sure, Not Well, Poorly."

Political identification was measured using a question asking what party the respondent had voted for in the last election.

The format for the questions about mobilization efficacy and institutional efficacy was: "I will read you a list of activities which one can carry out in order to influence the authorities. I will ask you to state the extent to which you think that each of these various activities is effective (has an influence). The list of acts (in order) were: "To act through a party, to demonstrate (with a license), to establish settlements [l'hitnachel] without government permission, to demonstrate without a license (but no violence), to occupy a government office (sit-in), to write to a political leader, to join an ongoing political organization, to use violence, to be active in a political campaign, and to disrupt traffic." The response choices were: "Very Effective, Effective, Not Sure, Not Effective, Not At All Effective." The acts which were used to build each scale are described in the text.

The measures of mobilization approval and institutional approval were similar. The questions were asked in a separate part of the questionaire, before the questions about efficacy. The format was: "There is a debate today in Israel about which acts that are designed to have an influence on the government are justified, and which are not." I would ask you to state the extent that you approve or do not approve of the following activities. The possibilities were: "Definitely Approve, Approve, Not Sure, Dissapprove, Definitely Disapprove." The list of actions was the same as before.

A score for mobilization attitude was calculated by multiplying the respondent's mobilization efficacy score times his or her mobilization approval score.

Leftism was measured using a 7-point scale in which the respondent was asked: "When thinking about leftist and rightist political attitudes where would you locate yourself on the following continuum." The number one (on the left side of the scale) had the word *left* under it and the number seven (on the right side) had the word *right* on it.

The mobilized action scale and the institutional action scale were based on the same set of questions: "I will present you with a list of political activities. Please state which of these you have participated in in the last three years. The possibilities were: 'Never, One Time, More than Once'." The list of activities is presented in Table 3–5.

The measure of need for influence was based on the extent to which the respondent agreed with the statement: "I feel an obligation to try and have an influence on what happens in this country." The response choices were: "Definitely Agree, Agree, Not Sure, Disagree, Definitely Disagree."

Organization membership was measured by asking the respondents if they belonged to any organizations in which they attended at least several meetings a year. They were given a point for each nonpolitical organization they mentioned.

A summary of the statistical attributes of the major questionnaire measures used in chapter 3 are presented in Table A–1.

CHAPTER 4: BEYOND THE NUMBERS

One hundred-and-twenty respondents from the original 1982 survey were contacted about a year after their initial interviews. Every attempt was made to contact an equal amount of interviewees from each action type (Inactives, Conformists, etc.). Due to financial restraints, most of those contacted came from the areas of either Jerusalem, Tel Aviv or Haifa.

Table A–1
Statistical Attributes of Questionnaire Measures

Variable	Mean	Std. Dev.	Range	Reliability[a]
Mobilization Efficacy	16.7	4.6	28	.74
Institutional Efficacy	14.1	3.1	16	.69
Mobilization Approval	15.7	4.0	28	.64
Institutional Approval	16.0	4.0	16	.71
Political Discontent	22.2	5.0	26	.76
Need for Influence	3.5	1.1	4	n.a.
Psychological Involvement	6.8	1.9	11	.76
Internal Efficacy	6.2	2.0	8	n.a.
Organization Membership	.16	.4	3	n.a.
Mobilized Action	.36	.7	4	n.a.
Institutional Action	.41	.8	5	n.a.

a. Reliability scores are based on alpha and are only calculated for attitude scales of more than two items.

n.a. = not appropriate

Apart from the political knowledge test, most of the interview schedule was "open ended." The respondents were encouraged to answer the question in their own terms, with as little prompting as possible. The interviews were recorded on cassette tapes and then transcribed onto paper. The full interview schedule is presented below.

General Selection

1. When you look around you, what are the problems that bother you most (in general)?
2. In general, are you satisfied with your situation today? Why?
3. What do you think are the most pressing problems that face Israel today?

4. Who is responsible for solving those problems? Do you think there is a reasonable chance that a solution will be found?

Political Thinking

1. Let us say that your were asked to describe your political opinions. How would you define them? (Go into depth.)

2. Are there, in your opinion, large differences between the big parties?

3. To what extent, do you think, the leaders and the parties represent the will of the people?

4. There is a debate about the level of democracy in various countries. What do you think are the traits that make a country into a good democracy?

5. What, in your opinion, is the meaning of the word "liberalism?"

6. What, in your opinion, is the meaning of the word "freedom?"

7. What, in your opinion, is the meaning of the word "equality?"

Political Action

1. What, in your opinion, are the traits which make a person a good citizen?

2. Were there any issues of political events that were especially important to you in the last year? If yes, did you do anything so that your opinion would be heard? What did you do? Did it help?

3. What do you think should be allowed and what do you think should be forbidden in order for a citizen to voice his opinions?

4. If a citizen wants to express himself, is there a way for him to do it?

CHAPTER 5: EXPLAINING COLLECTIVE ACTION

The information for this chapter was based on a content analysis of articles on protest which appeared in the newspaper *Ha'aretz* between the years 1979 and 1984. A parallel content analysis was carried out on articles from the newspaper *Yidiot Achronot* for the years 1979–1982 (Wolfsfeld 1985a) and no major differences were found which would contradict the results presented here.

The definition of a protest group is given in the text. Protests carried out by Arabs in Israel and in the occupied territories are included in all analyses in this chapter. Terrorist attacks were not included in the analysis, however, as they were considered a qualitatively different mode of political action.

As described in the text, the coding sheet for group behavior was developed in a pretest stage. The questions which were removed from this initial phase were found to be either unrealistic (the information was not available in the news articles) or unreliable (less than 85% agreement among coders).

As an additional precaution, many of the questions were given reliability indicators. "A" meant that the code was based on information which was mentioned specifically in the article, whereas "B" was used if the coder was almost certain that the fact was true. In the latter case the decision was based on either being strongly implied by the article or on some definite knowledge about the group. A "C" level of reliability was used when the coder was in doubt, i.e., when the fact was implied, but not strongly.

Any reliability codes of "C" were treated as missing cases in the statistical analysis. In general codes of "A" or "B" were taken to be true. The only exception to this rule had to do with the question of legality. To choose the most conservative definition possible, it was assumed that a protest act was legal unless it was specified otherwise or the group had carried out an act (e.g., throwing stones) which is known to be illegal.

The method for dividing the groups into ideal types (Ad Hoc, Community Action, etc.) is described in the text.

Any information which was not known was left blank and not included in any statistical analyses.

The coding sheet is presented below:

Group Characteristics
Name _____ ID _____

A.   Geographic Distribution
    1. Neighborhood   2. City-Wide   3. Area   4. National
B.   Type of Organization*
    1. New   2. Established   3. Political Party   4. Histadrut

C. Identity
1. Parents 2. Soldiers 3. Charidim 4. Arabs 5. Union
6. Ethnic Group 7. Druzim 8. Youth 9. Farmers
10. Neighborhood 11. West Bank Settlers 12. Seculars
13. Other _____

D. Group Goals
1. Political (Security/Foreign Affairs) 2. Political (Other)
3. Economic 4. Welfare 5. Education 6. Religious

Resources

A. Number of Members*
1. Less than 100 (includes 100) 2. Less than 1,000 (includes
"hundreds," "about a thousand" and 1000) 3. Over 1,000
(includes thousands.)

Actions

A. Type of Action
1. Meeting 2. Petitions 3. Press Release 4. Press Release
with Threat 5. Social Delegation 6. Press Conference
7. Press Conference with Threat 8. Strike 9. Sit-in
10. Hunger Strike 11. Demonstration 12. Vigil
13. Letters/Calls 14. Sanctions 15. Other _____

B. Legality*
1. Legal 2. Illegal

C. Disorder
1. No. 2. Blocking Street 3. Tresspassing 4. Occupying
Office (or stopping others' working routine) 5. Burning Tires

D. Violence
1. No 2. Physical Injury 3. Property Damage
4. Throwing of Stones 5. Blows 6. Physical Threat
7. Use of Weapons

E. Location
1. National 2. Jerusalem 3. Tel Aviv 4. Haifa 5. Galil
6. Occupied Territories 7. Other

F. Duration
1. Few Hours 2. One Day 3. Between a Day and a Week
4. More than a Week

G. Number of Participants*
1. Less than 100 (includes "about 100") 2. 100–500
("hundreds," "about 500") 3. 500–5000 ("thousands,"
"about 5,000") 4. 5,000

---

* Reliability indicator was used with these questions.

H.   Form of Mobilization*
     1. Reactive—The activity relates to some event in the recent
     past (e.g., government decision, press report, demonstration).
     2. New Issue—The activity does not relate to any specific past
     event. Brings out a new public demand.
Reaction of Security Forces
A.   Type of Reaction*
     1. No Reaction   2. Protection (of participants)
     3. Disengagement of Groups   4. Warning 5. Setting
     Limitations   6. Peaceful Dispersion   7. Dispersion by Force
B.   Arrests*
     1. None   2. Number _____
C.   Injuries to Protesters (Number)
     1. Light _____   2. Medium _____
     3. Serious _____   4. Death _____
D.   Injuries to Security Forces (Number)
     1. Light _____   2. Medium _____
     3. Serious _____   4. Death _____
E.   Methods Used
     1. Bringing Tear Gas   2. Use of Tear Gas   3. Bringing Clubs
     4. Use of Clubs   5. Bringing Water Hoses   6. Use of Water
     Hoses   7. Bringing Live Weapons   8. Shots in the Air
     9. Shooting into the Crowd
Detail of Article
A.   Date _____
B.   Page Number _____
C.   Size of Article (Standard ruler) _____

CHAPTER 6: BEYOND THE COLLECTIVE NUMBERS

The interviews in this section were carried out in an extremely
open-ended manner. As explained in the text, the group leaders were
asked to describe the nature of their organization and resources, the
background of the issues they were concerned with, and their experience with the press, other protest groups, and the authorities. A good
deal of emphasis was also put on the notion of strategy and most leaders were quite willing to talk about how actions were planned and exe-
cuted. Each of these interviews took about an hour, were recorded on
cassette tapes, and later transcribed.

CHAPTER 7: OUTCOMES OF COLLECTIVE ACTION

The protest groups described in chapter 5 provided the sampling frame for the smaller sample used in this chapter. The first leaders contacted were the ones who had carried out the most recent protests (1984). A total of sixty-nine telephone interviews were carried out. The interview schedule is presented below.

Organization
1. How many members would you say the group had at its height?
2. Did the group have the use of an office?
3. Did the group have paid workers?
4. Did you have a common treasury?
5. How did you keep in contact with the members?
    a. Telephone   b. Letters   c. Newspaper Ads
    d. Personal Contacts

Activities and Strategy
1. According to what was written in the paper, the groups carried out the following activities: (list). Were there any activities which were not reported? If so, what kind?
2. What made you choose that course of action?
    a. Previous Experience   b. Looking at Other Groups
    c. Seemed Like the Natural Thing To Do
3. Were there discussions about alternative strategies?

Success
1. What would you say was the major goal you hoped to achieve with your action?_____
2. To what extent would you say that the activities succeeded?
    a. To a Great Extent   b. Somewhat Succeeded
    c. Failed   d. Completely Failed
3. To what extent would you say that it was important for the group to achieve public suport?
    a. Very Important   b. Important
    c. Not Very Important
4. If it was important, to what extent do you think you succeeded in mobilizing public support?
    a. Succeeded   b. Somewhat Succeeded
    c. Failed   d. Completely Failed
5. Was there a particular office or official you tried to influence?
6. Did the group have the opportunity to make contact with him/her?

Other

1. Would you say that the press was more of a help or a hindrance?
    a. A Great Help   b. A Help
    c. A Hindrance   d. A Great Hindrance

2. There are those that claim that the only way for a group to achieve something is to make a lot of noise. To what extent do you agree with that statement?
    a. Completely Agree   b. Agree
    c. Disagree   d. Completely Disagree

3. Would you say that, in general, you were treated fairly by the authorities?
    a. Very Fairly   b. Fairly
    c. Not so Fairly   d. Not at all Fairly

4. If you had to do it all over again, would you do anything differently? If Yes, what?

NOTES

1. The Changing Political Culture of Israel

1. Gush Emunim ("Block of the Faithful") is the most obvious group to use these tactics and constantly portrays itself as the new pioneers in their attempt to settle the West Bank.

2. This figure is based on a survey carried out in 1982 for the present day study (see Methodological Appendix).

3. The continual survey is a project initiated by the Israel Institute of Applied Social Science Research and the Communication Institute of the Hebrew University. One of the major goals is the ongoing collection of social indicators about Israeli society. As the percentages presented in Figure 1–1 are based on calculating an average from a different number of surveys each year, it is important to note these variations. The following list gives the year followed by the number of surveys carried out: 1967 (3), 1968 (2), 1969 (2), 1970 (3), 1971 (1), 1972 (2), 1973 (8), 1974 (4), 1975 (4), 1976 (7), 1977 (during Labor rule − 6; Likud − 8), 1978 (22), 1979 (23), 1980 (16), 1981 (10), 1982 (10), 1983 (7), 1984 (2- before elections).

4. Respondents were asked how they saw politics. The choices were "very positively," "positively," "negatively," "very negatively." The percentage reported combines those answering "negatively" or "very negatively." Both surveys were carried out by the Israel Institute for Applied Social Science Research. The first was part of Asher Arian's election study, whereas the second was initiated by the present author.

5. In point of fact Gamson referred to those with high personal efficacy and low trust. But the difference is semantic rather than substantive.

6. Respondents were asked the following question: "To what extent do you think that you and your friends can influence government policy?" The response categories were To a Very Great Extent, To a Great Extent, To Some Extent, To a Small Extent, Not at all.

7. There is a danger here of committing an "ecological fallacy" of drawing individual conclusions based on aggregate data. The theory is more directly tested using individual level data in chapter three.

8. The question was asked in a national survey carried out within the

framework of the continuing survey of the Israel Institute for Applied Science Research and the Communication Institute, in December of 1984. Respondents were given the response categories of Agree Strongly, Agree, Not Sure, Disagree, Disagree Strongly. The stated percentage excludes those who were not sure.

9. This question comes from the major survey carried out in 1982. For deatils see Methodological Appendix.

10. These numbers may not represent the actual number of protest events, due to the selectivity of newspaper coverage. They do, however, represent a good indication of all political protests with any political importance. For more information see the Methodological Appendix.

11. Lehman-Wilzig (1983) claims that the level of protest and violence had actually dropped in the seventies. When this set of data is broken down into shorter periods, however, there is no consistent pattern. The data about collective action for this study came from the coding of articles about protests appearing in the newspaper *Ha'aretz* between 1979–1984 (see Methodological Appendix).

12. The level of disobedience in Israel is probably underestimated by these figures as only those acts which are explicitly reported as being illegal, disorderly, or violent are coded as such (see Methodological Appendix).

13. I am grateful to Bill Gamson for coining the term "uncivil disobedience."

14. Thus Kaase (1983) reported that the level of protest did not increase in four of the countries retested through the use of panel data in 1980.

15. In order to make the samples as comparable as possible, the data from *Political Action* was modified to include only citizens who were at least twenty years of age (as was the case in the Israeli sample).

16. In the original study *Political Action*, these items were considered examples of conventional participation. Here, they are seen as falling short of that concept in that none of these acts involved actually communicating demands to the authorities.

17. Although such survey questions are generally unreliable, it is unfortunate that Israelis who live on the West Bank, as well as Arab citizens, were not included in the national sample. This may lead to an even greater level of underestimation. See, for example the survey carried out by Weisburd and Vinitzky (1984) among settlers living on the West Bank.

18. The issue of petitions is a difficult one, both because it is a type of behavior which rests on the borderline between institutional behavior and mobilized, and because signing a petition takes so little effort or thought. It should be kept in mind that the results presented here would be quite different if those who only signed petitions were considered "Dissidents." In analyses which are presented later in the book a distinction is made between respondents who signed only one petition and those who signed more than one. Due to the nature of the *Political Action* measure this was not possible here.

2. The Analytical Framework

1. Tilly makes a distinction between group interests and group claims. His model of collective action suggests that shared interests create a need for organization which, in turn, leads to mobilization. The definitions in this study are somewhat different and the crystallization of interests are seen as part of the process of group mobilization.

2. Barnes and Kaase (1979) do not explicitly use the term repertoire, but it is an appropriate way to describe their work.

3. The study has nothing to say, for example, about the "free rider" phenomenon (Olson 1965).

3. Who, What, and Why: Explaining Individual Participation

1. The correlation coefficient used throughout this study is Pearson's r. Details about question format can be found in the Methodological Appendix.

2. The choice of the father for ethnic identification is clearly arbitrary. The need to make such a choice is indicative of the dangers of relying too heavily on the Ashkenazic/Sephardic distinction.

3. This technique of "Multiple Classification Analysis" is used throughout the book. It provides a relatively direct way of both testing for group differences and controlling for a variety of factors. The tests of significance (F) are based on an analyses of variance, after controls have been introduced.

4. An analysis of variance based on place of birth with only three categories explains more variance in psychological involvement than the original seven category analysis.

5. The sample was divided into three groups according to their self-identification: secular, traditional (partially religious), and religious. The religious had the lowest level of psychological involvement in politics (−.34), the secular the highest (.16), and the traditional Jews had a group score near the national average (-.04) (F = 15.55, p < .001). When one controlled for education, gender, and place of birth, however, the difference between the seculars and traditionals disappeared, but the religious remain significantly lower in their level of involvement.

6. It is also useful to rank these factors in order of importance. When a multiple classification analysis was performed with all of the variables in the equation, income proved to be the most important, followed by education, gender, place of birth, and religiosity (in that order).

7. The exact structure of all these indicators is given in the Methodological Appendix.

8. The two studies are actually quite compatible. Muller (1982, p. 7) himself calls for further research about the differences between conventional and unconventional political behavior.

9. There are some exceptions to this rule. The act of contacting a leader is often both specific and short term. This is indeed an unusual form of institutional action, as the initiation comes from the citizen. As further discussed below certain protest acts are also proactive: Gush Emunim is especially well-known for presenting governments with a fait accompli by creating illegal settlements.

10. Kaase (1983) makes a similar point by saying that the thrust of protest acts is, "... as much or more aimed at preventing some undesirable outcome, rather than at achieving a desirable one, while conventional participation is aimed at getting and not preventing something" (33).

11. It is rather interesting to note that the lowest correlation is with institutional efficacy. This can be attributed to the large number of Dissidents, who have learned enough about Israeli politics to be cynical about it.

12. Four of the questions were taken from Muller's (1979) measure of diffuse suport, whereas three others measure more specific dissatisfaction about the government with regard to its performance at the time of the interview, how it is dealing with the economy, and how it is dealing with security matters (see Methodological Appendix).

13. Even when party identification is removed from the analysis, education and religiosity are more powerful correlates of discontent then ethnicity, at least at the time of the survey.

14. There is of course a high correlation between these two scales despite the fact that they were presented in two different parts of the questionnaire. Some groups do, however, make a differentiation; college educated respondents were more positive about mobilization efficacy than mobilization approval.

15. This contrasts with the notion of expanding repertoires presented in *Political Action* (Barnes and Kaase 1979). Although it was assumed that most people move from experience with institutional action to the use of mobilized techniques, several pieces of evidence can be used to dispute this claim (Kaase 1983, Muller 1982).

16. Factor analysis is a statistical procedure which separates between variables which are correlated with each other and those which are not. It is assumed that there is an underlying factor which explains each set of correlations. In this case, principle components analysis and a varimax rotation were used. A factor loading of .40 was used as a cut-off point.

17. More specifically there were thirty-one respondents (3%) who participated exclusively in some type of political meeting.

18. It should be noted that the division used here is not the same as that presented in chapter 1. Questions used in that instance were designed to be identical to those used in *Political Action*, to allow a comparison. The questions here are somewhat more discriminating as they are used to distinguish between those who only took part in an activity once and those who took part more than once.

19. The difference between the four action types described in this part of the discussion were all found to be statistically significant (p<.001). Analyses of

variance were performed on the mean scores for the following variables which appear in Figures 3–5 through Figure 3–7: political discontent (F = 19.10), mobilization efficacy (F = 9.41), mobilization approval (F = 10.33), need for political influence (F = 14.17), institutional efficacy (F = 13.73), institutional approval (F = 16.49), psychological involvement (F = 37.54), internal efficacy (F = 15.64), and organization membership (F = 31.54).

20. Indeed Verba, Nie, and Kim (1978) see such organizations as central mobilizing forces which can significantly alter the level of individual participation.

21. As the authors pointed out, however, some dominant institutional systems can have the reverse effect of increasing inequality. This occurs when they only recruit people from the upper classes.

22. The formula is: $PR = ((X_i \, Yi)/X_i) \times 100$ where:

PR = Ration of over- or underrepresentation

X_i = The percentage of the entire population in the social group.

Y_i = The proportion of the same social group within a give category of participators.

(Verba and Nie 1972, 96)

23. Skeptics might claim that the reason for this finding has to do with the relationship between education and political discontent in Israel. When discontent is controlled, the relationship between education and mobilization action remains significant. In addition, a similar relationship was found in other countries (Barnes and Kaase 1979; Wolfsfeld 1986a).

24. It is important to note, however, the differences between women and the young. Women appear to reluctantly accept the use of protest; they do not score higher than men on either mobilization efficacy or approval. Young people are enthusiastic about direct action and seem to prefer those techniques. They do not, as a group, express significantly higher levels of blocked opportunities.

25. Figures based on Survey carried out by author in April 1982 (see Methodological Appendix).

26. The composite scores were created by multiplying the scores of each component to create on overall score.

27. The amount of variance explained (R2) is not overly high. It should be remembered, however, that this is one of the only studies which the attempt is made to explain actual behavior rather than behavioral intention.

28. Further analysis revealed that the results concerning Sephardic citizens are best related to a slightly greater participation in community work. It is important to remember, however, that this emerged only when all the other factors (especially involvement) had been controlled.

5. Explaining Collective Action

1. Groups with local interests may be ignored by the press and still have an impact. The number of such groups who are covered by the press suggest that the process of selectivity is not complete. It is a problem to bear in mind, however, in the interpretation of results.

2. This emphasis on events creates an additional problem for those interested in the outcomes of protest. With the exception of major conflicts, newspapers rarely report on how conflicts end. A conflict which is resolved is rarely news.

3. See the Methodological Appendix for a full explanation of the coding rules.

4. There are other aspects of group background which affect collective action. The social status of the group and the degree to which it is aligned with the political authorities should also affect a group's repertoire. Unfortunately, it was not possible to include these variables in the present analysis.

5. Interests can also have a dramatic effect on structure when they are generated by an outside force such as the government. Threats to an unorganized population will create a sense of identity and contribute to the building of structure.

6. Oberschall (1973) suggested the possibility of an integrated collectivity with strong communal ties. In part, these two traits are contradictory. A truly integrated population will have weak communal ties.

7. Physical goals are not, however, related to extensiveness. As detailed below, most communal groups seek physical goals and this limits the possibility for a strategy of extensiveness.

8. Most of the hypothesis testing in this chapter is based on a group level of analysis. This aggregation program of the *SPSSX* (1986) was used to create group scores. Measures of group action were based on the mean scores for a given variable (e.g., intensity).

9. It was not always possible to determine if a neighborhood group was organized around an established local council or an ad hoc group of residents. If the name of the group was simply "The residents of . . ." it was assumed to be organized by the council. If, on the other hand, the name was more specific (e.g. "Young couples of . . ."), it was coded as Ad Hoc.

10. The coding process was not blind and certain anomalies had to be resolved. Political parties and the *Histadrut* (the national labor union) were considered institutions and were removed from the analysis. In addition groups based on army ties were difficult to code and were also removed. Finally, although kibbutzim were a communal group who sometimes organized for ideological reasons (e.g., against the Lebanese War), they could hardly be considered a Sect. These few cases were also removed from the analysis.

11. It might be surprising to see the large number (44) of Sects in the sample. The reason for this is that it is not always easy to determine the relationship

between various groups. There were many different Arab groups who organized in the West Bank, for example, and each had to be coded as a separate group unless they were called by the same name.

12. The difference between the action types are all statistically significant (p.<.001). An analysis of variance was performed on the group means for all three variables: intensity (F = 22.02), extensivness (F = 6.81),and activism (F = 6.04).

13. Alternatively, the problem may be related to an inability to separate this group from Ad Hoc groups without more information about the nature of internal ties. See Footnote nine.

14. It was also thought that Ad Hoc groups would be more likely to have reactive interests than organized groups. This hypothesis was not supported by the data.

6. Beyond the Collective Numbers

1. The study of protest in Yamit was carried out before the bulk the research. Indeed, it provided many of the ideas which were later developed in this project. The extent of the observations and interviews were more extensive and reports about this initial study can be found in: Wolfsfeld 1984a, 1984b, 1984c.

2. The town council had also attempted to close the town during an earlier part of the struggle, but had failed. The council was split between those who wanted to oppose the withdrawal itself and those who decided to focus exclusively on the issue of compensation. Each found their place in either the businessmen's group or the Movement to Stop the Withdrawal from Sinai.

3. Many who identify with the left in Israel argued that the Yamit experience proved that setlements can be taken down, despite resistance.

4. Some have argued that the reason for the liberal policy of the police towards Charedi protests is related to the fact that the Ministry of Interior was under the control of the National Religious Party for so many years. There is no specific evidence to dispute this point, but the lack of arrests and trials appears to be a more general police policy.

5. The radical disagreed with the notion of the use of violence for fund raising. He argued that even the most radical of groups only receive a small amount of their budget from abroad and therefore have no need for such stunts.

7. Outcomes of Collective Action

1. The first leaders contacted were the ones who carried out the most recent protests (1984). A conscious attempt was made to find leaders from a variety of groups. Finding specific leaders proved to be an extremely time consuming task and this is the reason for the small sample size.

2. Intensity served as the covarient in this analysis.

3. The reverse process must also be considered and the suggestion made that some groups simply react to repression with violence. There is certainly an interactive effect between protesters and police which often leads to a cycle of escalation.

4. Innovation will also lead to publicity, but it is difficult to test in the present study.

5. It is worth noting that using a page number for a measure of publicity has some disadvantages. The most important of these is that the last page is usually considered more important than many of the pages in the middle.

6. Interests were divided into four categories: 1) Ecomonic 2) Education/Welfare 3) Political 4) Religious.

7. Shin (1983) reported a similar finding in his study of Korean protests.

8. For Gamson's reply see Gamson (1980).

9. O'Keefe and Schumaker (1983) also used the concept of threat and pointed out the difference between protest in democratic and nondemocratic regimes.

10. A new scale of violence was created to supplement the more general scale of intensity (which also includes peaceful acts of disorder). It was based on the percentage of violent acts carried out by each group. The correlations for each scale are:

	General Success	Public Success	Contacted Officials
Intensity	−.10	−.18	.06
(N)	(68)	(61)	(41)
Violence	−.23	−.37	−.11
(N)	(68)	(41)	(61)

REFERENCES

Adoni, H. 1979. The functions of the mass media in the Political Socialization of Adolesents. *Communication Research* 6:84–106.

Ajzen, I., and M. Fishbein. 1980. *Understanding attitudes and predicting behavior.* Englewood Cliffs. NJ: Prentice-Hall.

Almond, G., and S. Verba. 1963. *The civic culture.* Princeton, NJ: Princeton University Press.

Arian, A. 1971 *Consensus in Israel.* NY: General Learning Press.

Arian, A. (Ed.). 1972. *The elections in Israel – 1969.* Jerusalem: Jerusalem Academic Press.

Arian, A. (Ed.). 1975. *The elections in Israel – 1973.* Jerusalem: Jerusalem Academic Press.

Arian A. (Ed.). 1980. *The elections in Israel – 1977.* Jerusalem: Jerusalem Academic Press.

Arian, A. (Ed.). 1983. *The elections in Israel – 1981.* Tel Aviv: Ramot.

Arian, A. 1985. *Politics in Israel: The second generation.* Chatham, NJ: Chatham House.

Aronoff, M.J. 1977. *Power and ritual in the Israel labor party.* Amsterdam: Van Gorcum.

Barnes, S. M. and M. Kaase (Eds.). 1979. *Political action: mass participation in five western democracies.* Beverly Hills, Calif: Sage.

Bar-on, M. 1985. *Peace Now: The portrait of a movement.* Tel Aviv: Hakibbutz Hameuchad [Hebrew].

Bar-Yoseph, R. 1978. Representation and Involvement of Women in Public and Political Life. In the *Report of the Committee on the Status of Women.* Prime Minister's Office. Jerusalem: Israel Government Press Office.

Caspi, D., A. Diskin, and E. Gutmann. 1984. *The roots of Begin's success.* London: Croom-Helm.

Chazin, D. The strong hand. *Monitin.* April 1985. pp. 5–6 [Hebrew]

Coser, L.A. 1956. *The function of social conflict.* Glencoe, Ill: Free Press.

Danet, B., and D. Hartman. 1972. On protexia: Orientations towards the use of personal influence. *Journal of Comparative Administration* 3: 405–434.

Danet, B., (in press), *Pulling strings: biculturalism in Israeli bureaucracies.* Albany, NY: State University of New York Press.

Durkheim, E. 1951. *Suicide: A study in sociology.* Glencoe. Ill.: Free Press.

Eckstein, H. 1980. Theoretical approaches to explaining collective political violence. In T. R. Gurr (Ed.), *Handbook of Political Violence.* N.Y.: Frcc Press.

Etzioni-Halevy, E., with R. Shapiro. 1977. *Political culture in Israel.* NY: Praeger.

Fein, L. 1967. *Politics in Israel.* Boston: Little Brown.

Galnoor, I. 1982. *Steering the polity: Political communication in Israel.* Beverly Hills, Calif: Sage.

Gamson, W.A. 1968. *Power and discontent.* Homewood, Ill: Dorsey.

Gamson, W.A. 1975. The strategy of social protest. *Homewood. Ill: Dorsey.*

Gamson, W. A. 1980. *Understanding the careers of challenging groups. Americn Journal of Sociology 85: 1043–1060.*

Gitlin, T. 1980. *The whole world is watching.* Berkeley, Calif: University of California Press.

Goldstone, J.A. 1980. The weakness of organization. American Journal of Sociology 85: 1017–1042.

Gurr, T.R. 1980. On the outcome of violent conflict. In T. Gurr (Ed.), *Handbook of political conflict: theory and research.* NY: Free Press.

Gurr, T.R. 1983. Introduction, *American Behavioral Scientist* 26: 287–290. (Issue on the Outcomes of Collective Behavior.)

Horowitz, D., and M. Lissak. 1978. *Origins of the Israeli polity.* Chicago: University of Chicago Press.

Inkelhart, H. Value priorities and socioeconomic change. In S. Barnes and M. Kaase (Eds.), *Political action: Mass participation in five western democracies.* Beverly Hills, Calif: Sage.

Jenkins, J.C. 1983. Resource mobilization theory and the study of social movements. In R. Turner (Ed.), *Annual Review of Sociology* 9: 527–553.

Kaase, M. 1983. "Political Action in the 80s: Structures and Idiosyncrasies." Paper presented at 6th annual meeting of the International Society of Political Psychology. Oxford University. July 1983.

Kaplan, A. 1964. *The conduct of inquiry*. Scranton, Pennsylvania: Chandler Publishing Co..

Klingemann, H. 1979. Measuring ideological conceptualizations in S. Barnes and M. Kaase (Eds.), *Political action: mass participation in five western democracies*. Beverly Hills: Sage.

Kornhauser, W. 1959. *The politics of mass society*. Glencoe. Ill: Free Press.

Lehman-Wilzig, S. 1981. Public protest and systemic stability in Israel, 1960–1979. In S. Lehman-Wilzig and B. Susser (Eds.), *Comparative Jewish politics: Public life in Israel and the diaspora*. Ramat Gan, Israel: Bar Ilan Press.

Lehman-Wilzig, S. 1983. The Israeli protester. *The Jerusalem Quarterly* 21: 127–138.

Liebman, C.S., and E. Don-Yehiya. 1983. *Civil religion in Israel*. Berkeley, Calif: University of California Press.

Lipsky, M. 1970. *Protest in city politics*. Chicago: Rand McNally.

Lissak, M. 1964. Images of society and status in the Yishuv and Israeli society: Patterns of change in ideology and class structure. *Molad* 22: 494–505 [Hebrew].

Lofland, J. 1985. *Protest: Studies of collective behavior and social movements*. New Brunswick, NJ: Transaction Press.

Louis, K.S. 1982. Multisite/Multimethod Studies. *American Behavioral Studies* 26: 6–21.

Maslow, A. 1954. *Motiviation and personality*. NY: Harpers.

McCarthy, J., and M. N. Zald. 1977. Resource mobilization and social movements. *American Journal of Sociology* 82: 1212–1241.

McCarthy, J., and M. N. Zald (Eds.). 1979 *The dynamics of social movements*. Englewood Cliffs. NJ: Prentice-Hall.

Medding, P. Y. 1972. *Mapai in Israel: Political organization and government in a new society*. Cambridge, England: Cambridge University Press.

Merelman, R. M. 1986. Revitalizing political socialization. In M.G. Hermann Ed.. *Political Psychology.* San Francisco: Jossey Bass.

Milbrath, L. 1965. *Political participation.* Chicago: Rand McNally.

Milbrath, L., and G. Goel. 1977. *Political participation.* Chicago: Rand McNally.

Muller, E. N. 1979. *Aggressive politicial participation.* Princeton: Princeton University Press.

Muller, E. N. 1982. An explanatory model for differing types of participation. *European Journal of Political Research* 10: 1–16.

Muller, E. N. and K. Opp. 1986. Rational choice and rebellious collective action. *American Political Science Review* 80: 471–489.

Neuman, W. R. 1981. Differentiation and integration: Two dimensions of political thinking. *American Journal of Sociology* 86: 1236–1268.

Newman, D. (Ed.). 1985. *The political impact of Gush Emunim.* London: Croom-Helm.

Oberschall. A. 1973. *Social conflicts and social movements.* Englewood Cliffs. NJ: Prentice Hall.

O'Keefe, M., and P. Schumaker. 1983. Protest effectiveness in Southeast Asia. *American Behavioral Scientist* 26: 375–394.

Olson, M. 1965. *The logic of collective action.* Cambridge, Mass: Harvard University Press.

Paige, J. M. 1971. Political orientation and riot participation. *American Sociological Review* 36: 810–820.

Piven, F. F., and R. A. Cloward. 1979. *Poor people's movements.* NY: Vintage Books.

Rubinstein, D. 1982. *On the Lord's side: Gush Emunim.* Tel Aviv: Hakibbutz Hameuchad [Hebrew].

Schumaker, P. D. 1975. The effectiveness of militant tactics in contemporary urban protest. *Journal of Voluntary Action Research.* 9: 131–148.

Seligson, M. 1980. A problem solving approach to political efficacy. *Social Science Quarterly* 60: 630–642.

Shamir M., and A. Arian. 1983. The ethnic vote in Israel's 1981 elections. In A. Arian (Ed.), *The elections in Israel – 1981.* Tel Aviv: Ramot.

Shapiro, Y. 1984. *Elites without successors.* Tel Aviv: Am Oved [Hebrew].

Shimshoni, D. 1982. *Israeli democracy: The middle of the journey.* London: Free Press, McMillan Co.

Shin, M. 1983. Political protest and government decision making. *American Behavioral Scientist* 26: 395–416.

Sieber, S. 1978. The integration of fieldwork and survey methods. *American Journal of Sociology* 6: 1335–1359.

Simmel, G. 1955. *Conflict.* translated by Kurt Wolf. Glencoe. Ill: Free Press.

Snyder, D. 1978. Collective violence: A research agenda and some strategic considerations. *Journal of Conflict Resolution* 22: 499–538.

Sprinzak, E. 1981a. Gush Emunim and the iceberg model of political extremism. *Medina Memshal Veyehasim Beinleumim* (State, Government and International Relations) 17: 22–49. [Hebrew].

Sprinzak, E. 1981b. Illegalism in the Israeli political culture. *A Study Day – 1980.* Magnes Publication No. 6. Jerusalem: Hebrew University. [Hebrew].

Sprinzak, E. 1987. *Every man whatsoever is right in his own eyes: Illegalism in Israeli society.* Tel Aviv: Sifirat Poalim [Hebrew]

Statistical abstract of Israel. 1985. Jerusalem: Central Bureau of Statistics.

SPSSX users guide. 1986. Second Edition. NY: McGraw Hill.

Taylor, C. L., and D. A. Jodice. 1983. *World handbook of political and docial indicators.* New Haven. Ct: Yale University Press.

Tilly, C. 1978. *From mobilization to revolution.* Reading, Mass: Addison Wesley.

Turner. R. H. 1970. Determinants of social movement strategies. In T. Shibutani (Ed.), *Human nature and collective behavior.* Englewood Cliffs, NJ: Prentice Hall.

Verba, S., and N. Nie. 1972. *Participation in America.* NY: Harper & Row.

Verba, S., N. Nie, and J. Kim. 1978. *Participation and political equality.* London: Cambridge University Press.

Weisburd, D., and V. Vinitzky. 1984. Vigilantism and rational social control, the case of Gush Emunim settlers. In M. J. Aronoff (Ed.), *Cross-Currents in Israeli culture and politics.* New Brunswick. NJ: Transaction Press.

Welsh, S. 1977. Women as political animals. *American Journal of*

Political Science. 21: 711–730.

Wolfsfeld, G. 1984a. collective political action and media strategy: The case of Yamit. *Journal of Conflict Resolution* 28: 1–36.

Wolfsfeld, G. 1984b. The symbiosis of press and protest: An exchange analysis. *Journalism Quarterly* 61: 550–556.

Wolfsfeld, G. 1984c. Political communication and political violence, field notes from Yamit. *Jerusalem Quarterly* 31: 128–144.

Wolfsfeld, G. 1985a. Violent and non-violent forms of protest in Israel. Final Research Report to the Ford Foundation. Unpublished manuscript.

Wolfsfeld, G. 1985b, Political efficacy and political action: "A change of focus using data from Israel", *Social Science Quarterly* 66: 617–628.

Wolfsfeld, G. 1986a. Political action repertoires: The role of efficacy. *Comparative Political Studies* 19: 104–129.

Wolfsfeld, G. 1986b. Evaluational origins of political action. *Political Psychology* 7: 767–788.

INDEX

Activism
  of collective action, 104, 107–110, 112, 152–153, 159, 169
  and publicity, 152–153
Adoni, H., 42
Ad Hoc protest groups
  case studies of, 117–118, 124–131, 134, 139
  collective action repertoires of, 94, 98, 102–104, 108, 110, 113–114, 169, 191n.9, 192n.13, 192n.14
  outcomes for, 148, 151, 153, 158
Age, 33, 41, 47, 54, 67. *See also* Youth
  and political action, 71
  and psychological involvement, 47
Ajzen, I., 49
Almond, G., 1–2, 19–20, 24, 26, 29, 32–33
Arabs, 17, 86, 99, 103, 175, 181–182, 187n.17
Arian, A., 1, 7, 10, 15, 17, 23, 44, 49, 186
Aronoff, M.J., 10
Arrests of Protesters, 18, 123, 137, 144, 150–151, 161, 164, 175, 183
Associations, 101, 103–106, 108–110, 117, 127
Attitudes
  components of, 49, 50
  formation of, 32–33

  institutional, 49–52, 54, 56, 58, 60, 69, 167–168
  mobilization, 49, 51–52, 54, 69, 167–168

Background
  factors affecting collective actions, 96–114, 124, 170–171
  factors affecting individual actions, 39–47, 51–54, 62–71, 165, 168, 170–171
  stage, 4–5, 30–33, 148, 170–171
Barnes, S., 2, 24, 29, 32, 34–35, 41–42, 46, 51, 53, 174, 188n.2, 189n.15, 190n.23
Bar-on M., 17, 126
Bar-Yoseph, R., 42
Blocked opportunities, sense of, 19
  defined, 12
  measurement of, 60
  and the politics of provocation 18, 27, 82, 164, 166
  among protest groups, 112, 136, 155
  rise in, 13–16
  among women, 67, 190n.24
Businessmen in Yamit, 116–120, 122–123, 130, 147, 192n.2. *See also* Yamit

Campaigning, 23, 34, 50
  compared to other countries, 24, 26
  as institutional action, 58, 177

among political action types, 78, 81, 86, 87

Caspi, D., 23, 49

Charedim, 116, 139–148, 192n.4

Cloward, R.A., 32

Collective Action, 91–162. *See also* Protests; Protest Groups; Mobilization, patterns of,
associational, 101, 103–106, 108–114, 117, 127
communal, 100–103, 110, 112–117, 134–147, 151, 153
conclusions about, 169–170
outcomes of, 96, 149–162
repertoires of, 104–114
types of, 94–96

Community Action Groups, 102–103, 108, 110, 112–117, 134–140, 146, 151, 153, 158

Community work, 24, 26, 50, 56–58, 79–80, 87–89, 174

Conformists. *See* Political action types

Contacting leaders, 8, 22–24, 26, 56–58, 81, 89, 174, 189n.9

Coser, L.A., 106

Costs and benefits, 30, 34–36. *See also* Rational choice
of protest, 5, 18, 142, 145–147, 150–151, 161–162, 171

Cross-cultural comparison, 4, 6–7, 19–28, 175

Danet, B., 18

Democracy, 1
attitudes towards, 75, 80, 90, 130, 138, 180
in Israel, 2, 19, 164, 166

Demonstrations. *See also* Protests
attitudes towards, 76, 80–81, 85, 88, 89
as collective action, 22, 94, 102, 104, 105, 113–114, 117–118, 120, 128, 132–133, 136–138, 140, 142, 145, 159, 182

compared to other countries, 22–24, 26–27
illegal, 60, 81, 105, 132
participation in, 53, 58, 83–84, 87
rise in, 6, 16, 17
Sabra and Shatilla, 73, 88, 129, 132
violent, 143–144

Discontent. *See* Political discontent

Diskin, A., 23, 49

Disorders. *See also* Protests, illegal; Violence
attitudes towards, 76
extent of, 18, 95
level of, 163
measurement of, 182, 187n
and patterns of mobilization, 107
and success, 161, 162
types of, 94, 105

Dissidents. *See* Political action types

Don-Yehiya, E., 46

Durkheim, E., 29

Eckstein, H., 29

Education, 32–33, 44, 53, 68
measurement of, 175, 182
and political action, 64, 66, 165
and political action types, 75, 78–79, 81, 88
as a protest goal, 93, 98–99, 110
and psychological involvement, 6, 41–42, 47, 62, 188n.6

Efficacy, 89, 149, 186
compared to other countries, 6, 19–20, 22, 24, 26
group, 96, 136–137, 147, 172
institutional, 12–13, 15, 37, 50–52, 60, 69, 175, 177, 189n.11, 190n.19
internal, 19, 47, 51, 60, 62, 66, 70, 176, 190n.19
low sense of, 1, 15
mobilization, 51, 53, 58, 69, 177, 189n.14, 190n.19

and political action, 34, 74–75, 85, 89, 167

Electoral system, 1, 15, 20, 164–166

Equality. *See* Participation, equality of

Ethnicity, 33, 49, 53
and collective action, 98, 100, 105, 110, 135
measurement of, 175, 182
and political action, 67–68, 71, 165, 190n.29
and political equality, 41, 165
and psychological involvement, 44–46

Etzioni-Halevy, E., 1, 15, 17, 23

Evaluations of the political system. *See also* Strategy
components of, 49–51
interviews about, 71–90
measurement of, 176
of political action types, 55–56, 58–62, 69, 73
psychological involvement and, 47–48
rationality of, 3, 69
roots of, 51–55
stage, 4–5, 30, 34–35, 39, 49, 69, 170

Extensiveness,
of collective action, 104–105, 107–112, 132–133, 141, 152, 166, 169, 191
and publicity, 152–153, 162
and success, 159, 162

Farmers in Yamit, 116–120, 122–123, 146, 182. *See also* Yamit

Fein, L., 1, 15

Fishbein, M., 49

Flexibility, 36
of collective action, 104, 108–109, 113–114, 169

Galnoor, Y., 1, 10, 15, 23

Gamson, W., 13, 29, 32, 35, 98, 154, 156, 160, 186n.5, 187n.13, 193n.8

Gender. *See* Women

Gitlin, T., 130, 153

Goel, G., 29, 41

Goldstone, J.A., 160

Government
attitudes towards, 6, 12–13, 47, 49, 52, 56, 60, 79–83, 88, 125, 138–139, 175–177, 186
demands on, 2, 23, 48, 92, 102–103, 116–120, 126, 128, 132, 138, 145, 166, 189n.9
under Labor, 13
under Likud, 13, 49, 123
policy, 135, 138
responses to protest, 36, 54, 68, 119–124, 130, 134, 145, 147, 150–151, 154
system of, 15, 139, 166

Gurr, T., 154

Gush Emunim, 118, 147
identification with, 46, 84
illegal settlements of, 54, 186n.1
in Yamit, 118, 121
Peace Now and, 17, 103, 126, 131

Gutmann, E., 23, 49

Hartman, D., 18

Horowitz, D., 8

Identity, collective, 32, 98, 102–105, 117–118, 124–128, 134–135, 146

Immigration, 7, 9

Inactives. *See* Political action types

Income, 32, 41, 47, 62, 68, 165, 175
and psychological involvement, 6, 47, 188n.6

Inkelhart, H., 93

Institutional Action. *See also* Political action
attitudes towards, 50, 56, 60, 167–168
compared to other countries, 20, 24
definition of, 23
distinguished from mobilized action, 57, 164, 189

institutional recruitment and, 64
measurement of, 58, 175, 178
and political action types, 26, 58
roots of, 51, 69–70, 167–168
social background and, 66–67,
165

Institutional approval, 50–52, 60,
69, 190n.19
measurement of, 177–178

Institutional attitudes, 49–52, 54,
56, 58, 60, 69, 167–168

Institutional efficacy, 12–13, 15, 37,
50–52, 60, 69, 189n.11, 190n.19
measurement of, 175, 177

Institutional recruitment, 62–70,
165, 168, 171

Intensity, 36. See also Violence
of collective action 17–18, 104–
113, 121, 138–139, 151–153, 169
and success, 160–161

Interests, 52, 162
collective, 98–115, 121, 134, 146,
148, 169, 191n.7
crystallization of, 30, 32–35, 48,
171
measurement of, 47
and outcomes, 150, 153, 157–159
and political action types, 73, 86,
89

Interviews
methodology of, 35, 116, 150,
183–184
with political action types 4,
72–90, 168
with protest leaders, 5, 73, 124–
145, 154–162

Italy, 19–20, 26–27

Jenkins, J.C., 29

Jerusalem, 13, 116–117, 127, 178,
182
protest in, 93–94, 127–128, 139–
148

Jodice, D.A., 92

Kaase, M., 19, 24, 29, 32, 34–35,
41–42, 46, 51, 53, 174, 187–190

Kaplan, A., 2

Kfar Shalem, 134–139

Kim, J., 20, 23, 32–33, 41–42, 51,
56–57, 62, 64, 77, 168, 190

Klingemann, H., 176

Kornhauser, W., 29

Labor Party, 53, 86, 88, 129
historically 8, 10, 13

Law
breaking the, 18, 51, 54, 86, 94,
130–132, 144, 147, 151, 164
religious, 46, 143–145
respect for, 2, 18, 83, 89, 144, 147,
164

Lebanese War, 13
protest against 5, 73, 124–134

Leftism
identification with, 49, 74, 81–
82, 84, 86, 192n.3
measurement of, 178
of Peace Now, 126–127
and protest, 53, 124

Lehman-Wilzig, S., 15–17, 187n.11

Liebman, C.S., 46

Lipsky, M., 32, 151

Lissak, M., 8, 11

Lofland, J., 106

Louis, K.S., 37

Maslow, A., 93

Mass media, 2, 10–11, 36. See also
Newspapers; Publicity; Television
and protest groups, 90, 106, 117,
119, 122–123, 125, 130–134, 138,
144–145, 148–156, 164, 166, 170,
182, 185

McCarthy, J., 29, 34, 106

Medding, P., 8–10

Merelman, R.M., 46

Methodology, 3, 4, 37–38, 174–185

Milbrath, L., 29, 41

Mobilization
  patterns of, 93, 99–103, 108,
  112–114, 118, 124, 153, 171
  proactive and reactive, 33, 100,
  102, 112–113, 118, 146, 172
  of resources, 30, 32–35, 96, 102,
  109, 118, 169–171, 173
  stage, 33–34, 96–99

Mobilization approval, 51, 53, 58,
  189n.14, 190n.19
  measurement of, 177–178

Mobilization attitudes, 49, 51–52,
  54, 69, 167, 168

Mobilization efficacy, 51, 53, 58,
  69, 189n.14, 190n.19
  measurement of, 177

Mobilized Action, 23, 58, 102. See
  also Protest
  attitudes towards, 50–51, 53, 60,
  77, 81, 86
  compared to other countries, 20,
  24
  definition of, 23
  distinguished from institutional
  action, 26, 69, 70, 163, 164, 167
  equality of, 66
  measurement of, 58, 175, 178
  roots of, 69–71
  social background and, 41, 68, 71,
  190
  types of, 24, 172
  women and, 67

Movements, 102–104, 108–113,
  124, 126–127, 131–134, 151, 153,
  158

Movement to Stop the Withdrawal
  from Sinai, 116–118, 120, 122,
  192n.2. See also Yamit

Muller, E., 29, 34, 41, 50, 53, 56,
  177, 188n.8, 189n.12, 189n.15

Need for political influence, 1,
  11–12, 15, 33, 50, 52, 56, 60
  69, 190n.19
  measurement of, 178

Neuman, W.R., 74

Newman, D., 17

Newspapers. See also Mass media
  data from, 11, 17, 37–38, 92–93,
  150, 180–181, 187n.10, 191n.2
  reading, 8, 12, 20, 37, 41, 174, 176

Nie, N., 20, 23, 29, 32–33, 35,
  41–42, 51, 56–57, 62, 64, 77, 168,
  172, 190

Oberschall, A., 29, 32, 35, 100–102,
  104–105, 191

O'Keefe, M., 154, 156, 160, 193n.9

Olson, M., 29, 188

Opp, K., 34

Organization
  definition of, 32, 96
  and collective action, 91, 94,
  99–109, 116–119
  and resources, 94, 96–100, 104,
  107–108, 120, 125–126, 129, 146–
  148, 152–153, 156
  and success, 125, 129, 149–150,
  156–157, 162, 166, 170

Organizational membership, 58,
  60, 62, 70, 190n.2
  measurement of, 178

Outcomes of Collective Action, 5,
  96, 149–161. See also Publicity;
  Repression; Success

Paige, J.M., 12

Parents Against Silence, 124, 126,
  129–130, 146

Participation. See Political participation

Partisanship. See Political Identification

Peace Now, 17, 103, 118, 124–127, 129, 131–134, 136, 147

Petitions
signing, 22, 24, 83, 87–88, 120, 187n.18

Piven, F.F., 32

Police
reactions to protest, 18, 130, 132, 137, 141–142, 144–145, 147–148, 151, 177, 192n.4

Political Action (collective). *See* Collective action

Political Action (individual), 19
attitudes towards, 58–62, 69–71, 73–90
changes in, 17–18, 164
choices about, 38, 71, 156
compared to other countries, 1, 6, 20, 27, 163
definition of, 23
equality of, 62–69, 165–166
repertoires of, 2, 11, 36, 55–71
roots of, 5, 7, 55–56, 58–71
social background and, 62–71
strategies of, 54, 123
studies of, 19, 29, 30, 32, 50, 53
the potential for, 47–49
towards a theory of, 3, 4, 27, 29–38, 69–72, 166–173
types of, 23, 26, 29, 56–58

Political Action 19, 35, 56–57, 104, 174–175, 180, 187, 189

Political action repertoires, 4, 11, 35–36, 72, 90, 122, 164
of groups, 5, 38, 102, 104–114, 123, 158, 169–170
of individuals, 17, 20, 39, 55–71, 167–168, 188n.2, 189n.15
strategy and, 118–122, 127–133, 136–137, 141–143

Political action types (individual), 26–27, 39–40, 55–56, 58–69, 72–90, 168
Conformists, 26, 55–56, 58–68, 72, 77–81, 89, 168

Dissidents, 26, 55–56, 58–68, 81–85, 89, 168
Inactives, 26, 55–56, 58–68, 74–77, 89, 168
Pragmatists, 26, 55–56, 58–68, 72, 85–89, 168

Political culture, 1–2, 4, 46, 64, 168
changes in Israeli, 6–28, 67
of provocation, 89, 90, 162, 163–166

Political discontent
measurement of, 177
and political action, 51, 56, 58–60, 68–69, 81, 190n.19, 190n.23
rise in, 6, 11–13, 18, 20
roots of, 52–53

Political identification, 33, 48–49, 52–53, 84, 86, 128
measurement of, 177

Political interest . *See* Psychological involvement

Political knowledge 1, 34, 47, 75–76, 82, 87, 99, 169
measurement of, 176

Political leaders, 22, 24, 36, 77–79, 81–83, 85–86, 89, 92
attitudes towards, 6, 73, 75, 180
historically, 8–10
making demands on, 24, 92
relations with public, 15, 164, 166

Political meetings, attending, 24, 26, 57–58, 78, 87

Political orientations, 20–23, 39, 44–46, 50, 55, 58, 167–168, 171

Political participation, 8
equality of, 62–69, 165–166
obstacles to, 27, 50, 62
through political parties, 8–10
protest as, 164, 167
studies of, 3, 23, 29–35, 167–168, 172
conclusions about, 167–169

Political parties

attitudes towards, 15, 20, 24, 75–79, 82, 84, 86, 88, 180
changing role of, 6–12, 27, 166
and the electoral system, 15
as mobilizing forces, 64, 66–68, 165
identification with, 44, 49, 52, 53, 87, 177
membership in, 8, 10, 17, 57–58, 66–68, 174

Politics of Provocation, 18, 27, 148, 156, 163–165
defined, 2
participants in, 67, 82
roots, 4, 12–13, 20, 26, 39, 49, 60

Protest, 1, 29, 34, 110. *See also* Collective Action
attitudes towards, 53, 54, 56, 66–69, 78–81, 168
Charedi, 116, 139–148, 192n.4
compared to other countries, 20, 23
definition of, 92
distribution of, 94
early, 9, 11
goals, 5, 72, 84, 87, 93, 98–99
illegal, 18, 24, 57, 77, 84, 110, 161, 187n.12
innovation, 94, 104, 108–109, 113, 120, 133
institutionalization of, 96, 112
intensity of, 17–18, 104–113, 121, 138–139, 151–153, 169
at Kfar Shalem, 134–139
against the Lebanese War, 116, 124–134, 170
measurement of, 37, 92, 113, 175, 180–183, 187
as political communication, 90, 95–96, 164
rise in, 17, 164
roots of, 15–16, 24, 27, 49–53, 66, 70, 82, 96, 167
strategies of, 5, 12, 29, 35, 105–108, 118–122, 127–133, 136–137, 141–143, 151–154, 161, 169

success of, 5, 35, 77, 94, 120, 125, 128–130, 138, 149, 150, 152, 154–163, 166, 170, 184, 193n.10
in Yamit, 116, 118–123, 170

Protest Groups. *See also* Ad Hoc protest groups; Community Action Groups; Sects; Unions
case studies of, 115–145
competition and cooperation among, 122, 133–134, 137, 143–144, 147, 170
interests of, 93, 100–101, 105–109
leaders of, 5, 18, 37, 96–102, 100, 104, 108, 115–148, 146–148, 150–151, 154–155, 159, 161, 163, 171–172, 183–184
membership in, 98–100, 106, 118, 126, 156, 157, 172
organizational structure of, 32, 92, 96, 98, 100–103, 107–108, 116–118, 124–127, 134–136, 138–141, 146, 166
scope of, 92–95, 98, 105, 107–108, 140–141, 153, 156
traits of, 92–96

Psychological involvement in politics, 49
and attitudes towards political action, 51–52, 54, 168
compared to other countries, 6, 19–22, 24, 26
measurement of, 37, 41, 176
and the formation of opinions, 47, 48
and political action, 56, 60–62, 66–68, 70, 74–76, 78–79, 81–82, 84–85, 87–88, 167, 190n.19
as potential for political action, 41, 168
rise in, 12–13, 15–16
social background and, 41–43, 45, 47, 66–68, 165, 168, 188

Public opinion, 150, 151, 154
appeals to, 2, 100, 131, 134, 157–158
surveys of, 13

Publicity, 5, 119–123, 128–134, 138, 145–154, 162

Rabbis, 46, 139–143

Rational choice, 4, 27, 34–35, 71, 89, 146, 167, 171–173. *See also* Costs and benefits

Rationality
of collective action, 30, 146, 167, 171–173
of political action (individual), 34, 49, 60, 156

Recruitment. *See* Institutional Recruitment

Religiosity, 41, 42, 44, 46–47, 175
and attitudes towards protests, 53, 54
and collective action, 93, 98, 100–103, 106, 110, 117–118, 135–136, 182
measurement of, 188n.5
and political action, 62, 67–68, 78, 81, 83–84, 87, 165
and psychological involvement, 165, 188n.5

Religious court, 139, 142, 144

Repertoires, Political Action. *See* Political action repertoires

Repression, 5, 36, 113, 121, 144, 150–151, 162–164, 166

Resource mobilization theory, 29, 30–32, 35, 156, 169–170, 173

Resources
collective, 29, 37–38, 91–92, 98, 115, 135, 147
and collective action, 105, 107, 110, 114, 119
individual, 38, 48, 60, 62, 70, 73, 80, 86, 90
informational, 47, 74–75, 99, 176
instrumental, 99
measurement of, 182–183
mobilization of, 30, 32–35, 96, 102, 109, 118, 169–171
organization and, 94, 96–100, 104, 107–108, 120, 125–126, 129,

146–148, 152–153, 156
and political action (individual), 3, 30, 89
and success, 156–159, 161, 166

Rubinstein, D., 17

Schumaker, P., 154, 156, 160, 193

Sects, 103, 109–114, 139, 144, 151, 153, 158, 191n.11

Secular Jews, 46–47, 53, 68, 74, 84, 87, 102, 117, 118, 135, 139, 142, 165, 175

Settlements
West Bank, 18, 54, 84, 127, 177
Yamit, 116–118, 121–123

Shamir, M., 49

Shapiro, Y., 10

Shimshoni, D., 7

Shin, M., 54, 156, 193

Sieber, S., 37

Simmel, G., 106

Snyder, D., 9, 30

Socioeconomic status, 32, 41, 42, 168

Social Factors. *See* Background factors

Soldiers Against Silence, 124–126, 128–129, 133, 146

Sprinzak, E., 17, 18

Strategy, 5, 29, 35, 167, 171
of Charedim, 141–143
and interests, 101, 104, 108
and resources, 34, 110, 166
of extensiveness, 105, 108, 159, 162, 169
of intensity, 105–108, 151–154, 161, 169
in Kfar Shalem, 136–137
in protests against the Lebanese War, 127–133
roots of, 33, 34, 100
stage, 30, 33, 96
in Yamit, 118–122

Strikes, 33, 76, 85, 90, 92, 94, 106, 112–114, 160

Success of collective action, 53, 190, 150, 154–167
  intensity and, 35, 152, 160–162
  mass media and, 128, 130, 138, 150
  measurement of, 150, 154, 184
  organization and, 125, 129, 149–150, 156–157, 162, 166, 170
  rate of, 5, 154–156, 163
  repertoires and, 159–162, 193n.10

Surveys, 44, 46–47, 49, 53, 72–73
  comparative, 6–28
  methods of, 37, 38, 91, 174–179, 186n.3, 186n.4, 186n.8, 187n.9, 190n.25
  on political action, 37–71, 174–179

Taylor, C.L., 92

Tel Aviv, 93, 127–128, 135, 178

Television, 11, 119, 137–138, 145, 150. See also Mass Media

Threats, 76, 79, 81, 85, 132, 135, 159, 172
  by authorities, 36, 135
  group reactions to, 100, 112–113, 118, 120, 132, 135–137, 172, 191n.5
  individual reactions to, 53, 55, 73, 76, 79, 81, 85, 172

Ties. See also Identity, collective; Organization
  associational and communal, 101–114, 191n.6
  population, 96–101
  protest group, 124–126, 169

Tilly, C., 29, 32–35, 96, 99, 188

Turner, R.H., 104

Unions, 84, 98, 102–103, 117–118, 120, 134
  collective action of, 106, 109–114
  protest outcomes of, 151, 153, 158, 182

United States, 19, 22, 24, 64, 127

Verba, S., 1–2, 19–20, 22–24, 26, 29, 32–33, 35, 41–42, 51, 56–57, 62, 64, 77, 168, 172, 190n.22

Vinitzky, V., 18, 187

Violence, 131. See also Disorders; Intensity
  attitudes towards, 51, 53, 80–81, 83, 86–88, 90, 136, 147, 151
  Charedi, 139, 141–145
  decisions about, 130–131, 137, 147, 152, 171
  extent of, 18, 95, 187
  level of, 2, 18, 163, 187n.11
  measurement of, 107, 177, 182, 187n.12
  outcomes, of, 35, 151–153, 161–162
  participants in, 27
  and patterns of mobilization, 104–109, 112–114, 166, 169
  as political action, 36, 104, 164
  studies of, 29, 34
  types of, 94–95
  in Yamit, 118–124

Voting, 23, 44
  as political action, 23–24, 56, 74–75, 77–79
  as political identification, 177
  convincing others about, 47, 174, 176
  social background and, 44, 49

Welsh, S., 42
  West Bank, 121, 127, 131–132, 182, 187n.17. See also Gush Emunim settlements in the, 54, 84, 118, 186n.1

Wolfsfeld, G., 1, 34, 50, 123, 152, 161, 181, 190, 192

Women, 41–42, 62, 64–68, 165–166, 190n.24

Women Against the War, 124–125, 127–128, 133. See also Lebanese War

Yamit, protest in, 116–124, 146–147, 170, 192n.1, 192n.3

Youth, 8, 47
attitudes towards protest, 53, 54, 190
political action of, 64–68, 164–165

Yishuv, 7–9

Zald, M.N., 29, 34, 106

Zionism, 7, 9, 77, 78, 139